Larry Moffi

This Side of

With an Introduction by Paul Dickson

AN

ORAL

HISTORY

OF

MAJOR

LEAGUE

BASEBALL

IN THE

1950S

Cooperstown

Dover Publications, Inc., Mineola, New York

Photographs of Virgil Trucks, Frank Thomas, Gene Woodling, Mel Parnell, Andy Carey, Roy Stevens, Vern Law, Bob Cerv, Cal McLish, and Tito Francona are from the personal collection of each player and are reproduced with his permission. All other photographs are reproduced courtesy of the National Baseball Library and Archive, Cooperstown, New York.

Bibliographical Note

This Dover edition, first published in 2010, is an unabridged republication of the work originally published in 1996 by the University of Iowa Press, Iowa City, Iowa. A new Introduction to the Dover edition has been written by Paul Dickson.

Library of Congress Cataloging-in-Publication Data

Moffi, Larry.
  This side of Cooperstown: an oral history of major league baseball in the 1950s / Larry Moffi.
     p. cm.
  Originally published: Iowa City : University of Iowa Press, c1996. With new introd.
  Includes bibliographical references and index.
  ISBN-13: 978-0-486-47273-7
  ISBN-10: 0-486-47273-6
  1. Baseball players—United States—Interviews. 2. Baseball—United States—History—20th century. I. Title.

GV865.A1M646 2010
796.3570922—dc22

                                                                    2009033882

Manufactured in the United States by Courier Corporation
47273601
www.doverpublications.com

To my uncle

RUBY CHERNICK

and in memory of

ED WINSTEN

We might not have been

the greatest ballplayers,

but we were among 'em.

—MARTY MARION

Contents

ABOUT THE AUTHOR

Larry Moffi is a writer, editor and poet. He is the author of *The Conscience of the Game: Baseball's Commissioners from Landis to Selig* and co-author (with Jonathan Kronstadt) of *Crossing the Line: Black Major Leaguers, 1947–1959*. His *New and Selected Poems, 1980-2010* will be available next spring and he is currently working on an oral history of major league baseball in the 1960s.

Introduction to the Dover Edition

J ust before I started to write this introduction I had the opportunity to speak with Marty Marion who was then a few months shy of his 92nd birthday and still one of baseball's most exuberant ambassadors of good will. Marion was a shortstop with remarkable defensive skills who played on three World Series-winning teams. Our conversation reminded me that there are many people, myself included, who believe that Marion belongs in Baseball's Hall of Fame and that it is not too late, even now, for the Veterans Committee to put him there. As if he hadn't heard it a million times before, I told him so myself.

But there were many players in the late 1940s and 1950s who were genuine stars yet somehow fell short of enshrinement. These were the near greats—men whose statistics were lacking but whose influence on the game was significant. Larry Moffi's *This Side of Cooperstown* serves a grand purpose as an *ad hoc* shrine to those who didn't make it. In this book of magnificent stories told by the men who lived them, the likes of Mickey Mantle, Willie Mays and Hank Aaron have walk-on roles as these lesser stars are—under Moffi's direction—allowed to steal the show. Moffi's interviews with such luminaries as Carl Erskine, Del Crandall, Gene Woodling, Vic Powers, Virgil Trucks and others provide insight into the game and a time when baseball was in high bloom with more than 300 minor league teams in operation and relocated Major League franchises brought new fans to the ballpark. The West Coast was now in the game and expansion was in the air.

The era that Moffi describes in this book was a time of major change. It saw baseball go from day games to those played under the lights, from travel by train to jet aircraft, from Jim Crow to racial integration and from egalitarian iconoclasts, like Branch Rickey and Bill Veeck, to corporate men whose lives were devoted to the bottom line and the protection of the reserve clause. And radio, with its mostly southern broadcast voices, was beginning to give up some of its audience share to television.

Moffi traveled around the country to meet with these men and gain their trust just as the late Lawrence Ritter, who Moffi acknowledges as his inspiration, had done thirty years earlier with his pioneering work of baseball oral history *The Glory of Their Times—The Story of Baseball Told by the Men Who Played It.* This book is a worthy successor to Ritter and, for that matter, could sit on the same shelf as the works of Studs Terkel.

Moffi's skill as orchestrator of these voices is apparent in every one of these 17 interviews which, as they say, speak for themselves. He is a writer, editor and poet who brings his own experiences and sensibilities to this project. So please don't jump over Moffi's introduction in order to get to the players because you'd miss the story of the young Moffi growing up in the Italian section of Hartford, Connecticut listening to baseball on the radio in his father's hardware store, cheering for the big stars of the game. Even at an early age he is fascinated by "the others"—the journeymen and everyday players—the very guys who populate this wonderful book.

Then there is Moffi's moving postscript describing his poignant 1984 meeting with Roger Maris, some 23 years after he broke Babe Ruth's home run record. Maris was suffering from the cancer that took his life a year later, but was exceedingly kind to Moffi who ends the book by saying that this book is really for Maris and all the others no longer alive to tell their stories. Maris may be the ultimate example of the player who had a great influence on the game but never got elected to the Hall of Fame

As this was written Moffi was at work on the second volume of *This Side of Cooperstown* which will cover the baseball in the 1960s. Hot Dog!

Paul Dickson
September, 2009

Acknowledgments

To call this book a labor of love is an understatement. The only way I could have enjoyed it more would be to have actually taken the field with the players themselves forty years ago. This book is my version of a "fantasy camp."

I owe a lot of thanks to a number of people: Paul Zimmer, director of the University of Iowa Press, for supporting this book from the outset; Chuck Stevens, secretary/treasurer of the Association of Professional Ball Players of America, who provided me with addresses and phone numbers for all the players I contacted; Paul Mahon for keeping me on the right track; John Grady and his late wife, Nanse, who always understood why this book was important; Tim Boivin and Ed Winsten for taking time to read the manuscript; Ashley Paton for her careful indexing; Jennifer Eichel, patient travel agent; and Dennis Sampson and Louie Skipper, who provided necessary refuge when I needed it most.

And to the seventeen former players who shared so much of yourselves with me: I can never thank you enough.

Introduction

As infrequent as they were, some summer days while I was growing up I did *not* play baseball. Occasionally it rained. Also, every so often I would spend the day with my father in his store, the Acme Hardware and Supply Company, a deceptively important sounding name for a business that was doomed to die from the start, as were virtually all independently owned hardware stores of the 1950s.

In the Italian section of Hartford, Connecticut, along Franklin Avenue, there was a hardware store every five or six blocks; there must have been at least eight such stores along the two miles or so of Franklin Avenue between Main Street and Wethersfield Avenue. One of those sleepy stores belonged to my father.

They were the hardware stores that people like to wax romantic about nowadays, with an architecture unto themselves: bins of nails and bins of grass seed and dozens of smooth sliding wooden drawers with nuts and bolts and screws of every imaginable thread dimension and purpose. My father, like everyone else who tried to earn a living in the business, was something of an artisan. He owned one of the first-ever key-cutting machines. He replaced broken windows – people actually brought the entire sash into the store – using an L-shaped heating iron of electric coils that melted the old putty until the remains of glass popped from the frame. He threaded pipe using gobs of pipe-cutting grease and a heavy chain that secured the pipe to the worktable as he locked the vise-grip die into place, then spun it around until the fine threads were cut. Rarely – or so it seemed when I was there – did he ever do all three on a single day.

Eventually, all but one store went bankrupt, early victims of the mass merchandising that has become our addiction. There were plenty of days when my father made $10 or less in sales.

What has any of this to do with baseball in the 1950s?

Because business was always so slow, there was ample time for my father to lose himself in his real interest, baseball, specifically the Yankees, on the radio. Though back then there were also Dodgers games, Giants games, and Red Sox games broadcast daily. On any afternoon you could walk into the store and my father would be listening to one game or another, with Russ Hodges, Jim Woods, Vin Scully, Red Barber, Mel Allen, or Curt Gowdy calling the play-by-play.

When I think back to those days forty-odd years ago, I remember most the smells of Acme Hardware and Supply Company and the games we listened to on the DeWald radio tucked into its cubbyhole beneath the cash register, a virtual safe that took two people to lift and with color-coded keys for dollars and cents and a bell that actually rang. When I think about listening to those games with my father, the best part of my childhood comes to life again – the two of us hunched over the counter at the back of the store arguing over what Hank Bauer would do against Frank Lary with no outs, a runner on second, and the Yankees down 2–1 in the seventh.

You notice it wasn't Mickey Mantle batting against Bob Lemon. Or Ted Williams against Bob Feller. Or Mays against Spahn. Or Roy Campanella against Robin Roberts. It's not that I was biased against the superstars (I'm sure they weren't referred to as superstars yet). In fact, I rooted harder for them than for anyone else. Williams, Mays, Mantle . . . they represented the singular moments of ultimate glory or failure during the long season. But for some reason I've never been able to explain – and have never felt a need to – the game of baseball, the fabric of the game and its importance to me as I learned it from the radio and from arguing it with my father, consisted of all the *other* guys.

Who do I think of when I think of baseball in the 1950s? To name a handful, Carl Furillo, Sandy Amaros, Vic Power, Al Smith, Chico Carrasquel, Johnny Podres, Sal Maglie, Frank House, Bill Tuttle, Johnny Logan, Wally Post, Wally Moon, Ken Boyer, Gene Conley, Billy Bruton, Wes Covington, Frank Sullivan, Elston Howard, Bob Turley, Jim Lemon, Andy Pafko, Curt Simmons, Sam Jones, Gene Baker, Smokey Burgess, Brooks Lawrence, Whitey Lockman, and on and on – blue-collar, hard-working, reliable players who were there day after day after day. I'm not here to argue that the quality of baseball in the 1950s was better than during any other time. My *guess* is that it was, but I'm absolutely convinced that in no other decade of baseball were there as many consistently stand-up players as there were during that decade. I'd take any one of these guys, and all of them, on my team in any era.

Five years ago, when the idea came to me to travel around the country talking to baseball players of the 1950s who were *not* members of the Hall of Fame and who likely never *would* be enshrined in Cooperstown, I knew I was indulging myself, an attempt to revisit my childhood as best I could. (I've been to the site of the former Acme Hardware and Supply Company, and that doesn't work.) But I also suspected that if these players were as important to me as they seemed, then they were probably unequivocally important.

In case it's not already clear, the title of this book, *This Side of Cooperstown*, is meant to celebrate; it certainly does not mean to denigrate any of the former players included. No one was offended when I explained the criteria I had used in selecting players to talk to – that they were memorable in my mind as having made important contributions to the game, that they had played at least one year in the 1950s, and that they were not members of the Hall of Fame. What Roy Sievers told me undoubtedly holds true for the majority of most major leaguers in any era: "I didn't play ball to get into the Hall of Fame."

It should also be clear by now that this is not a book about the journeyman or the flash-in-the-pan. That the names of these players have not been inscribed on a Hall of Fame plaque does not diminish their accomplishments, which were considerable. Virgil Trucks was one of the best pitchers of the '40s *and* '50s. Vic Power was one of the greatest first basemen of all time. Frank Thomas was one of the most powerful sluggers ever. Del Crandall has to be rated as one of the top five or six catchers to play the game. And so on. Indeed, many of their achievements *are* historic and are chronicled in Cooperstown, of all places.

More than anything else, I chose the title *This Side of Cooperstown* because it evoked a vital landscape, specifically the baseball diamond, where the game belongs, where it has always lived for millions of kids and kids-turned-adults, and where its real value lies (as opposed to statistics and records and salaries and any other irrelevant shenanigans). Finally, I reasoned that although the greatness of their careers is undeniable, the stories of Williams, Mays, Spahn, and the twenty or so other Hall of Famers who played in the '50s are common lore to any baseball fan and are available as biographies or "as-told-to" autobiographies. The stories of those men who played beside the greats, however, remain untold, despite the fact that their names – Carl Erskine, Gene Woodling, Marty Marion, etc. – evoke some of the game's richest memories.

Was the game different back then? Of course it was: baseball has always been different "back then." And depending on who's talking, *different* is often synonymous with *better*. Concerning the '50s, I'd have to agree that the game *was* better than it has been ever since. And in light of the most recent players-versus-management nightmare, I'll trust the stories these players tell, my appreciation of their uncommon abilities, and my own quirky sentiments to support that argument.

I'm neither a historian nor a sociologist, but the history of the game and the significant cultural changes reflected in baseball during the 1950s are too obvious for anyone to miss. In the 1950s, the world of major league baseball was still somewhat simple. As there had been for five decades, there were eight teams to a league. Fields were grass and dirt. There were no divisions, no domed stadiums, and no free agency. A union was what fans in the bleachers paid their dues to, and ballplayers were tied inexorably to one club through the pernicious "reserve clause." There were no multiyear, million-dollar contracts. The schedule called for 154 games. There were day games during the week, "ladies' night" on Mondays, and doubleheaders on Sundays and holidays.

Uniforms were baggy. Gloves were small, and for fielding only. Batting helmets were optional. Pitchers pitched inside, and batters took that as a sign of respect. Relief pitchers walked from the bullpen. People smoked in the stands, and you could always afford – and purchase – tickets for decent seats.

But the changes that were taking place during the '50s were profound. Teams entered the decade traveling by train; they left in jets. Radio, the medium of choice since the late '30s, was suddenly second place to television, which relayed major league baseball coast to coast as the Saturday game of the week.

Salaries of a few select stars approached the $100,000 barrier. For the first time, there could be a slugger at every position. Whereas once the home run seemed the private domain of outfielders and first basemen, one glance around the infield told you there was a legitimate long-ball threat at every position – even at second base, where Bobby Doerr hit twenty-seven home runs for the 1950 Red Sox.

After decades in which no franchise had moved, Bill Veeck was squeezed out of St. Louis following the 1953 season, when the comic (or tragic) "Brownies" were moved to Baltimore and became the Orioles. That set in motion a chain of events that changed the game forever.

The Boston Braves relocated to Milwaukee. Connie Mack sold his interest in the Philadelphia Athletics, and the franchise promptly hopped to Kansas City in 1955. The born-again A's, though they played in the American League, acted more like KC's former American Association club, shuttling players back and forth to New York with the regularity of Pan American Airline's new Clipper service.

Of course, the biggest and most shocking moves came a few years later. The 1958 season began with the Dodgers no longer at home in chummy Ebbets Field but all aglitter in the cavernous Los Angeles Coliseum, home of Wally Moon's 250-foot "moon shot" home runs. The Brooklyn transplants would never be called – affectionately or otherwise – "dem Bums" again. And the Giants left baseball's oddest stadium, the Polo Grounds, on the banks of the Harlem River to take up residence in a minor league park called Seals Stadium, where they wondered when San Francisco's fog would lift and the winds die. Both the Dodgers' Walter O'Malley and the Giants' Horace Stoneham were mining California for all its gold. While it was always a foregone conclusion to the players that baseball was a business, now it was apparent even to fans – from Boston's Back Bay to sunny Chevez Ravine in LA – just how vast that business was.

As the United States entered the second half of the twentieth century, the social consequences of the Allies' victory in World War II slowly affected society, including that on the diamond. Eight of the ballplayers included here served during the war. As Carl Erskine explains: "The whole country had felt we had won victory in the war and we were getting back to the things of life that we wanted, wanted to enjoy, that the fear and all hardships of war were behind us. We had losses to think about. It was a pensive time right after the war. But there was a new momentum in industry and business in the country. Baseball had survived the war, and now it was rebuilding with new players. . . . And there was an acceleration of youth."

Competition for spots on major league rosters was never more intense. In the early 1950s, there were more than ten thousand ballplayers on more than 370 minor league teams in 52 leagues. Players, as Milt Bolling tells it, "slept with one eye open."

But the most pivotal effect of the end of the war on American life was in the area of civil rights for African Americans. Baseball, personified by Jackie Robinson and the Dodgers' Branch Rickey, led the way. Rickey's motivation involved both money and justice: some of the best players in the country were black, and fielding the best possible team was part and parcel to his business; but he was also a man of social conscience and responsibility who understood what was right and necessary. Robinson, a former three-sport star at UCLA, was an ex–army lieutenant who had challenged the racism of the military. Although there were players better than he in the old Negro leagues, Robinson was handpicked by Rickey for being temperamentally suited for the challenge and the inevitable resistance he would face from some white fans and players.

Robinson's breaking of the so-called color barrier with the Dodgers in 1947 is arguably the most influential event since the pitching rubber was moved from 50 feet 6 inches to 60 feet 6 inches in 1893. When the 1950 season opened, though, only five of the sixteen major league teams had integrated, and only twelve black ballplayers had made it to the majors. It would be another nine years before all sixteen teams were integrated, as the Boston Red Sox finally relented and brought up shortstop Pumpsie Green and pitcher Earl Wilson to the big club. By then, some of the greatest names in the history of the game – African Americans previously barred from "organized baseball" – were established stars: Ernie Banks, Willie Mays, Hank Aaron, and Frank Robinson, among others.

But the advance of integration of black ballplayers into the major leagues met with noticeable resistance off the field. Sleepy Florida spring training towns weren't the only ones that refused to change their Jim Crow ways and laws just because baseball had dismissed its unwritten rule. The Chase Hotel in St. Louis remained off-limits to black players until 1954, and even then hotel management refused to seat blacks in the dining room and barred them from using the swimming pool. In Kansas City, as Vic Power experienced, racial harassment was justified under the aegis of "routine investigation."

The stories that make up *This Side of Cooperstown* reflect all of the above.

.   .   .

I didn't write this book. It was spoken to me in stories – mostly about baseball in the 1950s, but going back as far as the '30s and extending into the '70s – told by ex–big leaguers, who in the telling opened up a great deal of what the game and their lives were about forty and fifty and sixty years ago.

For the most part, my questions were few and relatively inconsequential. Mostly I listened, in living rooms, dens, and kitchens between Pittsburgh and Southern California. Occasionally a player would come to my motel room, in St. Louis and in Paris, Texas. I met with Vic Power in a San Juan, Puerto Rico, shopping mall one day; the next day we drove into the mountains outside the capital to watch an American Legion baseball game, where the father of the local's third baseman played jazz riffs on his trumpet before the game, including a personal favorite, "I Love Paris."

Baseball abounds with stories, probably because baseball players are among the best storytellers ever. Why? My sense is that few people in the world enjoy what they do as much as ballplayers (at least those from the '50s). As Alex Grammas reasons, "If guys don't realize how lucky they are to be playing this game at the major league level then something's wrong with them." On the other hand, according to Marty Marion, even players in the '50s and '40s also "played for money . . . for a salary. We had a family to raise."

The stories contained in this book reflect much about the era in which these men played. They also reflect an uninhibited joy and love for the game. "You can't describe it to the average person," says Roy Sievers, but he and the other sixteen players are wonderful at doing just that.

These seventeen players, beginning with Marty Marion and ending with Tito Francona, provide a remarkable continuum of baseball history, from the era of Babe Ruth to the great Oakland A's teams of the 1970s – even to Michael Jordan – and from owners like Connie Mack, Branch Rickey, and Bill Veeck, to Bud Selig as a Ford dealer loaning cars to Milwaukee Braves players. There are also vivid reminders of landmarks of popular American culture: Ed Sullivan's "The Toast of the Town," a chorus line of Yankees dancing on "The Arthur Murray Show," and, of course, the Copacabana.

In all, I queried 119 former major league players, using the criteria previously described. Twenty-five said they were interested in sharing the stories of their lives with me. In a few instances, scheduling conflicts precluded our meeting; with others, I simply ran out of plane fare. This book could have been twice as long, easily. I went to Chicago twice to meet with Al Smith, who played with the Indians and White Sox, but an emergency and an illness forced postponement and, ultimately, cancellation of our getting together. I regret that very much.

But that's my only regret about this project. When I started out, I really didn't know what to expect, or what I would gather in the way of material, or how I would be received. By the time the interviews were completed, I had traveled more than thirty-two thousand miles, recorded more than one hundred hours of conversation and had been welcomed warmly wherever I went. Virgil Trucks even sent me a postcard from an Alaskan cruise he and his wife took two years ago.

What struck me most as I was transcribing the tapes was the mutual respect players genuinely felt for each other, for the legends as well as for the "merely great" players like Bill Mazeroski and Minnie Minoso. They also held tremendous admiration for unknowns, for the fans, and, refreshingly, even for some owners.

One thing I hadn't intended was to make this book a manual of how to play the game. Surprisingly, it is. Vic Power expounds on the aggressiveness required to play first base; Cal McLish on pitching to get ahead in the count; Del Crandall on what it takes to be a catcher; Alex Grammas on the quality of infields in the major leagues; and Dave Philley on "reading" pitchers. Best of all, there is nothing didactic to their instructions, which in their words actually sound possible. You could do a lot worse than learn how to play the game from these guys.

Of course, the nature of each player's stories reflects much about himself, his personality, and the particular way he sees the world. Virgil Trucks is as accomplished a storyteller as you'll ever want to meet. Andy Carey is a master of anecdote. Milt Bolling is brilliant in his insight. There is also an astute appreciation of players of today and how the game has changed (see, especially, what Carl Erskine says and also Dave Philley; I won't spoil those moments for you here).

■   ■   ■

Anyone who undertakes an oral history of baseball in any form must acknowledge what Lawrence Ritter accomplished thirty years ago with his innovative *The Glory of Their Times*. I kept Ritter's methods in mind as I edited the transcriptions of these interviews; namely, I omitted my own questions and comments as well as inevitable repetitions and irrelevant asides. For the most part, however, my editing was slight and was directed to maintain continuity and retain the energy and uniqueness of each individual speaking voice. What I hoped to accomplish was to put the reader in the chairs where I sat, in the position of hearing these stories.

Occasionally a player's memory failed, and I changed or added a name or corrected a score. However, there are moments of luxurious hyperbole that I chose *not* to correct to retain the speaker's sense of purpose and overall effect. I will leave it up to you, the "listener," to go with the flow or to turn to your reference books.

In terms of typographical notations, there are two things to keep in mind. I have used ellipsis points – . . . – to signify a pause in the speaking voice as opposed to omission of text. The use of italics, other than in titles, indicates the speaker's emphasis on a particular word or phrase.

Finally, while Ritter's classic will always be the prototype for any oral history of baseball, I feel compelled to acknowledge a distinction between the decades in which his work and this one were compiled. In the thirty years since Lawrence Ritter completed his trek across America, the fascination with baseball, its collectibles, and memorabilia has mutated from an innocent hobby to an industry. That any former player in the mid-1990s would grant six hours of interviews to a complete stranger is nothing less than remarkable to me. I understand the reluctance of some players to participate, and I wrote to each who declined making that clear. I feel very fortunate to have spent as much enjoyable time with so many enjoyable people.

This, then, is a book, as you will soon hear, about what is probably right with baseball in any era, even our current one, which seems so troubled.

Marty Marion

June 2, 1993, St. Louis, Missouri

Marty Marion was the St. Louis Cardinals' regular shortstop from 1940 to 1950. In 1952 and 1953 he was the player-manager of the St. Louis Browns. He also managed the Cardinals in 1951 and the Chicago White Sox from 1954 to 1956. Named the National League's Most Valuable Player in 1944, Marion had a .263 lifetime batting average and played on four Cardinals pennant-winning teams and on three World Championship clubs.

Let me tell you a story. When I got out of high school, my brother Johnny was playing with the Chattanooga Lookouts. Cal Griffith – he was old Clark Griffith's son – was the general manager up there. Anyway, my brother told me to come up there and he'd get me a job. So I went up there with him.

That's the Southern League. Pretty good league, Southern League, back in those days. Anyway, they signed me to a contract. I think they gave me a thousand dollars or something to sign a contract. We stayed there for about a week. And then the team had to go on the road. Well, when they were on the road I went back home to Atlanta, Georgia, where my girlfriend – who's my wife, now – was. I was lonesome. We were high school sweethearts. Been married fifty-five years. Wow! I been married to that gal all my *life*.

Anyway, I wasn't gonna stay there in Chattanooga, you know. Nobody told me. But when the team came back to town in a week, I went back to Chattanooga. Well, I went in the office and they said, "Hey, you were supposed to stay here and work out on the diamond here."

And I said, "Nobody told me."

So they gave me my pink slip. I only lasted a week. After I became famous I used to see old Cal. I says, "Cal . . ."

And he says, "I could kill myself."

.   .   .

I went back to Atlanta, Georgia, and they were having a tryout camp – the Cardinals – in Rome, Georgia, which is about ninety miles north of Atlanta, up toward Chattanooga. So this kind of a bird-dog scout there in Atlanta . . . great big old fat guy . . . he was getting a lot of the kids together.

"Let's go up to the camp," he says.

So we went up to the camp, and I played two innings of baseball, and the Cardinals called me and a kid named Johnny Echols over and said, "Hey, how would you kids like to make a trip to St. Louis?"

"Fine!"

So they invited me and Johnny.

He was a good third baseman for a rival high school, Boys' High, in Atlanta. A good-lookin' kid. Hell, the whole time we was up there, Mr. Rickey wasn't interested in me, he was interested in Echols. Echols was a good-looking ballplayer, kind of a polished kid.

So we came to St. Louis in '35. Tail end of '35. Hell, I was gettin' to be an old-timer by then. I'd already signed a contract and been released. And coming to St. Louis and try out.

Well, when Johnny and myself got on the train to come up here –
they paid our expenses, naturally; we didn't have any money – we said
that we're not gonna sign unless both of us sign. A little pact.

The Cardinals were playing the Cubs . . . that series when the Cubs
won twenty-one straight games in '35. And Phil Cavarretta had just hit
a home run the day before we got here, beat Paul Dean, I think, 1–0.

Anyway, we got to work out on the field. Sportsman's Park, which is
no longer there. And Mr. Rickey brought us in the office and talked to
us. And I'd just sit in the corner and listen to them, you know, and
finally they made us these kinds of offers.

"Want to play with the Cardinals?"

"No, I don't think so."

And we went back to Atlanta. And that winter, in February, Frank
Rickey – Mr. Branch Rickey's brother, a scout – he came down, driving
a big old convertible Buick. I remember that car like yesterday. Little
old short fellow. Fat kind of guy. Nice talker. Good man. Talked like his
brother Branch. Branch used to live right next door. Right before he
died, he moved right next door.

So he came down and he talked to us, and he talked to us, and . . .
Stayed about two or three days. And by that time, I was getting pretty
smart.

And I told Johnny, I says, "Johnny, I tell you what, let's take a four-
year contract." And this was before the days they ever had multiyear
contracts, you know.

I think they gave us $500 to sign. Something like that. Wasn't much.
I had it written down on a piece of paper – Johnny didn't have *nothin'*.
They'd pay us $250 a month for the first year, no matter where we
played; $500 a month for the second year, no matter where we played.
The third year we'd make $3,000 – that's the way it was written on the
piece of paper – no matter where we played. And the fourth year we'd
make $5,000.

So the first year I played at Huntington, West Virginia. In 1936. And
I was just a skinny little old kid. And I remember the newspaperman,
his name is Duke Rigsly. Huntington, West Virginia. Nicest man. And
I remember him writing an article: "Marty Marion looked like a girl
wearing her first pair of high-heeled slippers." But by the time the year
was over he said I was the best prospect in the league. So I really did
change, I really did come along.

The next year they sent me to Rochester. And I stayed three years in
Rochester. So my fourth year in Rochester, I was making $5,000. Hell,
that was good money for those guys. Way higher than anybody else.

I was in the Cardinal camp, I guess it was '39. I hadn't even made the team yet, the Cardinals. Anyway, one night at the Detroit Hotel in St. Petersburg, I walk in the room and who's sitting on the bed but old Johnny Echols, my friend from Atlanta, Georgia.

I said, "Johnny, what're you doing here?"

He said, "Well, the Cardinals released me."

I said, "They can't release you, you've got a four-year contract."

So, Echols had to meet with Mr. Rickey, and I went with him.

I said, "Mr. Rickey, you can't release us. We've got four-year contracts."

He said, "I don't know of any four-year contracts."

We said, "Well, that's what they promised us when they signed us."

And he said, "You know what? I can release Johnny Mize, Dizzy Dean, Ducky Medwick, anybody I want to. What have you got that we have to play you?"

I said, "Well, that's what you promised us."

So, lo and behold, we got a call from Mr. Landis, the commissioner of baseball. He was over in Clearwater. He always stayed over in Clearwater, that big old wooden hotel. Bel Air . . . something like that. He always stayed there. He called me and Johnny over there.

He was sitting on the front porch, and he says, "Tell me your story, boys."

So we just told him. He says, "You have any proof?"

I says, "I have this little piece of paper. That's all I got."

And he said, "Well, that's fine."

Well, he called Mr. Rickey, and he says, "Pay. You have to pay Mr. Echols."

He had it in for Mr. Rickey. Of course, I didn't know at that time. He didn't like the way Mr. Rickey was running all these clubs. He owned the whole Nebraska State League at one time.

■ ■ ■

Slats. Skinny. Burt Shotten gave me that nickname. See, when I joined the Cardinals in spring training, Mr. Shotten was the manager in Columbus, Ohio. And he took me back to Columbus.

I had a contract to go to Huntington, but Huntington didn't start for another month after spring training broke up. But Mr. Shotten liked me and he took me to Columbus with him.

I pitched batting practice for him, fooled around. I didn't play, I just fooled around for a month until my league opened. Then he sent me down there. But *he* called me Slats.

There was a comic strip back in those days, Slats and Abner, something like that. And Slats was the skinny guy. And also, Slats is like a board. I get mail all the time calling me Slats. Had one guy send me four baseballs the other day. "Marty, will you please sign, Marty 'Slats' Marion?"

I thought, "You must be out of your mind. Marty Marion's all you're getting."

I tell you, I never played shortstop in my life until I went to spring training, I think it was in '36. They had a tryout camp over in Bartow, where all the rookies came to Florida before all the others started.

In high school I played third base, second base. I never played shortstop. Hell, there was about fifteen third basemen there. Nobody was playing shortstop, so I just went over to shortstop and I said, "Hell, I'll play right here."

And I started fielding ground balls, and I guess they liked it, you know. And then that's all I played. That's how I got to be a shortstop. That easy.

Talking about Mr. Rickey and how smart he was . . . He always wanted to change guys' positions, and one time he came to me when he was still here with the Cardinals.

He says, "Marty, I'd like for you to play second base."

I says, "Why?"

"So you'll be more versatile to the team. You can play all positions."

I said, "Well, Mr. Rickey, I ain't gonna play second base. I'm gonna play shortstop. I'm a shortstop and I know how to play shortstop and I ain't gonna do it."

Surprised him!

■   ■   ■

Managing the Browns was quite an experience. It was tough, coming over from the Cardinals and all, but Bill Veeck paid me well. He paid me $10,000 more than I made with the Cardinals being a star. He didn't believe in underpaying you, if he could afford it. You got a pretty good contract playing with Bill.

I would say that Bill lived a good life. Drank that damn beer. Shirt open. My life is richer from knowing him, I'll tell you that. But it wasn't much fun trying to win with the Browns.

He said, "Marty, this is not baseball, this is survival."

We didn't even have any balls for batting practice the last two weeks of the season. Just had enough balls to play the game. Talk about poor teams!

Mr. Veeck was a showman. Wonderful person. When he was here in St. Louis, he was under very tough situations. He didn't have his mind on trying to get a winning ballclub. He didn't have any money. He wouldn't even talk to me when he was getting ready to sell a player.

He'd say, "Marty, it ain't your decision. It ain't about the ballclub. It's about us surviving."

Anyway, he was a great guy. He called me one time, we were in San Bernadino, California. I was the manager.

He says, "Marty, this is a tough day. Anheuser Busch just bought the Cardinals ballclub from Fred Saigh. You know what that means: we can't buck Anheuser Busch."

So I knew we was gone. That whole year, '53, it was just surviving. That was all. He had an apartment in Sportsman's Park. Nice apartment. He was a very *common* man. Good mind, always thinking. Publicity, you know. He knew baseball, too.

Veeck *loved* Satchel Paige. Bob "Sugar" Cain came to me one time and he says, "Marty, why do you let Satchel Paige do all these things and you won't let us do it? Satchel don't have to run, Satchel don't have to do this, Satchel don't have to do that . . ."

I said, "Well, Sugar, I tell you what, when you get to be sixty years old you can do that."

I fined Satchel one time $5,000. He almost got us killed.

It was about the tail end of the season and we were on our way to Boston. We had scheduled an exhibition game in Providence, Rhode Island, trying to pick up some extra money.

It was a night game, and I didn't know anything about what the Browns management had done. Anyway, they publicized that Paige was gonna pitch. Everybody in town knew that Satchel Paige was gonna pitch. That's all that people came out to see. Well, I didn't even know anything about it myself.

So, right before the game started all the newspapermen gathered around me – had a pretty good crowd – and they said, "When is Paige gonna pitch?"

I said, "Well, Paige isn't even here. I can't find him."

They said, "You promised to pitch him!"

I said, "I didn't promise to pitch him. Somebody else did, but I didn't. He *is* supposed to be here, though."

They said, "Well, where is he?"

I said, "You find him, I'll pitch him."

Well, anyway, some of the team guys said that he didn't even get off the train. He went on to Boston. Well, the fans were mad. Who wanted to see the *Browns* play? But Satch was different. Satch was a big draw.

Well, our traveling secretary came down and he said, "They're really mad!"

I said, "Well, you get the money and we'll go to the train."

And, boy, once that game was over we got out of there. We spent the night on the sleeper and got into Boston next morning. I walk into the Kenmore Hotel and who's sitting in the lobby but old Satchel.

I said, "Satchel, you almost got us lynched last night. That'll cost you $5,000."

"What'd I do wrong?" he wanted to know.

Well, I told him what happened.

"Grrrr, I'm sorry."

But Veeck didn't take the money. No way! He loved Satchel. Matter of fact, when I was with Chicago and we were about to win the damn pennant and Dick Donovan came up with appendicitis, Veeck called me up on the phone and said, "Marty, you want to win the pennant, sign Satchel."

I said, "Bill, I wouldn't sign Satchel Paige if you *gave* him to me. He would disrupt the whole team."

See, you cannot have a player like Satchel on the team with that kind of name and let him do one way and the team do another way. That's the only reason, though; Satchel could still pitch. But you cannot have a divided team and win. You've got to have everybody thinking the same way.

■　■　■

With the Cardinals, we had a good team. We didn't know how to lose. The reason Billy Southworth was a good manager was that he didn't bother anybody. He let them play. One time he took me out. I think we were winning by about ten runs. This was late when Billy was here and we were winning the pennant, walkin' away with it. He took me out for a pinch hitter. I remember that like it was yesterday.

I came back to the bench and I says, "If he can pinch-hit for me, Southworth, he can field for me."

I stormed into the clubhouse. He came into the clubhouse after the game was over and he put his arm around me and all this kind of stuff. *Buttered* me up. Oh, he was good at that. And that's why we won. Billy didn't want you mad at him.

He never took me out for a pinch hitter again.

Not that I was so great, but I was great enough to be among guys who were great and made a good team. You don't have to have a Musial on a team to win a pennant, or a Williams. You've got to have a lot of guys around him.

You take any great star: they don't win a pennant by themselves. You have to have all the qualities, and once you have that you've got to have the desire to win.

You know, you talk about ballplayers . . . We used to have a saying: You can always tell the good guys.

Ballplayers have little cliques on the team. And you'd say, "That son of a bitch. He wouldn't even speak to you when he was hittin' .300. Now he's hittin' .250, he's a great *guy*." We used to laugh about that all the time.

We used to say, "Well, you're gonna meet the same guy up and down, you better be nice to all of us."

It *is* so funny though. You could take some guy who was becoming a star—you know, an old country boy—you could see him change. Gettin' like he'd *met* somebody. Funny thing, you could always tell how well he was going by how he treated everybody. But you have to live with 'em every day, to know 'em.

I'll tell you what, don't *ever* trade for a guy you don't know about. And you never know a guy unless he's on your team. You think, you know, "That DiMaggio, he looks like a pretty good ballplayer. . . ." But he comes over to your team and he may be a troublemaker, he may not even fit in.

■　■　■

Desire? I didn't know I had it. But I was the kind of a player that, even though I was skinny and all, I just had a feel for the game. I just could *tell* when the team was going good. That you were going to win. Life is better when you win. Especially on a ballclub. Things roll better. You get more meal money. Everything was that much better.

Like the '42 team. Hell, I didn't think anybody could beat us. I don't care who they were. They start talking about these great teams in the history of baseball? Ain't nobody better than we were. *Guarantee* ya! All you had to do was put us on the same field.

Why, when they said the Yankees were coming to town in '42? You know, they had a great ballclub, helluva ballclub. Well, they didn't have a chance. That's the way we *felt*. And even though we were behind, always in the seventh inning of the game, we always thought we were going to win. We won a lot of games in the late innings. A team that don't quit and keeps battling.

Talent. You know everybody talks about he's got this and he's got that. Well, you don't win without talent. Don't tell me you can get a bunch of honkey donkeys.

Old Pepper Martin, I remember the time in spring training, our manager Ray Blades was having two workouts a day in spring training. Blades was about to kill us. He was a taskmaster.

We had a meeting one day, and Pepper got up and said, "Mr. Blades, I don't know why you work us so hard. You can't take an old mule and let him in the Kentucky Derby, I don't care how good he is."

That was Blades's philosophy. Work, work, work, work, and you'd be a better ballplayer. Well, that ain't quite true. You've got to have some God-given talent to be a good ballplayer.

Let me tell you something about managing. All this bull about managing. You give me the players, I'll win my share. You give *you* the players, *you'll* win your share. The hardest thing about managing is keepin' 'em happy.

Luis Aparicio. He had a good year in Memphis in 1955. I was the manager of the White Sox, and I wasn't that happy with Chico Carrasquel, who played shortstop. And they said this kid Aparicio was pretty good. So that winter we traded Chico to Cleveland.

So I took a chance on this kid.

I took him to Tampa and spring training. I worked pretty hard with him all during spring training. He had the feel. He had the good arm, the good hands. He could scoot. But he didn't know much about playing shortstop. I taught him how to set his foot and throw. He became very good at it.

I'll never forget, we opened up the season in Kansas City, and Luis was my shortstop. Well, I think I played him one or two games – I didn't play him very much – he just looked scared to death.

I said, "Luis, I'm putting you on the bench. I want you to sit next to me, and you just watch it for a couple of days. I'll get you back in there."

He was just in over his head. He didn't feel right. Then I put him back in there after two or three games, and he played there the rest of his life.

Just had to get that little confidence. That's all he needed. He could have beat his brains out for two or three months out there before he found himself. Sitting on the bench helps.

He was a great shortstop. When he finished up he was about as good as any of them.

Billy Pierce. You pitch him twice a week and he couldn't get anybody out. You pitch him once a week, he couldn't get beat.

One time, I was pitching him first game of a Sunday doubleheader, and boy we packed 'em in. We must've had 55,000 people in Comiskey Park. About the seventh inning, the Yankees had the bases loaded and we were ahead by a run, and I went out to take Billy out. You never heard such a booing.

Anyway, Hank Bauer was the next hitter, and Hank was a very good hitter against left-handers, so I wasn't gonna let Billy pitch to Hank with the bases loaded and him getting tired. Brought old Dixie Howell in. He was a right-handed sinker-ball pitcher, and he pitched to Bauer and Bauer hit a shot right at Minoso. If it'd been one way or another, it would've cleared the bases, but it was right at Minoso, about the hardest hit line drive I ever saw. Then we coasted through the next two innings and we beat the Yankees—and the next game, too. We beat them four straight!

And all the newspapermen came in the clubhouse after the game saying, "You got more guts. . . . I'd've *never* taken Billy Pierce out."

I said, "That's why you're not the manager."

That's why baseball's so famous, everybody loves to manage a baseball club. I had one guy—never met the guy in my life—had nice handwriting. Every day I walked in that ballpark, there'd be a letter from him. Big thick letter. I read the first one. The rest of them? I didn't ever open another.

He would rant and rage and didn't know a bit of what he was talking about. But every day I'd get a letter. See, that made him happy, somewhere.

Stengel? The first year I was with the White Sox, Casey selected me to be one of the coaches on the All-Star team. 'Cause he says, "Old Marty, he knows those National Leaguers."

We played in Cleveland that day. He has the pregame meeting and he says, "Here, Marty, here's the scorecard, you take care of it." And he walked out, didn't have anything to do with it. He said, "You talk to 'em about it."

Now, Whitey Ford was starting, and I said, "Granny Hamner is a good high-ball hitter."

Well, I'm sitting out on the dugout steps looking out and Whitey's throwing Hamner a high ball. I said, "Whitey, get the ball down."

But Whitey strikes him out on three high fastballs. Boom, right by him. And Whitey just shook his head, "I was trying to pitch low, but the ball just got high."

. . .

We played for money. We played for a salary. We had a family to raise. But we had this old Brownies party the other night and one fella got up and said, "We must have played for the love of the game because we sure didn't make any money."

When I came up, Mr. Breaden owned the Cardinals, and that was his livelihood. He had owned an old Studebaker franchise here in town. They told me that after he died he didn't have any money. Baseball was his living.

I was watching a movie today, old Robert Mitchum was playing in it. Kind of a slap-silly thing. He was playing an ex-marshal, you know. They fired him as a marshal and he wasn't even a part of the town anymore. He wasn't respected anymore because he wasn't what he was. Same with a ballplayer. You go down to the ballpark and if you go into the clubhouse and say, "Hi boys!" they say, "Who's that old fossil?"

Me and nine other guys used to run the Stadium Club restaurant at the ballpark for eighteen years. Saw a lot of baseball. Can you believe it? All those years, saw a lot of baseball. So when somebody says, "You mean you don't go to the ballgame? You get in _free!_" They're surprised.

I don't even ask 'em for a ticket. You're really not welcome. . . . It's hard to say you're not welcome – you're excess baggage to the present club. You don't feel like you're part of the club.

See, I'm a famous Cardinal, right? You would think they'd like to see me once in a while. Nahh, no way.

I've been in baseball at least twenty-seven years. I didn't ever save anything. The only thing that I have in my whole possession – in 1944 I won the Most Valuable Player of the National League. And that award is the only thing. I don't have any uniforms, I don't have any gloves, I don't have any balls, I don't have any shoes. I wished I'd've saved those things. They're worth a lot of money. Dumb, dumb me. But it wasn't worth a nickel back in my day.

The game is not tough. Baseball is not a tough game to play. It's an easy game to play. You don't have to be in great physical condition, you don't have to be a superstar. It's just a nice game, if you can play it. But you gotta think.

When I say _think_, that's the wrong word. Because Frankie Frisch told me one time when he was managing and I was in the minor leagues and with the Cardinals in spring training.

Frankie heard some player say, "I think . . ."

And Frankie said, "Stop right there. That's your first mistake. Don't think. I'll do the thinking."

Instinct. Instinct is the great thing. Where to get the ball, where to throw the ball. You have all these plays in front of you, and you have to know exactly what that guy is gonna do before he does it. Instinct. You don't teach instinct.

Now, practice helps improve your instinct. Some guys can play ball and some guys can't. We had so many good players when I first came out they could've sent me back to Rochester and brought somebody up that's just as good as me.

I think Dizzy Dean made the best statement in the world. Dizzy says, "I don't know, I might not have been the greatest pitcher, but I was among 'em."

And that's the way we feel. We might not have been the greatest ballplayers, but we were among 'em.

Virgil Trucks

May 26–27, 1994, Birmingham, Alabama

Virgil Trucks pitched in the American League from 1941 to 1958, excluding military service in 1944 and all but one game of 1945. In addition to spending twelve years with the Detroit Tigers, Trucks pitched for the St. Louis Browns, the White Sox, the Kansas City Athletics, and the Yankees. He won 177 major league games, lost 135, and compiled a 3.39 lifetime earned run average. A member of Detroit's 1945 World Championship club, Trucks won game 2 of the '45 Series. In 1952 he pitched two 1–0 no-hitters.

I've always loved baseball since I was knee-high to a duck. Baseball has always been in my blood. I used to watch my father play when I was seven, eight years old. And being the type of father he was – iron hand – he'd spank my fanny and send me home, because I had no business being on the field. But I'd always linger somewhere where I could watch.

I used to stuff cotton into his baseball shoes and walk around the house with them. I felt like a ballplayer myself, though I was only eight years old. I'd just mimic him in every way I could.

I played on the same sandlot team with my father. He pitched and I played the outfield. There were three other brothers I had, and we all played on the same team. That was on the sandlots of Birmingham.

Most of the time we played pretty good ball. It was a good brand of sandlot ball. When I was coming up, Birmingham, Pittsburgh, and Detroit were probably three of the greatest cities in the world for sandlot ball. A lot of guys at that time could have gone on to play pro ball in the minor leagues, but they never left home. They couldn't stand being away from home, and some of them were married and their wives said, "Either you stay home or you stay out."

My parents never saw me play in the major leagues. I offered to pay their transportation, but I don't think my father ever went above the Mason-Dixon line. Not to my knowledge. He just didn't want to go that far just to see a ballgame. I don't think he would have gone if he was pitching.

But he loved baseball, no doubt about that. He pitched till he was sixty-three years old, right here in the sandlots of Birmingham. He pitched that long.

.   .   .

A guy by the name of Eddie Goosetree, who was a scout for the Detroit Tigers, signed me. You know, I was always a Tiger fan ever since I can remember. I don't know why, I'd never been above the Mason-Dixon line myself. But Detroit was my team: Charlie Gehringer, Mickey Cochrane, Hank Greenberg, and Rudy York, who's a native Alabamian. Guys like that. I just seemed to like the type. In fact, that's why that Tigers tatoo is on my arm. I did that when I was sixteen years old, before I got into the major leagues: crossed bats, balls, and the word *Tigers*. So it's strange that I would wind up with the Tigers. I almost didn't.

Goosetree signed me off the sandlots of Birmingham. At that time I was just partially pitching, mostly playing infield and outfield. Goosetree signed me for a $100 bonus, as an outfielder. My dad had to sign the contract; we both signed it. This is in 1937. I was working for Stockham Pipe Company here in Birmingham and playing on their ball-club. But we had to work eight hours a day, five days a week. I was making $20 a week.

Anyway, he signed me. But they didn't want to send my contract in that year – I found this out later – and this was the first part of the season, sandlot had just started. He wanted to keep it until the end of the season, then afterwards turn in the contract, because they didn't have any place they could send me.

After that signing, it was May 15 or something, and I'm working and a guy by the name of Bruner Nix from Jasper, Alabama, was managing a semipro team up in the Valley League. He was a catcher. They had Shawmutt, Riverview, Fairfax. So he'd heard about me being able to throw hard, and he was gonna make me a pitcher. And he *did* make a pitcher out of me.

So he come down, and he heard that I was working at Stockham and he got hold of me, somehow, at ten o'clock in the morning. They had me come out from the shop and had me meet him in the office. He told me what his plans were: "We only play three games a week, it's semipro ball, but we can pay you."

I said, "What kind of pay?"

"Twenty-five dollars a week and free room and board."

Well, I wanted to play ball. At Stockham you only played on the weekends.

He said, "I can give you that and would love to have you come join my ballclub."

I said, "Well, I owe them some courtesy of talking to them before making a decision." But I thought it was great.

I still owed Stockham something, because they *did* give me a job, and you needed a job in those years. I went to the manager and I told him that I had been given an offer to go play semipro ball. I told him what I was offered and said, "If you make the same agreement – give me $5 more a week – I won't go."

"I can't give you any more money," he said. "That's all I'm gonna give you, that's all you're gonna get."

So I said, "Bye!"

It was the greatest move I could have made. I went out and said, "Okay, Bruner, I'm ready. Give me a chance to go to the house and get my clothes." I was married at the time.

I got my clothes and I went with him. I didn't have a car. We go up

VIRGIL
TRUCKS

16

to Shawmutt and he makes me a pitcher right away. And because he was a catcher, he had some experience. That season I won twelve and lost one, had a terrific year.

Now Andalusia came into play – that's Class D ball, down in south Alabama. They had had a split season – they won the first half and Union Springs had won the second half. So now they've got to have a playoff to see which one wins the championship.

My season is over. I'm back home here in Birmingham, I've got no job, I don't know what I'm going to do. Anyway, I get a call from Andalusia, a Dr. Gresham. I'll never forget it. He was one of the owners. In those days, the local people owned the ballclubs, even double-A and A ball.

Dr. Gresham said, "How would you like to come down and play in the playoff with us?" Well, I didn't know how this worked. But in those years, they could get a green rookie who had never played any pro ball – no matter what position he played. They could get two on each club and let them be eligible for that playoff.

He says, "We'll give you $35 a game, and even if you don't pitch a game we'll give you $35 for the series. You're gonna get paid."

Why wouldn't I take it? I had nothing else to do. I said, "It sounds okay to me, Doctor."

He says, "I tell you what, I'm gonna be in Montgomery, tomorrow. Meet me there."

So I took a bus and met him at the Travis Jackson Hotel, and he drove me back to Andalusia. Comes the opening day I pitch the opening game. Won 5–0.

Now, it gets to the point where it goes down to the last game, and I pitch that one and I win it 3–0.

They give us this outing at Fort Walton Beach, Florida. At that time Fort Walton Beach wasn't anything but some little cottages along the beach there, but they took the ballclub down. So, there's about ten businessmen that owned the ballclub. Dr. Gresham was one of them. Mr. Henderson was the president.

We're down there and there's nothing really to do but walk along the beach or go swimming. There was no activity at Fort Walton Beach in 1938, I'll tell you that right now. I could have bought the whole beach for probably $2,000, but I didn't have two cents.

I went into one of the bigger cottages where the owners were staying. There were about five of them sitting around playing poker. I had never seen a poker game before. Every once in a while a chip would fall off on the floor. I'd never seen a chip before. I knew *nothing* about poker.

So it'd fall off on the floor and I'd just pick it up and they'd say, "Ah, stick it in your pocket." So about two hours later they break up the game, and I've got two bulging pockets of chips.

They started to laugh and said, "Take them over to that guy."

"That guy" was the banker. I found out all this later, you know – I didn't know what a banker or anything else was. So I take them over to the banker and I say, "Here's the chips they told me to give you." So I laid them all up there and I start to walk away.

He says, "*Wait* a minute, get your money."

I say, "What money?" thinking they're gonna pay me for the two games.

He said, "You've got some money coming."

I said, "Okay" and he wheeled off and he gave me $75 or $85. I took the money and left. So now the party's over and we all drove back to Andalusia. And one of them – it might have been Dr. Gresham – said, "How 'bout coming by our office about noon?"

I said, "Dr. Gresham, I've got to catch a bus."

So he said, "Okay, well come by around ten o'clock and we'll give you your money, pay you for your games." I was bug-eyed. I thought they'd already paid me from that money they were paying me from those poker chips.

I met them at ten the next morning. They're all sitting around there and the first thing he said was, "Here's a check for $70 for the two games. And then the bus fare; we're gonna just round it off to $100." Well, bus fare was only about $10.

Then they said, "How would you like to sign with us? We'll give you $500 to sign with us."

I'm thinking, $500? I've already signed with Detroit. That didn't matter to me, I see $500. So they talked me into it and I signed a contract with them. And they give me that. I've got over $700 in my pocket, and that's gonna take care of me for about two years as far as I can figure it. I didn't care what happened to Detroit. I loved baseball and all I wanted to do was play.

Anyway, I get back home and get through the winter. I'm surviving well, didn't have a job or anything. So it comes January when the contracts start coming out, I get one from Andalusia and I get one from Beaumont in the Texas League, which is the Detroit farm club. Oh, man, I don't know what to do now. The Andalusia contract was for $75 a month. That's all they could pay you; that was the league rule in those years. And I get one from Detroit to report to Beaumont for $200 a month.

I'm thinking, Gee, what do I do. They're both gonna come after me for the money, both of them for the two contracts, and I can't pay them and they may put me in jail. I was just a kid, I didn't know anything. Anyway, I sent them both back with a message: "It's not enough money." And they sent them back to me.

This happened a couple of times, from both of them. So I called up Fob James – not the governor, his father – who was the manager of the Linett ballclub. I'd met him when I was playing for Shawmutt. I said, "Could you use another ballplayer this summer?"

He said, "Definitely you."

Same kind of situation and same type of pay I had the year before but with a different ballclub. So I went up there. I'm still getting the contracts and I'm still sending them back. I'm working out and I'm ready to go, the season is about ready to open.

Paul Richards comes through, managing the Atlanta Crackers at the time, and I pitched against them and shut them out for six innings. I'd never pitched against a pro ballclub above Class D.

When the game was over, I ran into Paul. He'd had a flat tire in the car he was driving. They were fixing the flat and he said to me, "Hey, you belong to anybody?"

I said, "I think I belong to Andalusia."

He said, "Well, I'm gonna get in touch with them and see if I can get you from them."

Meanwhile, I get the contracts back again and I return them unsigned.

So I decided to go to Fob James and confess, see what I could do about this. I was worried! He said, "That's no problem."

I said, "Which club do I belong to? I don't know which club to sign a contract with."

He said, "Come back and see me in about an hour, and I'll let you know which club you belong to."

So, within an hour I went back and he said, "Your contract is the property of Andalusia."

I said, "Fob, how can that be? I signed a contract with Detroit first."

He said, "Well, they pigeonholed your contract and they kept it, and the Andalusia contract got in before theirs did."

So now Andalusia is gonna open in two days. Yam Yaryan, who was the catcher and manager for Andalusia, called me on the phone and says, "We want you down here."

I said, "Yam, you're not giving me enough money. You're only offering me $75 a month, that's not enough money."

He said, "Well, we can't pay you any more, it's in the rules. I'll tell you what I'll do: We'll give the $75 in the contract and we'll pay you $50 a month under the table, so that's $125."

I said okay.

He wanted me to pitch the opening day and he drove up to get me. On the way to Andalusia the car broke down, and we didn't get to the ballpark until about an hour before the game. We went in and put our uniforms on, and I shut them out 3–0 on opening day.

But on that day, Detroit sent Eddie Goosetree, the same scout that signed me to that first contract, down there to watch me, and if he didn't sign me he was gonna lose his job. They offered the Andalusia ballclub $10,000 for my contract. Now that was unheard of in those years. Opening day, 1938 in Andalusia, he bought the contract back from Andalusia for $10,000, with the stipulation that I stay at Andalusia the rest of the year. And that's how Detroit got me back.

So I stayed there the rest of the year. Had a terrific year, struck out 450 hitters. Struck out 420 in the regular season and 30 in the playoffs, 15 in each game. Won twenty-six and lost six. Pitched two no-hitters that year. I mean I just had one *tremendous* year. Of course the last guy to strike over 400 men – 412 – was Old Hoss Radbourn in the late 1800s. So I broke his record. He was in the major leagues but then they pitched from 50 feet 6 inches, not 60 feet 6 inches.

The next year they sent me to Beaumont. Stayed there two years, and I went to Buffalo the last year. I went to spring training with Detroit in '41. They sent me out to Buffalo on the last day they had a cut. They brought me back at the end of the season and I stayed from then on.

I went back to Andalusia two years after I finished playing ball. They wanted me to come back, the old guys that were still there. They gave me a helluva dinner and everything. They gave me the scorebook from the year I broke the strikeout record. While I was there for the dinner, the president of the club told me, "You know, we didn't want to sell you, but we owed $10,000 for our lights, and you paid for our lights."

．　．　．

The first few years I was with Detroit I stayed in the Detroit Leyland Hotel. Most of the ballplayers stayed there. They gave us a rate, I think $2.50 a day. Nice big room. Each one of us had an individual room, because we paid for it, the ballclub didn't. From the Leyland to the ballpark it was only six or eight blocks.

When we went on a road trip we'd leave what clothes we weren't taking in the closet. And if they needed our room while we were gone, they'd move our clothes downstairs. When we came back we may have gotten another room, and they'd put our clothes there for us when we returned.

Most of the guys stayed there if they were from out of state and didn't have anyone with them. Rudy York, I know, lived there. When I first went up he was there.

Rudy York led the league in hotel fires. I think that's one of the reasons they wrote those laws in, that you couldn't smoke in bed, because of him. But he would.

I remember one night at the Leyland. I'm up at about the eighth or tenth floor and he's on about the fourth floor. So I hear the sirens coming, it's about two o'clock in the morning. I say, "Uh, oh. Rudy done set another fire." And sure enough, it was Rudy's room. He always got out, but he got burned several times on his hand. Because laying down with the cigarette in his hand and falling asleep, it'd set the mattress on fire. He got burned two or three times like that. Sure did.

He set one in Boston, after he went over to the Red Sox. He didn't intentionally do it, but he was good at it.

TNT – Trout, Newhouser, and Trucks – got its start in the '45 World Series. I had just got out of the war in time to pitch the last game of the season, which I didn't win.

In those days, because of the war, if you got out of the service and your team was in the World Series, you were eligible to play. That was another trivia question, you know: Who won more games in the World Series than he did in the regular season? It was me.

I heard that one day on the radio. It was the wintertime and I was driving some place, and I heard that question. I had no idea who it was. Then they gave my name.

I went into the service in February '44 and got out on September 26, 1945. It's a strange thing – all the athletes that were in the service, no matter what branch of the service they were in, if they were professional athletes before they went in, their papers had to be approved by Washington before they got out. I don't know what the reason was.

I'd come over from Guam to San Francisco and then to Norman, Oklahoma. I went up to see the captain in July or August, and he listened to my situation. He can't sign my papers, but he can send them to Washington and if they okay them then I can get out. That went on up until September. Finally the captain's secretary, a lieutenant, came to me and he said, "Your papers are still on the captain's desk. He hasn't sent them to Washington yet."

I said, "What? What can I do about it?"

He said, "You can request to see them. You can request a captain's mass and tell him your situation."

So I did, and I got to see him the very next day. He says, "How will you benefit by this?"

I told him, and he sent a TWX wire to Washington. The next morning a wire came back and I was discharged. He could've done that two months before. Anyway, I was off that base by one o'clock that afternoon.

I go from Norman to Oklahoma City and I'm heading to St. Louis, where the Tigers were playing the Browns, the last series of the season. I have nothing but that blue uniform. Everything else I dropped on the base. I didn't take anything except my shaving kit.

I get into St. Louis the next morning and to the Chase Hotel, where the team is staying, and talked to Paul Richards and Steve O'Neill, the manager. Then, I said, I've got to have some clothes, so I went down to a shop and bought a couple of suits off a gas-pipe rack and some socks and things I needed to get me by. Bought a suitcase. Anyway, the twenty-sixth was Saturday and I started that ballgame.

I'd been down at Norman for six months, and all I'd done every day was run. I found a minor league catcher that was stationed there and he would catch me every day I wanted to throw. That's all the training I had, and they start me in that last game. I was winning 2–1 when I went out of the ballgame. Newhouser came in and they tied it up and then went ahead. Then in the eighth or ninth inning, Greenberg hit that grand slam home run to win the game, and the pennant.

If we'd've lost that ballgame, we'd've had to play the second game of a doubleheader. Washington was already in Detroit waiting to have a playoff game. If we'd've lost it, we'd've had a tie and would have had to play Washington in a playoff. But we won the first game and they called the second game off because it was raining.

Greenberg put us into the World Series that year. He hit that home run in the last game of the season. He also hit a home run in my 4–1 World Series win. Greenberg won it for me. He was a great person, too. I hated to see them get rid of him. He met Carol Gimbel, and I tell you something, I liked Carol Gimbel. She was just an ordinary person. She'd walk to the ballpark and back. They had an apartment about ten blocks from the ballpark, and she'd walk back and forth to the ballgame every day. Real nice lady, she really was.

We were a very, very close ballclub. On an off day we might go down to some little tavern by the ballpark and sit around and have a pitcher of beer. Five or ten of us. Always. We were very, very close. I never heard any harsh words on that ballclub as long as I was in Detroit. I never saw one ballplayer get on another one. Never.

. . .

In the five games I won in 1952 with Detroit, I think I gave up a total of five hits, two no-hitters and a one-hitter. We had a good team but we didn't score many runs. Both of my no-hitters were 1–0 ballgames. And one of them I won in the last inning with two men out and two strikes on the hitter, Vic Wertz, who hit the home run. And in the Yankee game, it was in the seventh inning. Walt Dropo and Steve Souchock got that run in. If you got two runs or three, you better hold them because you weren't going to get many more than that. You better not give up any more 'cause you're not gonna win.

Of course you know we finished last, the only time in the history of the eight-team league that Detroit had finished last. We won 50 games and lost 104. We couldn't score any runs.

My first win was in May. That was the no-hitter against Washington in Detroit. And Bob Porterfield, pitching against me, had given up no hits until the seventh inning. That was probably as easy a no-hitter as anybody could have pitched. Every play was routine. There was nothing that resembled a hit. I struck out eight or nine. Of course, the last hitter I had to get out was Mickey Vernon, and you know he's no easy out. I struck him out. That was the last out in the top of the ninth, Mickey.

Vic Wertz came up in the bottom of the ninth with two men out and two strikes and two balls and hit the ball in the upper deck for the win. I greeted him at home plate like it was a World Series game. This was May 15, so it was a full month or more that I hadn't won, and I took my turn every time. I never missed a turn.

The next month, Washington came in again. Their lead-off hitter was Eddie Yost. And the first pitch I threw he hit a single by George Kell into left field, and that's the only hit they got the rest of the ballgame. I set down the other twenty-seven men, no hits. Yost was usually a first-ball hitter, and if he didn't swing at the first pitch he would usually walk. So I guess I didn't put enough on that first pitch as I could have.

Then the season goes on, and the last win I had, on August 25, was a no-hitter. We're playing the Yankees in Yankee Stadium. As you know, in the early part of the ballgame, Rizzuto hit a ground ball, a two-hopper to Johnny Pesky, right at him, but Pesky fumbled around with it – it wasn't stuck in his webbing, he was just trying to get it out of his glove – and he still threw Rizzuto out. But Bill Grieve, who was one of the worst umpires in baseball as far as I'm concerned, called him safe. All of us argued it.

I looked over to the scoreboard and there was an error up there. I didn't pay any attention to that; I just wanted to see how they were ruling it. So then we go on and the next time I come out of the dugout I look up at the scoreboard and there's a hit up there. Well, I'm still not paying any attention to it. It didn't bother me.

Anyway, in the fifth or the sixth inning, unbeknownst to me, John Drebinger, who was the official scorer that day, called down to the bench to talk to Pesky. And Pesky said, "In the first place he was out, in the second place the ball did not stick in my webbing" – because if it does it's a base hit – "I just couldn't get a grip on the ball."

Well, that's an error.

So I go back out, the sixth inning, and I look up and there's no hits up there again. They've taken it off and put an error back up there. Now in the seventh inning I come up to bat. I either walked or got a base hit, but I'm on first, and Grieve says to me, "There's your no-hitter, now go and get it."

I says, "You . . . I'm not trying to pitch a no-hitter, I'm just trying to win a ballgame."

Later they came out and announced why they made the change, that they talked with Pesky. And the other sportswriters got on Drebinger about it. I found out later. John was a good friend of mine, a real nice guy. They told him in the fifth inning – they didn't wait till the seventh when they actually announced it – that that wasn't a base hit, it was an error.

So anyway, it goes on and I get the rest of the guys out, and I have another no-hitter.

There were several good catches in that ballgame. Irv Noren pinch-hit and hit a slicing ball into left center field and Johnny Groth made a backhanded catch of it. And some other pinch hitter hit an identical ball and Groth made a good catch of it. Other than that, there wasn't any really hard hit balls. Except the ninth inning.

It was Yogi and Mantle and Bauer I had to get out in the ninth. Mantle I struck out, Yogi popped up, and Bauer hit a line shot to Gerry Priddy, the second baseman. If the ball had been hit either side of him, it would have been a base hit. Self-defense is what you'd call it. He had to catch it or it would have killed him. One hopper in his glove and Bauer had hardly got out of the batter's box when he threw him out.

That was my last win. Probably at that time I had something like five wins and eighteen losses. So now, after I lose the nineteenth game we still had about three weeks to go. Freddie Hutchinson had become manager halfway through the season – they fired Red Rolfe and he replaced Rolfe. I could have probably lost twenty-five or twenty-six, with any luck at all. So I went to Hutch and I said, "Look, I've never won twenty games and I sure don't want to *lose* twenty before I win twenty."

He agreed. I said, "How about letting me go to the bullpen from here on out, so I can't lose the twentieth. I'll be your mop-up man so I won't have a chance to lose."

And I didn't. Who knows, I might have pitched another no-hitter. But I just did not want to lose twenty games.

Ted Lyons, who was the pitching coach at that time, said, "Hey, forget this season. It was a bad season for all of us. Probably next year you'll turn around and win twenty." Not thinking that I'm gonna be traded.

Sure enough I was traded, and I did win twenty games the next year. Between two clubs. I was 5 and 4 with the Browns and 15 and 6 with the White Sox.

I figured they must have been really angry with me to have traded me to the Browns. The thing about it was, if they traded you in those days and they kept you in the league, they usually traded you to the worst ballclub in the league, because they didn't want you to come back and hurt them. But I did. I pitched against them opening day and I beat them 11–0. I think I beat them a couple or three times that year.

But it just always inspired me after that. Every time I faced the Tigers I wanted to beat them just as bad as I could do it. And yet those were my fondest memories, with the Tigers. And here I am, still a Tiger fan.

I know the reason I was traded was the situation with Spike Briggs, Jr. The old man was a great fella.

When I was traded, I was in Henry Ford Hospital. I'd just had my gall bladder taken out, and I read it in the paper. I wasn't too elated, I almost had a setback. I never thought I would be traded from Detroit. In fact, Spike Briggs, Jr., had told me just the year before that I would never be traded.

I used to play catch with his kids, including Walter O., III. They really liked me, and they were sad that I was traded. And I wasn't playing catch with them for identity or to keep me with the Tigers, it was just that they were nice kids. I'd play catch with them just about every day after school let out when they come out to the ballpark and shag fly balls. One of them was his cousin, they called him Lefty, and there was Walter O., III, and a friend.

Well, Spike Briggs, Jr., was known to be an inebriator and he would imbibe. And Bill Veeck knew that.

When they had their winter meetings out in California, Veeck pulled it over on him. He gave up Johnny Groth, me, and Hal White to the Browns for Owen Friend, Bob Nieman, and J. W. Porter. Veeck pulled a fast one on him, because he got him up at two o'clock in the morning.

Charlie Gehringer was the general manager at that time, and Charlie told me later, he said, "I told him, 'Don't make that deal. Stay away from Veeck,' I told him. 'If you don't keep away from him he's gonna get half your ballclub.'"

Of course, Gehringer, being a rookie general manager, wasn't too well versed on that subject either. And being a quiet man like he was, he didn't talk too much. I got to play with him a couple of years before he retired, and he only said two words the whole season long. Spring training he said, "Hello." And when the season was over he said, "Good-bye." And that was about the sum of his conversation.

. . .

The first two guys I met when I went with the Browns were Art Richman and Milt Richman. They covered the Browns and they were in spring training with us. Two great guys. In fact, I heard from Art not too long ago, at Christmas. You know what that son of a gun does? He sends me $50 and says, "Go out and take Ethel to dinner and have a drink on me." And he said, "If you see Whitey, have a drink on me." Meaning Hal White. So we did.

But that's the way Artie is. You know that he got that ball that Bill Buckner missed in the World Series? Do you know that he got something like $90,000 for that ball? Some actor out in California bid on it at auction. He took guys out to dinner and he spent most of it and he gave some to charity, but that's the type of guy Art Richman is. He's one fine man, just a great person. Always has been and always will be.

Of the five trades I was involved in, Bill Veeck was the only man that ever told me that I was being traded to another ballclub. I either read it in the paper or heard it on the radio. That was it. But Veeck called me the day he traded me. We had an off day and I was home.

He told me, "Virg, I've got to meet the payroll, and the only way I can meet it is I've got to sell you and Bob Elliott to the White Sox for $100,000."

I said, "Bill, I'm sorry. I enjoyed playing for you, I enjoyed playing here."

He said, "I know that, we enjoyed having you. Wish you could stay, but I've got to meet the payroll. I've tried to move the ballclub to Baltimore, but they won't let *me*."

And they wouldn't.

He said, "I've never really sold a ballplayer in all the time I've been in baseball." He picked up a couple of ballplayers in the trade.

Then he was out of baseball. Of course he came back later with Cleveland and the White Sox. He was a great man. To me, that was an honor right there, calling me and telling me that I'd been traded.

That first year I was with the White Sox I won twenty ballgames. But back when I was with Detroit, I had an agreement with Gehringer that if I won fifteen games or more I'd get a $3,000 bonus. So I didn't think anything about it, especially since I'm now playing for the White Sox. When the season was almost over, about three games before the end, Chuck Comiskey, the owner, and the general manager, Frank Lane, sent word for me down to the clubhouse that they wanted to see me after the game.

After the game was over they said, "Well, we really appreciate what you've done for us and we're going to give you a $1,000 bonus."

I said, "I really appreciate it. But I'll tell you what, Chuck, Gehringer gave me a verbal contract that I'd get $3,000 if I won more than fifteen games. I realize that I'm not playing for Detroit, I'm playing for you guys, but I thought it would carry over." He well knew that I couldn't prove it. In those days the only thing you could put in writing in a contract was the salary, you couldn't include bonuses or anything like that.

So they say, "Well, we'll call Gehringer, and you come back after the game tomorrow and we'll let you know."

Well, he already said he was gonna give me $1,000, so that was acceptable to me. After the game was over I went up there and he said, "Okay, we'll tell you what, we'll give you the $3,000." Of course they were thinking, too, that they might be able to sign me for a little cheaper. Because I had a good year, they knew they were going to have to raise my salary. And they did. They gave me what I really thought I should get according to those years.

I really couldn't complain. I liked the White Sox, and they were good to me. And then comes the next year and I won nineteen games and *could've* won twenty again. And this is an odd story I'm gonna tell you now.

I'm gonna pitch the last game of the season in Baltimore. The season was gonna end a day early, on a Saturday, because the Colts had a football game on Sunday. I already have my nineteen wins and I see Richards, the Baltimore manager, and he says to me, "Can you pitch tonight?"

I said, "Why?"

He says, "Well, we got a rookie going, and the last time he pitched he walked about eight and they knocked him out of the box in about the third inning."

It was Digger O'Dell, that was who the pitcher was. It was his second or third start in the major leagues.

I said, "I can pitch if Marty Marion will let me." Marty was managing the team then.

I'd had more than enough rest. This was about the fifth day since I pitched last. I thought it was good of Richards to give me that information. I asked Marty and he said, "It don't matter to me if it don't matter to Pierce."

Billy and I were going to pitch the last two games of the season. Billy said it didn't matter to him. Of course, he didn't know what I knew.

Okay, so I pitch that game and we lose 2–1. Gil Coan hit a home run inside the ballpark to beat me. Next day Pierce pitches and we won 11–0.

.   .   .

When I was playing we actually made our living in the off season by barnstorming, in the '50s, until television got real big. People watching television didn't have the time to go out and see a barnstorming team no matter if they *were* major league ballplayers.

We were in Whitville, Tennessee, and we were going to go out and play golf. Sherm Lollar and myself and Hal White and one other guy. We'd always play during the day, because we played all night games. So we get out there and Clint Courtney wants to play with us. Courtney hadn't played a golf game in his life, but he wants to play.

I said, "Courtney, you're left-handed, and they don't make those clubs anymore, but you can go with us."

He said, "No, I'm gonna play."

So we talk to the pro and he lends Courtney a set of left-handed clubs and three balls. So we go out on the first tee and everyone hits, and we're all in pretty decent shape. Then Courtney says to me, "Give me one of them little ol' pins."

I said, "What little ol' pins?"

He said, "One of them little ol' pins you set the ball on."

We laugh and we give him a tee. Well, he hits two balls into the pool before he finally hits one down the fairway. After the first hole we ask him what he shot and he says, proudly, "Give me eleven licks!"

He was a funny guy, a great guy. And he was a pretty good catcher. I liked pitching to him. I'll tell you, he was a scrappy little catcher. He was just like they say in his nickname, Scrap Iron. He *was* scrap iron. He wasn't afraid of nobody.

I'll never forget, we were playing the Yankees in St. Louis when I was with the Browns. He was the catcher. I wasn't pitching this day.

Gil McDougald's on third, one man out. A ground ball is hit to the third baseman, and he's playing in, naturally. So the play's at the plate and McDougald just ran over Courtney, didn't slide or nothing. He just really undressed him—the ball went one way, the glove went another way, his glasses come off. But he just started gathering up his stuff: "Don't worry, I'll get somebody, I'll get somebody."

Anyway, that puts the Yankees ahead by one run. So sure enough, Courtney leads off the bottom of the ninth with a ball off that screen in Sportsman's Park. Really, you've got to be a *fast* man to go to second on that. Courtney rounded first and he never let up and he's out by the time he's halfway down there. Rizzuto caught the ball and put the tag on him, and he hit Rizzuto right in the chest with his spikes and he knocked him out into left field almost. Man, I thought he killed Rizzuto; he was moaning and a groaning.

Reynolds was pitching, and before Courtney was even off the ground at second base Reynolds had gone out and poked him. I mean, we had a *helluva* battle. Benches emptied and everything. And when they all untangled, Courtney's down the bottom of the pile and again he's undressed. The glasses—can't find them, they're crunched. His uniform is torn and he's got no cap on and one shoe is missing. And he comes off the field as happy as can be. "I told you I'd get somebody."

They made *me* out to be mean and all that stuff. I was just an outgoing pitcher. I just wanted to win, and I didn't care how I won. That's the name of the game in the pros. If you're gonna stick around, you're gonna have to be a little bit mean as a pitcher.

I never wanted to hit anybody, though, because throwing the ball one hundred miles per hour it's not a good thing to do, to come close to somebody. Although I hit one guy in the head one time, and he ducked into the ball. That was before the helmet. It bounced off his head and into the stands. That was in St. Louis. He was a good buddy of mine, Jim Rivera. Sure did. It knocked him down, and he shook his head and he went to first base. They took him out for observation.

Of course, I pitched up and down inside. They knew that. They stood up there loose. And I can say this – I don't think you can find a record of this – but no hitter ever hit two home runs off me in one ballgame. Never. They may have hit one, but they ain't gonna hit the second one. They knew they weren't gonna hit the second one. 'Cause you can't sit there and hit somebody when you're standing lightly on the ground. They knew that I would come close.

The hitters knew the pitchers that would brush them back. You take, for example, Billy Pierce for the White Sox. I never, ever saw him brush anybody back. There's no telling what kind of pitcher he would have been if he had had what I call the fortitude to knock somebody down, or come close to him.

The only player I ever saw Pierce hit was a guy he had played with before, and it was strictly an accident. He hit Johnny Groth in the head, and that was the end of Johnny Groth's career. He could never stand in the batter's box any more after that. And Billy had no intention of hitting Johnny in the head or anyplace else. I would venture that any ballplayer you talked to at that time would say it was strictly a slip. It was not intended to hit Groth in any way. We knew that. Even Groth knew that.

If Pierce didn't have such exceptional stuff he wouldn't have lasted in the major leagues.

. . .

I met Satchel Paige when we were with the Browns. Of course, he's from Mobile and later played here in Birmingham. We became close friends. I'd trust him with my life. He was one of the finest guys you'd ever meet in baseball. Oh, he was funny.

One time, we were out in Phoenix, going up to Mesa to play the Cubs, and we were sitting next to each other on the bus. He always sat beside me. At that time there was Tucson, Phoenix, and Mesa, nothing in between. I said, "You know something, Satchel, I'm gonna get me one of them little coyotes out there and I'm gonna make me a pet out of it, put it on a leash, walk him around."

He said, "Man, you can't do that!"

I said, "Why not?"

He said, "Why that's the meanest animal you ever saw. He'll bite your head off."

I said, "Satch, I'll get him when he's first born, a little puppy, and I'll train him and he'll be just fine. I'll put him on a leash and I'll even let you pet him on the head."

He said, "Yeah, I'll pet him on the head, if it's about two foot from the rest of his body."

He was something else. Really a great guy. In his house in Kansas City he had a little bandstand, and he had a piano. He'd sing and play the guitar. He was really an entertainer.

For some reason he and Larry Doby didn't get along. I never asked Satch, and I never wanted to ask Satch, because that was between them and let them handle their own problems. Anyway, Satch didn't like him.

I'd sit out there in the bullpen with him on days I didn't pitch. He's gonna be in the ballgame, he always *was* because the Browns pitching staff isn't gonna last nine innings.

Anyway, we were sitting in the bullpen in Cleveland. Doby's playing center field and Satch yelled out to Doby, "Hey, Doby! You know what, I'm gonna be in that ballgame sometime today and you know that. And when you're up there to hit I don't want to see you digging them cleats in. And I mean it, don't dig them cleats in. Because when I'm out there pitching I want to see *all* them cleats."

That meant he was gonna get down and loose. And Satch *would* knock you down. He'd knock anybody down. He knew how to pitch as well as anybody.

Again when I was in training with the Browns, we were in San Bernadino and we were coming back north, working our way back after we finished training. We stopped off in Phoenix and we were going to play the White Sox there. We were staying in a hotel in downtown Phoenix, and Hal White and I said to Satchel, "Satch, you're going to go to dinner with us tonight."

He said, "Man, I can't go to no restaurants around here."

I said, "You can go with us!"

He said, "No."

He couldn't even eat in the dining room of that hotel. They sent his meals up to his room. I didn't know that, I thought he ate wherever he wanted to eat. At the time I hadn't spent much time with Satch. We'd gone out to a bar in spring training, had a couple of beers, but that was about it.

Well, we were going to go out to The Flame restaurant, one of the nicest restaurants in Phoenix. Hal and I went down to the restaurant about 4:00. They didn't open until 5:30, but the door was open. There was a lady at the desk and we asked if we could see the manager. He came up and we explained who we were.

I said, "We've got one black player on the club and we would like to come over here and have dinner here with him."

The manager said, "Look, I've had this restaurant for ten or twenty years, and I have blacks working for me, but there's never been a black person walk in through that front door."

Well, this seemed useless and I'm not gonna argue with him. But, I said, "Look, this man is a fine gentleman. You can put us off in a corner or someplace, I don't care where you hide us."

And it was a pretty big restaurant. A lot of the tables were on little daises. Probably four or five daises off the main floor. I said, "Stick us wherever you want to, I don't care. We just want to have dinner."

Well, he agreed. I guess he figured he might have a problem if he refused a guy to eat there. These things were beginning to change about that time. Well, it hadn't changed there.

We were elated. We went back to the hotel and told Satch. At about 5:30 we met in the hotel lobby and walked over there. We were all in suits and ties – you had to in those days. The restaurant was across the street and less than a block from the hotel. We walk in and already there's a bunch of people in there.

The manager was waiting for us when we came in, and he puts us in center stage, right in the middle of that place on about the third dais up from the floor. We're sitting and we can hear people whispering and buzzing all over the place. Satch was the only black guy in the place, probably the only black guy they'd ever seen. The whispering and buzzing continues, and finally they found out who he was. And you know, they came over to that table and I bet you he signed maybe 250 to 300 autographs, for everybody that was in that building. And they never asked for mine once or for Hal's. We never signed an autograph; they didn't want it. After they got Satch's, boom, they were gone.

I felt great about that. And everywhere I went from then on, Satch went.

Then we were coming through Alpine, Texas. There's a man there that owns Alpine, Texas. It's a small town, but he has a big cattle and oil ranch. He owns miles of property and he had a ballclub that he paid, like a semipro club. He loved baseball. His name was Mr. Cokernaught – Mr. Coconut. So he had this ballclub, and we're with the Browns and we stopped to play there. We just stopped our train car right there on the rails and stayed there for a day and a half using the train as our hotel.

So we went in and played the game, and for every opposing player that got a hit he'd give a dollar. And if you got a home run you got $100.

He was giving money away like crazy. I think we left there with $2,000 or $3,000. I didn't get to pitch – it wasn't my turn – but he gave pitchers $50 for every strikeout. Satch pitched an inning or two. Oh, man, he gave away a ton of money.

We stayed there that night and left the next day. And Mr. Cokernaught gave Satch a big Stetson hat and a pair of cowboy boots, the best boots you could buy and the best hat.

And Satch puts on that big hat and Whitey and I kidded him about it, he looked funny. We were going to Kansas City, where he lived. So when we get to Kansas City, Whitey and I go to a five-and-dime store and we get two little cap guns and a holster. So we go over and put them in his locker. We know he's gonna come in wearing those boots and hat. And we put a note on there saying, Welcome home, Tex.

He looked straight over at Whitey and me with a big grin – he knew just who did it – and from then on we called him Tex.

Fantastic person. He is one of the guys that made me have a good time. I enjoyed being with him and being around him. He was just a peach of a guy.

I told him, "You know, Satch, it's too bad you couldn't have been in the major leagues when you were twenty-one, twenty-five or even thirty. Any of those years that you could've come up would have been great."

He said, "Man, I didn't really care if I came to the big leagues. I was barnstorming all over the world. Everyplace – Europe, Japan. I was making around $100,000 a year. I wouldn't have made any money. I was better off right where I was. I wasn't worried about them not putting me in the major leagues, because I was making more money outside."

Satch deserved more, but he got what he got by going out and earning it himself. The barnstorming trips and such. He wasn't dependent on anybody. He knew how to make a living himself and he done it. Of course, he had great ability.

■　■　■

When Bill Durney, the general manager of the Miami Marlins triple-A club found out I was released he wanted to know if I'd come down and play with the Marlins. He was the general manager of the Browns when Veeck was there.

I told him, "Bill, I'm not in shape to play yet, and I don't know if I'll be able to get in shape, and I don't want to impose on your ballclub. You've got young players down there who need to be playing, and I don't need to be playing." Although I loved the game and would love to have gone.

He said, "Look, I want you to come down here. You can be an asset to our ballclub in other respects."

I said, "I don't know."

He said, "I'll tell you what I'll do. I'll send Mr. Stohrer's plane up there – Stohrer owned the ballclub then – and you get on it and come down and look over the situation and we'll talk."

So they sent his plane up and I got on it and went down there and went through the thing. I went back to Lakeland, where I was staying at the time, and he called me and said, "What do you think?"

I said, "Bill . . ."

He said, "I tell you what, I'll give you a $5,000 bonus. Come on down, and if you decide you don't want to play after that the bonus is yours."

Well, I got nowhere to go. I don't have a job, and I'm not ready to retire at forty-two years of age, so I said okay. I stayed there for one month, I think. I pitched one inning. I still wasn't in shape. So I said, "Bill, I'm hanging them up, I'm sorry. I'm just not interested in playing."

I thanked him for everything and went back to Kansas City, where I was living then. Satchel was also living there, and we were close friends.

There was this guy who wanted Satch and me to go on a barnstorming tour. Satch says this guy, from Beloit, Wisconsin, would pay us $600 a week and all expenses, though they wouldn't be much because Satch and I would drive with the promoter.

They had a busload of Cubans. They were all from Cuba, none of them could speak English. That was the ballclub, other than Satch and I.

We open our first game somewhere in Oklahoma. Satch and I pitched every night. He pitched an inning and I pitched an inning, because that's all these people wanted to see was Satch and me.

We went down into Mexico, and we'd gone about 3,000 miles and the promoter hasn't come up with $600 a week yet and this is a month, month and a half later. He'd paid us in little dabs, $50 one game, $75 another, but he didn't pay according to our agreement. So Satchel went to him and he says, "Hey, Dempsey." His name was Dempsey Holland. "I want my money."

He says, "I don't have it."

Satchel says, "You pay tonight or I'm gone."

So that night he didn't have the money, and Satch gets on a bus and goes all the way back to Kansas City. I stayed with the team.

We went out to the West Coast and we traveled up to Bellingham, Washington. Went over and played in Victoria, British Columbia. He had something like eighty-five ballgames booked. We were gonna finish up in New York. When we got to Beloit, his hometown, the manager of the club, a Cuban, got the message from Fidel Castro that they better get back now or they're not going to be let back in. That whole busload left from Beloit and went down to Miami to get back to Cuba.

Well, I've got no place to go, except back to Kansas City. I thought for a while. I knew Danny Murtaugh in Pittsburgh. The Pirates were in first place at the time. This was about the first of July. So I called Danny. By then I was in real good shape – I could throw ninety miles per hour. But nobody's gonna give a forty-two-year-old ex-ballplayer a job. Only as a batting practice pitcher. So that's what I asked him for. I can still throw sliders, curveballs – anything that the hitters want to see that they'll see in the game, I can throw those pitches.

He says, "I tell you what. I'll talk to Joe Brown, the general manager, and Joe will give you a call."

The next morning he called me and told me he'd give me $750 a month. I travel with the ballclub, I get the same expenses they get, and he pays my plane fare home at the end of the season. I said, "Well, that's fair enough for me."

So I went into Pittsburgh and I threw batting practice for them the rest of that year. They won the pennant and the World Series, you know. I got a World Series share – I didn't get a full share – and a World Series ring. And he wanted to know if I wanted to come back and I said, Sure.

Went on for three years like that.

In '62 I go back. They had traded Dick Stuart. Every off day in '60 and '61 I played golf with Stuart. I just beat him every day. So I go to Joe Brown – I was living in Pittsburgh then – and I said, "Joe, you've got to give me a $1,000 raise."

He said, "I don't have to give you nothing. I can find coaches out there on the street for a dime a dozen."

I said, "But you have to!"

He said, "Why do I have to?"

I said, "Well, you traded Dick Stuart, didn't you?"

He says, "Yeah, you know I traded Dick."

I said, "Well, I made $1,000 a year from him playing golf. Now I'm losing money by you trading him. Give me the $1,000."

You know he believed that so well he gave me a $1,000 raise. I absolutely got a $1,000 raise. I had no idea I was going to get any more money from Joe Brown – he was such a skinflint and it was such a cheap ballclub.

But I said thank-you and walked out. That's the honest-to-God truth.

Frank Thomas

June 30–July 1, August 16, 1994, Pittsburgh, Pennsylvania

Frank Thomas played the outfield, third base, and first base in the National League from 1951 to 1966. He spent eight years with the Pittsburgh Pirates and another eight with the Reds, Cubs, Braves, Mets, Phillies, and the Colt 45s (today, the Houston Astros). A .266 lifetime hitter with 286 lifetime home runs, Thomas hit thirty or more home runs three times in his career and twice drove in more than one hundred runs in a season.

I was a little bitty guy when I was a kid. I didn't start growing until I was a freshman in high school, only five foot three inches. My freshman year in high school I shot up to six foot. I grew nine inches in one year. Like a tree. My dad would say, "Well, what I did was I made a box, a square box, and I stood him in it and put horse manure in it and I put a chain around it so he couldn't run away and it made him grow."

I got my first baseball from Josh Gibson with the Homestead Grays. I asked him, "Can I have a baseball?" And he gave me two. Everybody was running all over the place chasing me, trying to get the balls from me, so I just went on out of the ballpark and ran home.

I saw Gibson hit two balls over the 457-foot sign at Forbes Field. He could hit! He was a *great* hitter. Great hitter. I can't recall if Gibson was a real hero to kids. He was just a ballplayer.

I never had any idols, like a lot of players. All I wanted to do was just play baseball, that's all I wanted to do. I'd leave the house at seven thirty in the morning on a Saturday and I wouldn't come home until nine thirty, ten o'clock at night. Come home with my pants torn and my dad would say, "Go up to your room! No dinner!" Mom would bring dinner up anyway, as mothers always do.

But that's all I wanted to do was play ball. Just let me play. I'd play with one group, and once they quit I'd go play with another group. I used to walk three miles to go to the Oval – Schenley Oval in Pittsburgh – and go out and play. And I used to play with older people. We used to play with Dad's pick handle and a baseball we'd taped up. I played shortstop without a glove because I couldn't afford one. . . . Lot of fun, lot of fun.

My dad was from the old country, Lithuania, and he really didn't know much about baseball. He came over when he was very young and got himself a job. His marriage was planned for him – back then that's what they did. My mother was fifteen years younger than my dad. And it was a tough life for her, him being fifteen years older.

One day Father Lucien, who was a Carmelite father, came to our school and started talking about the seminary and what a great life it was, this and that. So I went up there for a summer and I had a great time playing ball. And I thought, well, maybe I had the calling. I was thirteen.

Jack Butler, who played for the Pittsburgh Steelers, was in my class in the seminary. And he left probably a month before I did. He went into professional football and I became a professional baseball player, from the same class in the seminary. And both of us were good. He was a helluva football player. We had intramural competition at the seminary, him on one side and me on the other, and we had great competition. They used to make me bat left-handed because I hit the ball so far right-handed.

They say when you leave the seminary and you don't become the priest that you thought you wanted to be, you can still do things in the world to be a good example to people. When I decided to leave, I realized that I could do just as much for people being an athlete out in the world. I can remember when I first left the seminary and I went and signed a contract. It was like a miracle when I left. I left in January, and I signed a professional contract six months later.

You know the story. The Pirates offered me $150 to sign, and my dad said, "No, my boy worth more than that." Then Cleveland, George Susce with Cleveland, asked me if I'd come to Cleveland for a week and spend time with his son and work out at the stadium. Laddie Placek then drove me back to Pittsburgh and said to my dad, "We'll give you $3,100."

My dad says, right away, "You're gonna sign."

Well I said, "No, I'm going to think about it."

Because at that time I wanted to play in my hometown. I thought it would be great. So I went back to the Pirates and told them, "I've been offered X amount of dollars from Cleveland, and I'll tell you what—Mom and Dad have a mortgage on their home for $3,200; you pay the mortgage on the home and I'll sign the contract." And that's the way it was. Roy Hamey signed me.

My dad was always the type that thought playing baseball was not a place where you could make a livelihood. Because back then they weren't paying that much money. And then when I got to the major leagues, he came out to the ballpark and I hit a home run against the Giants to win the ballgame. Afterwards, as we were coming out of the clubhouse and down the ramp at Forbes Field, he came up and gave me a big kiss as if to say, "Okay, I agree with you now. You picked a good life and this is what you want to do."

■　■　■

Five years in the minors. Well, back then, most of the players were kept in the minor leagues anywhere from four to five years. Then you were a proven ballplayer. You had the experience. You knew.

I went from double-A to the major leagues—I skipped triple-A. I played at New Orleans in the Southern Association, which was a good league. A lot of players came from that league: Pete Runnels came from that league, Eddie Mathews came from that league. And at Waco, Texas, in the Bi-State League was where I got the reputation of catching bare-handed, because of the pitcher Bill Pierro. He died of a brain tumor.

I'm out in the outfield, and he was popping off saying how fast he was.

I said, "I'll catch your fastball bare-handed."

He said, "Like hell you will."

I said, "You go down to the bullpen and warm up."

He said, "You can't catch it even if I'm not warm."

I said, "Well, let's walk off 60 feet 6 inches and you rare back and you fire and I'll catch you. But I know what'll happen. After I catch you, you'll say you're not warm."

And that's how it happened. And I said, "Go down to the bullpen and get warm, and whenever you're ready come back again and I'll catch you."

I caught five of them.

Hank Aaron and I, we got along well. He's the greatest hitter I ever played with, without a doubt, but I used to tease him all the time. I caught *his* fastball. We were playing in St. Louis, and we're warming up between innings and he'd throw the ball and I'd drop the glove and I'd catch it. Then I'd move closer. He threw three of them, and he started throwing them harder and I'd catch them. Finally he took one and he threw it up in the stands and said, "You won't catch that one!"

But I guess Don Zimmer was the toughest one I had to catch. He drew a line 60 feet 6 inches and he threw me a spitter. When I caught it he threw his glove up in the air and said, "You made a believer out of me."

I look back now and I could very easily have hurt myself.

. . .

I came up in '51 and at the end of the '52 season, so I had too many times at bat to be the Rookie of the Year in '53. I hit 30 home runs and drove in 102 runs in 128 ballgames. When they sold Ralph Kiner in '53, they took the Greenberg Gardens down. If they had left the Gardens up for me, I honestly and truthfully believe that I would have hit 500 home runs in my career. Because I was strictly a pull hitter. In '58 when I hit the 35 home runs, I hit 26 on the road and nine at Forbes Field. That kind of tells you. You're playing 77 ballgames in your home park and you only hit nine home runs? That's the difference. It was a good park to hit in but not for a home-run hitter.

When I first started out I had raw ability, and it just took some maturing and somebody to take me aside and work with me and make me a good ballplayer. I had coaches that when I was playing would say, "Watch the ball. Quick with the hands, quick with the hands." I'd hit everybody to right field, right center, and center field. I couldn't pull the ball to left field, I stood away from the plate. Then I had Rip Sewell work with me. I moved closer to the plate. I developed my wrists and my forearms to where I was quick with my hands. I used to hit the ball out in front.

I respected pitchers that pitched inside, that brushed me back, because I felt that they had respect for me. Stan Musial gave me the greatest compliment you'd ever want to give. He said Frank Robinson and I were probably the greatest two pull hitters he'd ever seen in baseball.

I used to take a lot of batting practice. The first two, two and a half weeks of spring training I'd be down in that cage after everybody'd go home after the ballgame. I'd be down there hitting, because I wanted to toughen up my hands. I wanted to build up my wrists and my forearms, I wanted to be quick with my hands, and I just hit and hit and hit until my hands bled. Then I put tape over them and I kept hitting. I think if you like something – you *love* something the way I love baseball – that you'll do anything.

I practiced fielding too. I mean, when they moved me in to play the infield, I used to take two hundred ground balls a day. I'd play anyplace, as long as I was in the lineup and got my four swings a day.

I was the first Pirate that was on a *Sports Illustrated* cover. 1958, July. Only cost twenty-five cents back then. The caption on the bottom reads, "Nobody knows him but everybody wants him." My kids turned it around: Everybody knows him and nobody wants him.

I was always the type of person, I would go out and I would do my job and I agitated quite a bit, probably one of the greatest agitators in the game of baseball. But all in fun, never to hurt anybody.

I wasn't an agitator with Branch Rickey. I just felt that, well, he might have been a great baseball man but as a human being I had no respect for him. I just couldn't respect the man because of the way he treated me. Like I was dirt under his feet.

I had a good year at New Orleans, led the league and everything, and I asked him for a $1,000 raise. He gave me the same salary. When I talked to him he said, "I can't pay a major league salary to minor league ballplayers."

I said, "Well, I thought you got paid on what you've done."

He said, "Oh, you have to be a major leaguer."

I said, "Well, I'm in the minor leagues. How can I be in the major leagues if you keep me in the minor leagues?"

So I signed, and then in '53 I hit the 30 home runs and drove in 102 runs, which is still a rookie record with the Pirates. The first thing out of my mouth was, "I'm a major leaguer and I want to be paid accordingly."

He asked me what I wanted and I said $15,000. And he said, "Well, you go along with what I'm offering you, twelve-five, and you have another good year and I'll take care of you."

I said, "Fine."

So I had another good year, 1954, and what do you think he offered me? The difference on what I had asked for the year before.

"No," I said, "that's not the way to treat somebody when you're saying you'll take care of them. I went along with you for two years, and all of a sudden now you're going to treat me this way? I don't think you're being very fair to me."

And I held out.

Well, my dad was a real good friend of Chilly Doyle, who was a writer for the *Sun Telegraph*. They were in the service together. My dad would ask me, you know, "How's contract negotiations coming?"

I'd say, "Well, I'm having a few problems."

Then, at church on Sunday, my dad would see Chilly and mention that I was having problems.

Rickey was always the type of person that said he never divulges anybody's salary negotiations. He was a liar. Because I'm watching TV one day and it comes right out on TV: If Thomas doesn't get $25,000 he's not going to sign. The Twig – that was the nickname we had for Rickey's son – and him and I were the only three people who knew what I asked for. And then it came out in the paper the next morning, and it was Lester Biederman, who was with the *Press*.

Rickey, Sr., was down in Florida; Twig and I were up here in Pittsburgh. So there was only one person that told Les Biederman what I had asked for – it had to be the old man. So I called the Twig up and I said, "Well, I guess your dad's a liar."

He says, "What do you mean?"

I said, "He told me he never divulges anybody's salary negotiations and it came right out on TV?"

He says, "Well, it was probably Chilly Doyle."

I said, "No, it was Lester Biederman from the *Press*."

Finally the dad comes home and I said to Twig, "Well, let me talk to your dad, I can't get anywhere with you."

He says, "I don't think Dad wants to talk to you."

I said, "Well, I think you should give me that courtesy."

So he took me down to his dad's office. I walked in and he just knocked everything off his desk and said, "Do your negotiating with the newspapers and that's how we'll do our contract negotiations. I'll write you a letter with an offer, you tell the paper what you want, and I'll read it in the paper. We'll do that."

So after he was ranting and raving I said to him, "Are you finished?"
"Yes."

I got up and I said, "I had nothing to do with what was in the paper. My dad is interested in me the same as you're interested in your son."

I walked out, and that was the extent of my negotiations with him.

You know they always say this about him, about not going to the ballpark on Sunday and all that stuff? That's a bunch of baloney, he did things that . . . He wasn't a very Christian person to individuals he was dealing with. I just had no respect for him after the way he treated me.

Dick Groat will tell you something different because he was nice to Dick. Dick and I would always have arguments about that. I used to say to him, "He treated you great, Dick, and you would feel that way, but he treated me like I was dirt under his feet."

I just had no respect for him. He treated Dale Long the same way. Dale and I were always very good friends and we always talked about that before he passed away. But that's the way life is. He was doing his job and he was trying to hold me down. And, like I said, I don't think he was very fair to the ballplayers. He treated us like slaves. And most of the general managers – John McHale, George Weiss, Joe Brown – they all popped out of Rickey.

I mean, when I was traded to the different clubs I knew exactly how to negotiate with them because I had the experience with him. You know, you walk in to him, and he'd say what you *didn't* do. So the next year you go and you do what he says you didn't do, and he says the exact same thing, "Well, you did this, but you didn't do *this*."

It's like what he said to Kiner when he gave Kiner the same contract one year.

Kiner said, "I had a good year."

Rickey said, "What place did we end up?"

Kiner said, "Last."

Rickey said, "We can end up last without you, too."

. . .

It's a dream that every boy has that ever picked up a ball and a glove to get to the major leagues. I enjoyed playing *baseball*. I mean, I didn't care where I played. When I was traded, people'd ask, "Because of the trade are you depressed?"

No. My philosophy on trading was that the club that got me wanted me more than the club that let me go. What else is there? I started to get traded after the '58 season. They got some good ballplayers for me, and then later on I started to get traded because you reach an age where they want to protect their kids and you get expendable, and usually you're going to a club that's fighting for the pennant, because they're looking for experience down the stretch drive. I mean, I went from the Mets to the Phillies, they were fighting for the pennant; I went from Houston to Milwaukee, they were fighting for the pennant. My last hit with the Phillies was a home run, my last hit with Houston was a home run. I got traded both times – I said I better quit hitting home runs.

I always kid around with people that my claim to fame was that I was traded for Don Hoak, Harvey Haddix, and Smoky Burgess, who played a big part in Pittsburgh winning the pennant in 1960. But actually, when I was traded from Pittsburgh after the '58 season I was traded with a bad hand, but no one would believe me.

Tom Acker from Cincinnati hit me on the fists, broke the bat, and part of it lodged back into my thumb. That was September third that happened. And the rest of the season I only hit three more home runs. I had thirty-two home runs at the time.

After the season was over, the team doctor operated on me, and I said to him about a month and a half after the operation, "You didn't get what was in there. It's still there, I can still feel it."

He said, "That will heal."

I said, "Well, you're the doctor, I guess you know what you're talking about."

And I went to Cincinnati and I only hit twelve home runs. You re-member the movie *The Lost Weekend*, with Ray Milland? Well, I had a lost year. I mean, it got so bad, when I used to call home collect they wouldn't accept the charges. And when I came home, my kids were burning my bubble gum card. That's when you're having a bad year.

You don't go from thirty-five home runs to twelve unless there's something radically wrong with you, not when you're in the prime of your life. So after the '59 season the Cubs were interested in me, but they wanted their doctor to examine me. I explained to the doctor. He took X-rays and he operated on me.

After I got out of anesthesia he said, "I don't know how you did as well as you did, how you hit twelve home runs with that type of hand."

I had tumors growing around my nerve. Every time I would pick up a bat it was like cold water on the nerve of your tooth. I had tears in my eyes, but I never asked to get out of the lineup. Put me in the lineup, I played.

I did everything: I put a doughnut around it, I taped it, put a sponge on the bat, put a sponge on my hand . . . It just didn't pan out. And then after that season I went to the Cubs and I hit twenty-one home runs there, and then the next year I was traded to Milwaukee, where I hit twenty-seven home runs. The following year I hit thirty-four home runs. So it just goes to prove that I was hurt.

I remember that when I was traded to Cincinnati I told Gabe Paul, "You got damaged goods."

He said, "No, you're concerned about the trade."

And that's the year I was having trouble with Joe Brown with my contract. My last conversation with him, I said, "Joe, if you're going to trade me – and I know you'd trade your mother if you got a good deal – let me know first."

Well, I was in Europe doing a clinic for the air force. Joe Garagiola and myself, Early Wynn, Nestor Chylok, and Del Wilber from the Red Sox. Seven o'clock in the morning, the phone rings.

"Frank Thomas?"

"Yes."

"How do you feel about being traded?"

"Who was I traded to?"

"The Reds."

I'm burning. After I came back and went to get my stuff at the ballpark, one of the guys in the front office asked me when I heard about the trade.

"The next day," I told him. "In the morning, a radio man called me."

He said, "Well, Joe probably tried to get in touch with you."

I said, "He didn't try very hard. Gabe Paul didn't know where I was and he got in touch with me."

I lost a little respect for Joe because of that.

But it was the same way with McHale. I went to Milwaukee in 1961 and I ended up hitting twenty-seven home runs. I hit two with the Cubs and twenty-five with the Braves, set a record for a left-fielder. In June, he said, "We want to sign you for next year."

I said, "John, this is June! I may go bad and you'll be sorry. And I may go good and I'll be sorry. But I'll sign before I go home."

Two weeks before the season's over he called me into his office and said, "We'd like for you to sign before next year."

I said, "First of all, let me ask you one question. What are your intentions for me come 1962?"

"We're counting on you very heavily to be our left-fielder."

I said, "I tell you what, for you giving me the opportunity to play regular again, you bring out whatever contract you want me to sign and I'll sign it. I can't be any more fair than that. But if you have any intentions of trading me, please don't let me sign. Let me dicker with the new club I'm going to."

That was in September. In November, I'm up hunting and my wife calls, "You just got sold to the Mets."

I called McHale four times. He never returned the call. When I saw him in spring training, I just went up to him and I said, "You lied to me. I lost a lot of respect for you. You didn't even give me the courtesy to answer my calls, to talk to me about it. Because you were ashamed, because you lied to me."

And I just walked away from him.

When I was traded from Chicago, we took a bus from Chicago to Milwaukee, and I got off the bus and the manager says, "You're changing clubhouses."

We go from New York to Philadelphia, and when we get off the bus Casey Stengel says, "You're changing clubhouses." They don't even give you the courtesy to sit down and talk to you.

■ ■ ■

Every once in a while I get my scrapbooks down and go through them. I was good, if I have to say so myself.

I got to meet the other Frank Thomas at the All-Star game. And he told me, "You're big."

I told him, "Not as big as you."

He said, "Let's not talk about weight."

I told him, "Thanks for keeping my baseball card and name in circulation."

But I reached my boyhood dream. I was fortunate enough to play eighteen and a half years professionally at something that I love. Just putting on a major league uniform and staying as long as I did in the big leagues is the greatest thing that anybody would ever want. I reached my dream, something that the good Lord gave me the talent for. Not too many of them make it. Many are called and few are chosen . . . in any profession. You're outside. You meet all kinds of people.

You're in an office, I mean, how many people are you going to meet?

FRANK
THOMAS

———

46

You've got friends all over the world. I used to send out thirty-five hundred Christmas cards, my wife and I and the kids. We're down to about four hundred now. Sherman Jones, who used to play with the Mets, he says that I'm the only one that sends him a Christmas card. And I've been sending them to him ever since '62. Dave Dravecky's uncle in Ohio, George Judy, who pitched for the Tallahassee Pirates in 1948 . . . I still send him Christmas cards.

But it's really not an easy life. It's not as glamorous as a lot of people think it is, and it's not much of a family life. The only time it was really a family life was when I played in Chicago – you could eat dinner with your family.

And the wives, the life that they have to lead, being a mother and father, both, to the kids. She's a special woman, a ballplayer's wife. But I never brought anything home from the ballpark. I left everything there. This was my family, and I couldn't put them through the things I was going through. I mean, I went o for 41 one time. My wife would say, "Well, how'd you do today?"

I'd say, "I went o for 4." And I just left it at that. But what's so *nice* about the game of baseball is you forget about what you did yesterday because today's a new day.

I used to go and visit Children's Hospital and I'd see these kids in traction and still big smiles on their faces, and I'd say, No way am I going to be down, because I have my health and I can do something about it. They don't, and they *still* have smiles on their faces. That's just the type of person that I've always been.

I was respected because every clubhouse that I would come out of the kids would say, "Line up and he'll stay and he'll sign autographs for everybody." That's what I was noted for. When I came out of the clubhouse, they lined up and I signed until everybody was finished.

That was the reputation that I got. I've received beautiful letters from kids that are grown up now. I just got one not too long ago from a guy in Chicago, a cop who's working with kids now. It took him twenty-five years to sit down and write me a letter.

He said, "I can remember in Wrigley Field, when you had everybody line up. It took me all this time to get enough nerve just to sit down and write you and say how much I appreciate what you did for me when I was a little boy at Wrigley Field."

It's little things like that come back to you.

One time I was asked to visit a little kid in the hospital who was dying of leukemia. This kid wouldn't eat, wouldn't smile for anybody, but when I poked my head in his room a big smile came over his face. The nurse said, "I have somebody here who would like to talk to you. Do you know who it is?"

He said, "Yeah, it's Frank Thomas, my favorite ballplayer."

I went over and I shook his hand, and we talked baseball for about an hour. I had taken him an autographed ball by the Pirates and an autographed yearbook. I had all the players sign it to him. When I was leaving he said, "Would you do me a favor."

I said, "Sure. If I can't do it we'll find a way that it can be done."

He said, "Would you hit a home run for me?"

I said, "Well, we're going to Chicago tomorrow, and you listen to the ballgame, and when I hit the home run you'll know it's for you."

Well, the first time up I'm squeezing the sawdust out of the bat and I eventually struck out. The next time – and I believe in faith an awful lot and the good Lord – I just made a little sign of the cross on the on-deck circle and I said, "Dear God, not for me but for the little boy whose life you're taking. Let his last wish be a very memorable one."

I got the count to 3 and 2 and hit the next ball out of the ballpark. As I was rounding the bases I was wondering what little Stevie was thinking in that hospital bed. And I got my answer when I went into the clubhouse after the game. On my stool was a telegram from his mother, and it said, "Dear Mr. Thomas, no sooner than you hit the home run, Stevie passed away."

I've had other memories. I hit three home runs in one game. I hit the fourth home run in succession in one inning, the first one that ever did it. I played for some great managers – Casey Stengel, Danny Murtaugh, Freddie Hutchinson, Charlie Dressen, Leo Durocher.

I remember when Durocher picked me for the All-Star team in '55. I wasn't having a really good year at the time, but he said, "In my book, you'll always be an All-Star. You always hustle, you always give 100 percent."

And that's true. I always knew that deep down I gave 100 percent every time I was on that field, and no one could say that I didn't. I always had the reputation. I ran back and forth from my position – I used to beat infielders into the dugout many times. That's the only way I knew how to play. I always felt that that's the only way to play the game. If you can't give 100 percent of God-given-talent for two and a half, three hours, you shouldn't be between those lines.

I may have made, at third base, maybe two or three errors in a ballgame, not because I wanted to make the errors but because I was trying. If I could go into that clubhouse every day and as I was taking off my uniform say to myself, "I gave a 100 percent of the talent given to me," I didn't care what you or anybody else said.

It had its peaks and valleys, wondering would I make it and then just having the desire and determination and motivation to continue on when things were bad.

It's a great game, a great game, no matter what happens to it. No matter what happens to the game of baseball, it will overcome every obstacle in its way. It's so big. It's just the national pastime.

Gene Woodling

February 21, 1993, Clearwater, Florida

Gene Woodling played outfield from 1943 to 1962, excluding his military service in 1944 and 1945. In addition to playing six years with the Yankees, Woodling played with the Indians, Orioles, and Washington Senators and with the National League Pirates and Mets. A .284 lifetime hitter, Woodling played on five consecutive World Champion Yankees teams (1949–1953), compiling a .318 lifetime World Series batting average.

Baseball was a job to me, and I thank my lucky stars to this day that I was able to be a ballplayer. I had about forty years in the game. You find a better way to earn a living, then you tell me. Heck, I never had to work all my life. Of course, I found that out. My wife and I bought a farm, you know. That's work!

We grew up in Akron, Ohio, right on top of Goodyear. Right on *top* of Goodyear Tire and Rubber Company. Goodrich, Firestone, General Tire, Goodyear . . . Akron was the rubber capital of the world.

My father worked at Goodrich. Most everybody did. We used to call them the slave shops. When I first started playing ball, I didn't even know what the scout was talking about cause I just played in my neighborhood. I only played a few games of high school baseball. I come from a family of swimmers, which was an odd thing. I had three brothers, and my brother next to me was a national champion swimmer at Ohio State. All four of us were competitive swimmers and none of us ever lost a meet. The funny part is, you come back after your career is over, you put in twenty years in the big leagues, and you get put in your high school hall of fame for swimming.

I played everything else in high school but baseball. I was a good athlete, and I come out of a neighborhood of good athletes, which is very fortunate. You're gonna do what your buddies do. They were Depression days but, hell, you didn't know you were poor. Everybody was poor. That was quite a neighborhood I come out of. Predominantly Polish-Hungarian. God, whatever house you were in you'd eat. Didn't have nothing, but I had fun. You only get one whack at that, you know.

My wife and I, we've known each other since we were kids. We grew up together. We just had our fiftieth wedding anniversary last October. I don't wish Depression days on people, because we went hungry and stuff like that, but it's a lesson you've got to live through. And if you have success later on in life, why, it's real easy to handle it. You get a little out of hand, you just remember East Akron and you close the pocketbook again.

Of course, being a ballplayer is the biggest difference. You know, these guys, I don't know whether they realize it today, but even in my day, what was there – about 200 million people when I was seventeen years old? And there were only 400 ballplayers. Christ, you figure out the percentage on you becoming a major leaguer!

What really happened was the swimming coach became the baseball coach. And he more or less forced me. With three brothers, Christ, he practically lived in our home. He just said, "Play ball." So I played ball.

Bill Bradley signed me with Cleveland. When I started, rubber shops were paying about $10 a week. I made $80 a month my first year. Hell, that's $40 more than working in the rubber shops right there. Bradley also signed Tommy Henrich. Tommy was from Massilon, right there, and then Denny Galehouse. There weren't many ballplayers from my area. Weather kills you. Springs are so late. And back in my day they didn't have any teams. Of course, it's a great football and basketball area, northeastern Ohio. Still is.

• • •

I was seventeen years old and they sent me to Mansfield, Ohio. The Ohio State League. Class D. Well, my minor leagues, I led four leagues in hitting my first four years. And you only get moved up a notch: .398 and then I went to the Michigan State League. The second year, Class C, I hit .394. And then I went to Wilkes-Barre, Pennsylvania, and I had a bad year: I hit .344. Led the league. And then I came to the big leagues with Cleveland and Boudreau said I couldn't hit. Shit!

I trained right here in Clearwater with Cleveland, 1946. I had a good spring training. I came from A ball, Wilkes-Barre, to the big leagues in the last month of the season in 1943. Then I went in the navy, like everybody, until '46. And I was with Cleveland in '46, all year. Got traded to Pittsburgh for Al Lopez. You never know in that business. I was just with Pittsburgh in the spring, and then I got optioned to Newark, which was the Yankee chain. Then got sold in a trade with a bunch of people to San Francisco, and fortunately, there was Lefty O'Doul, and I had a heck of a year out there in 1948.

Man, you talk about going first class. Fagan, the sugar magnate, he owned the ballclub. I never went like that anywhere in the big leagues. We trained at Sonoma Mission Inn, which was one of the most exclusive resorts in California. We had our own airplane. You'd play a week in a town out there, have every Monday off, and always fly back to San Francisco for Monday with your family.

If I was to single out one guy that helped me more than anyone else in my career it would be Lefty O'Doul. "Holy mackerel!" Lefty says. "There's no way you shouldn't be in the big leagues." That's what he said to me out in San Francisco.

Anyway, we were in spring training and Lefty got to horsing around with me, and he says, "God, we got to get you back to the big leagues." So I get in the batting cage and he says, "Move up close to the plate." So I did. And then he says, "Put your feet together a little bit." And by doing that – you never want to change the position of a guy's bat, you'll crucify him – when I drew back I had to go into that crouch. And I went on to have a great year. I hit .385 and led the league. I've got to single out Lefty, and he did it so unassumingly.

Casey Stengel was with Oakland that year. Casey probably had one heck of a lot to do with me going to the Yankees, because I played a tune on his ballclub. And of course I went to the Yankees the following year, and I stayed.

Casey, oh my! Casey knew people. Let's face it, a manager's job, baseball-wise, isn't that tricky in the big leagues. But handling guys is a *big* job because it's pressure business. You're handling twenty-five temperamental people. He knew who to leave alone – some guys, you get on them and they go out and die on you. The greatest thing about Casey as a manager was that he knew ballplayers. He got outstanding mileage out of a lot of guys, a guy like Billy Martin.

Martin wasn't rated a good ballplayer; he was surrounded by good ballplayers. But Billy gave you 110 percent. Billy played hard. But being surrounded by good players *will* make you a better player. Casey got good mileage out of his guys; he got good mileage out of me. Hey, two clubs gave up on me. Of course, once you played with the Yankees, your chances of playing somewhere else and getting opportunities are still gonna last.

Casey used to stare Hank Bauer and I out. Like Crosetti said later, "You two dumb square-heads," that's what he used to call us, Frank. Of course you've read all that stuff about Bauer and me, but we'd get out on those trains and we'd drop down to .275 and we were worried about being shipped out. We were worried to death.

You'll hear a lot of things about the way Bauer and I fussed at Stengel, but that was all a part of winning. Nothing personal in it. Sure I got mad at him. I admit it. And I called him some names, but the more I called him an SOB the more I played. He knew people.

And I tell you, fortunately, when I ended up my career, I was forty years old, with the Mets and back with Casey again – he got me again!

The first day we were there – he always drew crowds wherever he was – he got me over there with all the writers, and he says, "This'll stop all this baloney about me and him. There's no way I didn't think he was a real good ballplayer, and there's no way that Gene didn't like me."

He said, "You mean to tell me I'm not going to like that guy? All he got mad about was he wanted to play. How can you get mad with a guy who wants to play."

It just sort of cleared the air.

Oh, he was funny. Especially when I was with the Mets.

"Woodling can play all he wants over here." And he'd sit there and he'd just wink at me.

I tell you one thing, he was probably the best public relations guy that's ever been in sports. He sold the game. He wasn't easy to play for, but the other stuff was all for the public. Image. You know. And he did a heck of a job. He really sold baseball. But you know, I tell people later on, and they read all that garbage about Casey and me, and I says, "How can I hate a guy for making me successful?"

He put money in my pocket, he gave me a chance to play in the big leagues. Nobody else did. And he made a better ballplayer out of me, let's face it.

My youngest daughter was born on Casey's birthday. We were in Chicago and Casey got word of it, and he come down the bench and he says, "You better name that girl Casey."

Of course you can imagine what I said. No way! Now that same daughter had a daughter and her name's Casey. Yeah, she's named after Casey Stengel. She sure is. If he'd be alive today . . . She's nicer than Casey, but she didn't make me any money.

You read a lot of things. There are books and books. I've got chapters about me and Casey. I never read any of them. They mail them to me. I say, "I don't have to read any of them, I was there."

. . .

You don't really think that much about it when you're doing it. It's when your career is over . . . I'd be working out there by myself on the farm, in the fields, and you get to thinking and reminiscing out there and you say to yourself, "Gee, we won five pennants and five World Series in a row." All records are made to be broken, but that's a tough one.

It was great playing with DiMaggio. We didn't bother him. I played on the left field line, Bauer played on the right field line. If you run into Joe DiMaggio you're gonna go home and go to work.

Everything they've said about him as a ballplayer is true. Never said much. I think he was shy. But he was great. And I played three years with him.

Houk's and my lockers were over by DiMaggio and the writers weren't allowed around him. No way! And they'd come over by us, and that Houk – he was ornery anyway – he'd push them over there. And Joe used to just look up . . .

He paid me one of the biggest compliments when he was having that heel trouble. That helped. They asked him who should replace him while he was gone. He mentioned me. Not too bad is it? And they did. They put me in centerfield.

But they had reasons for moving me around in New York. That left field in Yankee Stadium, that was tough. And we played day ball. We only played two night games a week. They said I played it better than anybody else. Well, maybe I was luckier. The three decks there and that humidity and people smoking. And that sun?

I tell you what I did, and Houk can vouch for this. I came out when pitchers were having batting practice and went to left field. As many balls as I could field out there, I did. Houk had to be there early, because he was the bullpen catcher, so I'd go out there with him, and I was able to do those things.

I tell you, there wasn't too much I didn't know about left field. And you know, I never said anything while I was there. I didn't try to make excuses. That was my job. That's what I was supposed to do. But don't anybody kid you that I didn't drop some, and don't anybody kid you that I didn't get hit. Cause I did, probably not as much as the other guys.

Oh, Norm Siebern, I felt sorry for him. I'm gonna tell you. We won a lot of ballgames when they'd shoot somebody out there in the late innings for defense. I don't care if you put the greatest outfielder out there, he ain't gonna adjust. And we won a lot of ballgames like that. They just weren't gonna do it. The old man would be happy when they defensed out there, cause he knew it, too. It isn't because I said it. It was said many, many times before I got there: It was the worst outfield to play under those circumstances. Boy, I tell you, along about three, four o'clock, it was tough. And then World Series time it was even worse.

Charlie Keller talked to me an awful lot, cause he had to play it, and did a good job. He helped me a lot.

I used to say, "Charlie, you're too damn nice to be a ballplayer." And he really was.

Bobby Brown . . . we used to torment him. He was in the middle of the year taking his internship and we presented him with an old rusty knife. He was a good hitter. Fielding? He come down here one spring and fielded ten thousand baseballs, and we went up there and opened the season against the White Sox. I'll never forget it. First ball hit was to Bobby Brown and I'm chasing it in left field.

I used to kid him. I'd say, "Bobby, if I ever get sick, you get to the airport as fast as you can, get the fastest jet you can, and go the opposite way I'm going."

In '54 we went into Cleveland to play a doubleheader on a Sunday – if I remember right, and I'm pretty sure I do. If we'd have beat them we'd have won another one. That was the only difference, right there. But hey, how'd you like to have five guys won ninety-three games between them? And then Boston had good clubs. Detroit. You know we only won one of ours by any margin. All the rest of them were the last day of the season, two days before. One of them was six or seven ballgames. We never run out and beat everybody. It was always a close battle because, hey, Cleveland wasn't easy to beat.

Where we beat them was on defense and speed. They could match us in pitching, naturally. They could match us with the bat. Think of Cleveland's clubs. But on defense and speed we were outstanding. And this is something we never were given a lot of credit for on the Yankees. We had outstanding speed and defense. Oh, man!

We didn't hit into double plays. You know why? Casey said, "I did not want those guys that took one swing and made two outs."

And he got rid of some good guys. Look at Jackie Jensen. He'd go up there and hit a line drive and make a double play. We didn't hit into any double plays. Casey, he ran his ballclub.

Dan Topping and Del Webb? I shouldn't say this . . . Oh, I'll say it anyway, what do I care: Owners are not like they were. You lost the Yawkeys. You lost the Wrigleys. You lost the Toppings and Webbs. These were guys that enjoyed the game of baseball. Sport! To them it was a hobby, and they never interfered. Never interfered. Topping and Webb? We'd see them in spring training, and the only reason they did that is they threw a big shindig for the ballplayers and their wives. And then, naturally, World Series time. That's it! Weiss run his business upstairs. Stengel run his business downstairs. That's the way it was.

Frank Crosetti. One of the nicest guys ever been in baseball. Very serious minded fella and a great coach. Frank wouldn't go to anything. No World Series parties, none of the gingerbread stuff. He was just all business. I come, I do my job, and I go home. We'd win four games in a row or something and we'd be riding high, and Frank would walk through the clubhouse and say, "Don't get gay when you're full of shit." That stops you.

But he went first class. A lot of times we'd take our wives with us on a trip and we'd go up to Frank, "Frank, where's a good restaurant to go to?" He knew all the good restaurants.

I tell you something about memorizing things as a hitter. He came up to me one time and said, "Gene, when you're up at home plate" – and this guy had to work at hitting, he was with Gehrig and Ruth – "when

you see the second baseman shift, you know you're gonna see a breaking ball you can pull more."

I never thought of those kind of things. Christ, it opens up a big
hole. When you know what's coming it makes a big difference, and
Frank was one of the first guys to make me aware of that. And boy, I
used it. Like with Nellie Fox. Every time they were going to throw me
a breaking ball or change up on me, Fox used to cheat early. And Jesus,
I knew it. This is hitting. It has nothing to do with swing this way, stand
this way. This is the mental part I was talking about, and Frank's one of
the first guys to ever teach me that. He's good people.

Jackie Robinson and those Dodgers in '52 and '53? They had us
down one year and we had to win both games in Ebbets Field. We had
to win them both to win the Series. And that's hard to do. And we went
out and won both of them.

That was a good group of guys. There were twelve of us that played
through it. Unfortunately there are only nine of us left. Eddie Lopat just
passed away, and of course Collins and Raschi. We're all getting up there
in age. Reynolds, Chief, he's had some health problems. Chief and I
have known each other since we've been in baseball. I see a lot of Hank
Bauer. We go to card shows. We're the same age, within two weeks.

■ ■ ■

I lasted a long time. I played in three different eras of ballplayers.
You know, I even played with the Brooks Robinsons.

Now I'm gonna tell you a story. Eddie Robinson and Paul Richards
come into the locker room after a night game, and Eddie wants to
know if I could come out the next day and look at a kid that Eddie's
bringing in. Just give an opinion. So I said, sure. Well, this kid – Brooks
Robinson – couldn't run, he couldn't throw, he couldn't hit. I said,
"You got me out of bed to see this? You ain't going to sign this kid."

Brooksie? He'd have never been a ballplayer if it was up to me. He'd
have been back in Arkansas, a chicken farmer. You know, I could outrun him. Easy. And his arm! He could stand right there and throw and
he couldn't break that window. But he was quick.

■ ■ ■

The years take care of things. Where I'm remembered the most is
Baltimore. And the reason is, well, I got booed out of town.

When I got traded from the Yankees to Baltimore I got a thousand
calls, and I said, "What do you want me to do, roll over and die?" I says,
"Baltimore is in the big leagues, ain't they?"

Hey, you cannot get sentimental over any city you play for or any uniform. If playing with the Yankees was gonna make me a good ballplayer I would've gone home and went to work.

Yeah, I went down there from the Yankees and I didn't hit. The trading deadline was around the fifteenth of June, and Paul Richards says, "I better get you out of here before they kill you."

He traded me over to Cleveland and then he brought me right back three years later. And I wasn't young. I had good years when I came back. A few base hits change all that, you know. It's funny, coming back the second time under those kind of conditions – I think it leaves a little bit of a mark. You know, people will remember. And then just last June I was put in their Hall of Fame.

Ballplayers gauge things differently than their public. Everybody looks at batting averages and RBIs, and that doesn't have nothing to do with it. There's a lot of guys drive in 110 runs, maybe 25 of them mean something to win or lose. Here's a guy that drives in 65 runs, and maybe 40 of his have something to do with winning. Now who would you rather have? And that's the way you base it.

I had what I considered my best years, as far as winning ballgames and what a ballplayer's supposed to do, in Baltimore. I had a reverse career in Baltimore. And the people . . . We made a lot of good friends. I was there about eight years, including coaching. We won a pennant and World Series. It's the only place that I ever played ball where I walked down the street and people knew me. They knew me! They don't even know me in Akron, Ohio. And New York?

My best year, by far, was 1959. It just seemed like every time you wanted to win a ballgame, I was the guy. I know everybody remembers the World Series, the Yankees. That was all great, don't mistake me. And then the Cleveland year was an outstanding year, but it wasn't the kind of year like the years I had in Baltimore – to me, personally – because I won a *lot* of ballgames. I played a tune on the Yankees.

Yogi used to look up and say, "You're making the old man mad."

They were talking about me one time – I forget where I was, Cleveland or Baltimore – and Casey says, "You know something about that guy? There's very few guys get traded in the same league as often as he did and stayed around."

I got traded in the same league and they're supposed to know all about you. They knew all about me, all right. God, I had a good career against Cleveland. You're talking about four twenty-game winners. Then I go out against a team like the St. Louis Browns, against a guy who'd win two and lose eighteen, and I couldn't get a base hit off of him. You can't pinpoint hitting. No way. It just happens and you don't know why or nothing. I wrote hitting books, too – that's only for money.

* * *

The whole time I was in Baltimore – the second time – the writers weren't allowed near me. There was a friction. You trust people. I was brought up to trust people. You try to be decent to a guy and help him earn a living, and the next day in the paper they crucify you. These interviews: Oh, God, they were terrible. You *build* up resentment. Of course, when they wrote that about me leaving Baltimore, that hurt. Cause it didn't matter where I played I was never accused of not doing my best, and they did. So I came back the second time, whew, and Lee MacPhail and Paul Richards? No way they even *tried* to do anything about it.

They both said it: "Hey look, you guys caused that. The guy does what we want him to do."

And I was having good years. I could've given them a lot of good information. But they got to write about it anyways. If you do good, they gotta do it; if you do bad, they gotta do it. So it doesn't really matter. Publicity don't keep you in the league, base hits do.

I had a writer come up to me one day and say, "Hey, we can help you. . . ."

"Yeah, you can help me! The day I don't get base hits I'll be back in Ohio."

There's been a lot of bad ballplayers and there's been a lot of bad writers, too. I'm not saying they're all bad. John Steadman in Baltimore, he's a great one. I'll tell you a story.

I roomed with Billy Klaus, and John got close to Billy. And I got deeper and deeper in trouble with this pension business – I was the leader of our pension plan for seven years – and getting some bad publicity, and Billy says, "Why don't you let this guy clear the air for you."

I says, "Nah, come on, he'll be like the rest of them." But I was getting so deep then, what did I have to lose. So I did, and he cleared the air. All over the country.

And John was a guy you could trust. If you told him not to say something he would never do it. And he had common sense enough to take a quote and not turn it around. He was a sentimental writer, more or less.

I'd say, "John, I read your articles and you make me want to cry. What are you trying to do, make some damn martyr of me?"

He's the only writer I'd go out to dinner with. That's how much I liked the guy. John and his wife and me and Betty, we'd go to dinner together.

I didn't have many friends among the writers, but *they* created the problems. Anyone who creates problems, you got to stay away from them.

Frank Lane? How do guys like that get in baseball? Ruin your families. I made him trade me. From Cleveland. I had a real good year in 1957 at Cleveland. It's my home. I was man of the year, and he comes into that banquet and says, "Well, Gene better not unpack his bags."

Well, I got news for you, that's the wrong thing to say to me. I told him, "You trade me or I ain't going to let you into the ballpark." That's it. That's the way I am. That guy wasn't going to ruin my family. No way! Nobody messed with my family. No baseball people.

You know, years ago, it's funny, I was one of the guys that broke the thing you couldn't bring your families to spring training. I'm over there in that navy and these guys are around here enjoying everything, and I'm away from my family and I come home, and two weeks later I'm going to spring training and I can't bring my family? No way! Baseball didn't mean *that* much to me. So I just brought 'em.

And they told me, "You've got to take them home."

So I said, "Okay, I'm going home with them."

I didn't care. Go home and go to work.

.   .   .

I was natured this way: When I go to the ballpark it's all business to me, no nonsense. You don't tell me to hustle. That's an insult. I never wanted to hear a ballplayer saying, "Nice hustling." That's an insult. You're supposed to do that. And I did.

Down at Washington? Mickey Vernon got me down there because he knew I'd stir up a lot of ballplayers, and I did. That's one thing about that Washington ballclub, they didn't loaf. We'd get beat 15–2 or something, but we played.

.   .   .

Baseball takes you away from a lot of things. It takes you away from everything but baseball. I don't know about these ballplayers today, but if they're living better than Gene Woodling is right now . . . I'll take odds on that.

I made good money for my ability. I didn't set any records, but I think I ranked pretty high when it came to that eighth and ninth inning and winning ballgames. And I made them pay me for it. I was a stand-still guy. I wasn't easy at contract time. I needed no agent. I had my agent right here. My wife.

I tell you the easiest guy I signed with was George Weiss. I'd tell them, "I'm not signing here unless I sign with George Weiss."

Weiss *knew* the facts. If you came in and told the facts, the truth, he would never deny you. Except that he never wanted to sign contracts. He had an assistant, because he'd always give in. This is the truth. George Weiss, you didn't fool him.

Of course I didn't have to fool them. I went in with the facts. Hey, when you had the kind of year that I had in Baltimore in '59 and they're gonna offer you a $2,000 raise, that's absolutely ridiculous. That's the only time in my career I held out. Not into the season, but I was up there in Ohio when spring training started, and pretty soon Paul Richards called me.

Paul says, "What's going on?"

I says, "Paul, I ain't moving from this farm. You better talk to MacPahil."

I says, "You think I had a pretty good year last year?"

"You better believe it."

I says, "Well, $2,000 bucks?"

You know what Paul says right then? "You come down."

I says, "*Wait* a minute, Paul. Now there's been ballplayers been told to come to spring training and then you get out there and they give you the hose. No way.

"It isn't that I don't trust you. You've had the greatest faith in me. But it's gotta be done before I leave the farm."

And then, I got down there and I wouldn't sign the contract.

We got up to Baltimore and I still wouldn't sign that contract.

Opening day. You couldn't play without a contract.

Finally, Paul came out and says, "Hey?"

I said, "I'm gonna sign it, Paul. But sometimes you have to teach somebody a lesson."

I signed a few minutes before opening day. The contract was there and the offer was right, but I told Klaus, "Well, that guy shouldn't've done what he did to me."

Ask Mantle sometime. He'll tell you: "If that guy tells you he's gonna do something he'll do it. You can bet your last dollar on it."

He'll tell you – Sic Woodling on them.

Carl Erskine

April 27, 1993, Anderson, Indiana

Carl Erskine pitched for the Brooklyn and Los Angeles Dodgers from 1948 to 1959. He appeared in five World Series, including that of 1955, Brooklyn's only World Championship season. Erskine won 122 games, lost 78, and compiled a 4.00 lifetime earned run average in his twelve National League seasons. A twenty-game winner in 1953, he pitched two no-hit games, in 1952 and in 1956.

Betty and I were just kids when we were called up to Brooklyn in 1948. Betty may not have been out of her teens yet. I think she was still nineteen. We had one small child.

It was very scary for us – Betty had never been out of Madison County, Indiana, and I'd been in the navy, but only a short time. So right away we found that neighborhoods were close-knit, the way it had been back in our hometown. We were surprised: "Gee, these New Yorkers are family oriented. They're sensitive to family. If they like you and you respond well, you become almost a part of their family."

Well that was what we found in Brooklyn. And having lived there ten summers, we put down a lot of roots. To this day, I still correspond with people who babysat for us, who are now married and have kids of their own, maybe even grandparents themselves. A lot of those people are still around. Some of the places we shopped in Brooklyn, the old butcher's shop . . . Joe Rossi, and his family . . . we've stayed in touch. There has just been a lot of linkage.

I went back to a wedding in Long Island last summer, Betty and I. And we drove back to East Nineteenth Street in Brooklyn to see if we could find the location of our old pediatrician, Dr. Morris Steiner, who's well into his eighties and retired. Betty remembered the address, after all these years, and how to get there.

We drove over to Brooklyn and down East Nineteenth and found Dr. Steiner at home and stayed and had dinner with him. Just had a great visit. Those ties were genuine, and they have lasted all these years. Even though when I had a bad day in Brooklyn I was not immune to a few catcalls – "We brought you out of the minor leagues for this?" as Phil Foster said.

Poor performance was not appreciated in Brooklyn. And the fans let you know it. With one exception: Gil Hodges. They never booed Hodges.

To this day, baseball people shake their heads and can't believe it, because I did hear DiMaggio booed in the Stadium. I heard Musial booed in St. Louis. But I never heard Hodges booed in Brooklyn.

They caught the spirit of Gil as a genuine person doing his dead-level best all the time. Through the bad slumps he had occasionally – though he always fielded well, slumps never affected his fielding – he was such a quiet strength on the field. And the loud, leather-lunged Brooklyn fans understood that, and they refused to boo Hodges.

Plus, Hodges did something that I think really endeared him to the people of Brooklyn. He pulled up stakes in Indiana and moved, permanently. Married a girl and lived in Brooklyn. That really made Gil a part of their life. I think all that together . . . the people in Brooklyn refused to boo him. But that was an exception.

It was a love affair, as you've heard stated before . . . the fans in Brooklyn. It just seems that Brooklyn was sort of the orphan borough in New York. Brooklyn didn't have much political clout. A few good restaurants . . . the St. George Hotel . . . It just didn't capture "New York." Manhattan and the Bronx, they were the uptown folks. Brooklyn was the orphan borough.

And they never had any consistent success in baseball. They'd win a pennant occasionally, never a World Series. Then, in the late '40s, the team that Branch Rickey put together began to gel, and Mr. Rickey was very selective of who he kept.

The centerpiece of that team was Jackie Robinson – the strong personality, strong player, first black. We became a team that drew extremely well on the road, as well as home, and we started to win. And we either won, or were close to winning, for a decade.

The team stayed together. There were very few trades of the nucleus of that team. We traded for Andy Pafko, to find a left-fielder. There was the trade that brought Preacher Roe and Billy Cox to us in the early '50s; both of them became stars for the Dodgers. But Jackie was signed, Campy came through the minor leagues, Newcombe came through the minor leagues, Furillo, Snider, Reese . . . they all came through the system. That nucleus just stayed together for all those years.

Suddenly, Brooklyn became a city that had respectability on the baseball field and the identity of a championship team. Or a near-championship team, still being human enough to have these tragedies that happened in 1951, 1950 . . . losing on the last day, losing in a playoff after a big lead. There was a tragedy in the personality somewhere that was like life itself. And somehow the souls in Brooklyn embraced this team even greater.

But I can tell you that the team agonized over the loss in '51. Not because of ourselves. I know every one of us felt this deep, deep hurt for the Brooklyn fans that the hated Giants overtook us with a thirteen-and-a-half-game lead and beat us in a playoff on this dramatic home run by Thomson. That was bitter, very bitter. It's still bitter . . . in the sense that the team felt they had really let the Brooklyn fans down.

The Giants played great. We didn't fold as much as it was a miraculous finish for the Giants. It was a very historic time, a historic moment in baseball. Still, the bitterness we felt was more for the fans than for ourselves. But then, as Duke Snider pointed out, a team so devastated with that kind of loss might have just gone down the tubes. But what *did* happen to that team? We won the pennant in '52 and '53. We were close in '54. We won it all in '55. And we won the pennant again in '56. That team was a *great* team, and destined to be a winning team and a contending team. So even with that bitter disappointment, the team went back to spring training in 1952 and had an outstanding year.

Went back in '53 and, to my surprise, Dressen wanted to tinker with this lineup. He wanted to bring this kid, Gilliam, in to play second and move Robinson to third. Well, we thought he was out of his mind. Why tinker around with this team that had a great 1952 season? Well, we had a better season in '53.

I think that if you ask the Dodger players who were there "What was your best team?" most would say that team. The numbers generated by that team in '53 . . . I think three players in the middle of that lineup all had 120 to 140 RBIs. We won 105 games. Then again, we lost in six games in the World Series to the Yankees. But the magic year in '55 was the one that vindicated all the other failures and gave the Brooklyn fans the success that they had dreamed about . . . to be World Champions. And we did it against the Yankees. And we did it in Yankee Stadium.

I think all that together was just the culmination of this beautiful support that the Brooklyn fans had given us all those years. To this day, there's this element of carryover. There's a group in Brooklyn that has a countdown on the actual date of that victory, the final seventh-game victory in '55. They have a countdown to the very second when Reese fielded the ground ball and threw to Hodges for the third out. That was always a lot of fun: Pee Wee contended that he made a beautiful throw and Hodges said, "I saved you, again, Captain. It was in the dirt."

I think that down in the gut of every player there who wanted to win, wanted to get this World Series win, that the ultimate prize was that we were able to present to the borough of Brooklyn, which had been promised over and over . . . with the good teams that had won the pennant in my years. I think every player felt that. I treasure the World Series ring I got from 1955, but I think the bigger prize is to still get letters to this day from Brooklyn fans who write about the thrill of being World Champions over the Yankees in 1955. It meant something deep. ·

·   ·   ·

I think there was a chemistry that writers and players have tried to identify. What made this chemistry the way it was?

Just my own observations. Number one, it was right after World War II. The whole country had felt we had won victory in the war and we were getting back to the things of life that we wanted, wanted to enjoy, that the fear and all hardships of war were behind us. We had losses to think about. It was a pensive time right after the war. But there was a new momentum in industry and business in the country.

Baseball had survived the war, and now it was rebuilding with new players. The Dodgers had a farm system that had 790 players – something like that – under contract. And there was an exhilaration of youth. All of that was in this mix.

Number two. Mr. Rickey – a gifted man in how to select talent, how to scout, innovative ways of teaching baseball – was coming into his own with another dynasty. He'd been in St. Louis, and now he'd come over to Brooklyn and was going to pick up this team that'd just been also-rans and try to make a real consistent team out of it.

Competition for jobs was fierce in spring training: one-year contracts, and all this talent. Well, out of that, Mr. Rickey selected and selected and selected – kept a few veterans, but he basically had a youth movement on, moving guys up quick. Through his handling of the various personalities and selecting, keeping, and training, he ended up with a team in the early '50s that influenced baseball for years to come.

I mean that in this sense: Mr. Rickey not only had players, but if you'll look at who stayed in baseball after the '50s and were the coaches, scouts, managers, broadcasters . . . they were shot through with Brooklyn people. What you might say is shot through with Rickey disciples. I see a fifty-year era coming to an end when Tommy Lasorda retires from baseball. He was a Rickey disciple. He's about the last one, because the scouts who were under Mr. Rickey, who stayed in the organization, and some of the people who worked for him have all retired. Now we're into free agency. Makes the farm system much, much different. Scouting is different. His system doesn't fit today's baseball the way it fit in his era, or in the eras up to free agency. But I see Lasorda as the carryover from Mr. Rickey's influence.

He had a lot of teaching ideas and teaching aids that are still used in spring training and have gone through all of baseball. But that was part of the magic of the era.

Baseball just had a rebirth at that time. Jackie, being the first black, opened up a new area of talent and a new area of fan interest. Most people wouldn't remember that some ballparks were segregated in the early years. Black fans sat together and the white fans sat together. That didn't last long, but in the beginning it was that way. Well, that was a major social change in our country, to see this integration take place in the right way. Jackie deserved to be in the big leagues. He proved it. He proved it right out in front of everybody. He didn't have any political help, he didn't have any financial help. He had to do it. That's the right way, that's affirmative action at its best, and maybe the only real way that you should have affirmative action. But Jackie deserved to be there, as did many other great black players.

Also, technology came into the picture. Baseball went from a day game to a night game. It went from a train game to a plane game, from radio to TV. And from East Coast to West Coast. That all happened in the '50s. Those things made it a very special time for baseball.

People ask, "Don't you wish you were playing today, with all the big money?"

Yeah, I wish I could still play. I'd love to play. I love to make money. I'd love to be in the game in any era. But I tell you why I think our era was special. I look back to the early 1900s, the '20s and the '30s, before I came on the scene. The guys who played in those years, and the owners in baseball in those years, set the stage for this golden era of the '50s. We could not have enjoyed that had it not been for the guys that played for virtually nothing, and franchises that had to get established, and owners who had to invest in stadiums. All that had to take place. I don't think you can have an appreciation of life if you don't look back and see who set the stage for you to have this opportunity. That makes it real easy for me to say, "No, I don't wish I was playing today."

I'm glad that players today are getting a big piece of the big pie. It'd be a shame if they didn't. We got our share in the '50s, and we're beholden to the guys that got such a small piece before us. And I think that really is why I'm grateful for my time.

■ ■ ■

We negotiated from a very weak position. We couldn't go anyplace else if we didn't agree with the salary, so it wasn't true negotiation. It was really the owners talking to you about what would you be happy playing for this year. Well, I wanted $30,000 after I won twenty and lost six. I was making eighteen and I wanted thirty. I couldn't get it. I got ten-five. They took me to twenty-eight-five but gave me some extras. They paid my family's spring training expenses, and see these gold inlays? That's part of my 1954 raise. Bavasi agreed to let me have some dental work done on top of my salary. And that's a part of it, I'm telling you, what you see in my mouth is a part of my '54 raise.

But did I feel cheated? No. I was happy. And believe me, the owners played on this fact. Maybe you think we were naive. The owners said, "We need the reserve clause because it keeps baseball stable. It keeps these franchises stable. It keeps the wealthy clubs from owning all the players. Otherwise the weak franchises would disappear. And baseball needs to keep the franchises healthy."

We bought in to that. We wanted the game to stay healthy. And so only occasionally did somebody test in the courts the reserve clause. But when free agency began, baseball business was done differently, and had to be. It was just a different era. And then TV pumped in all these new revenues, and bigger parks. My goodness, sixteen teams when I played; now there are twenty-eight teams in the major leagues.

Why did that happen? Well, one major reason was the jet plane. You couldn't go to San Francisco from New York, or anywhere else in the National League or American League, without the jet plane. You couldn't do it by train. Well, technology opened that up. Mr. O'Malley, when I retired in 1960, offered me a job with the Dodgers to be kind of a liaison in Japan, where we had played and were very popular. Mr. Suzuki, who was with the newspaper over in Tokyo, was the one who helped set it up. Mr. O'Malley wanted me to go talk to Mr. Suzuki and begin to discuss the time when the next generation of jet plane came along and would shorten the time again . . . when Tokyo and Osaka and some of those cities could be major league franchises. He was just thirty-five or forty years ahead of his time, but that'll happen some day . . . Mexico City, probably Havana. I think you'll see a team in Europe. So it's just a matter of time. Maybe in my lifetime we'll see a *real* World Series. It's indicative of what's happening, and we're slow to want to change that. It's now a world economy, and we're slow to embrace that. But baseball is part of the changes, and I think there's real reason to believe that baseball, as popular as it is, will be worldwide.

▪ ▪ ▪

When the Dodgers left Brooklyn in '58, they left behind a broken spirit. In this sense: There was always this subtle inference that this is your team. In Cleveland or in St. Louis, the people who live in those cities and support the Indians or the Cardinals have an identity of ownership.

It was interesting in Brooklyn – Duke points this out in his book, too – when the wives would go shopping and we were playing a day game, they never missed a pitch, because you'd walk down the streets of Brooklyn shopping at all these open-air stores, the radios were on everyplace, and you heard pitch by pitch by pitch, no matter where you walked down the street. And that's true. That's the way the games were received in Brooklyn.

Mr. O'Malley got a bad rap, because he made lots of logical efforts to keep the team in Brooklyn. But Brooklyn had very little political clout, and the powers that be – I think Robert Moses – in the city of New York wanted to move him – the team – to Flushing Meadows, where the Mets are now. Mr. O'Malley did not want to move to Flushing Meadows. For whatever reason. He wanted to build a stadium in the downtown area of Brooklyn, which would mean reclaiming some downtown properties near where the Long Island Railroad's lines converged. But the city fathers wouldn't buy that.

We went to Jersey City, Roosevelt Stadium, and played a few games, just to test the waters. Then the romance started from the West Coast. And with the jet plane making it possible, the Dodgers were the first team to fly. Mr. O'Malley was a very futuristic person and a good business mind, and when LA made him that offer with the property and the location in downtown LA, and to open the West Coast . . . If you were a stockholder for the Dodgers, you'd want to put Mr. O'Malley in the Hall of Fame. But if you were a Brooklyn fan living in Brooklyn, you hung him in effigy because "he stole a part of my life and he had no right to because he told me that I owned a part of this team."

Brooklyn fans to this day, many of them, don't even acknowledge that there is a Dodger team, other than the Brooklyn Dodgers. Some of that's abated. I know that Peter O'Malley and Terry, his sister, agonize over the image their father has with some people in Brooklyn. Because Mr. O'Malley did everything he could to try to keep the team in Brooklyn, short of just caving in and not having any say and letting the city fathers tell him where to put the stadium, how to build it, and so on.

Mr. O'Malley owned the team. After all, he brought the Dodgers, in Brooklyn, the only world championship in 1955. He was the owner–general manager at that time. So I think it's an unfair indictment to nail him with that.

But in the last analysis, he did make the decision to leave. And he did influence Horace Stoneham to move the Giants, because the owners in baseball said the only way they would approve a move to the West Coast is if two teams go. So I'm sure Mr. O'Malley had a strong influence on Horace Stoneham.

■   ■   ■

In a way, moving from Brooklyn was outside the players' realm of concern. We'd read the newspaper accounts and knew there were rumbles and knew that Mr. O'Malley was trying to relocate us . . . somewhere . . . away from Ebbets Field.

When we went to spring training in 1958, it had already been announced that we were leaving. But we went back to the same training site. Our spring training felt just the same as it always had. Vero Beach, Florida. Dodgertown.

We played our exhibition games around Florida. Came time for the season to open, and instead of us moving north the way we'd always done, playing our way north with some big league team – usually the Braves – and ending up in New York for opening day in April . . . instead of that, when spring training ended we boarded a plane and flew to San Francisco to open the season in Seals Stadium. I think it was only at that time did it really hit the players that we were not going back to New York. We were not going back to Brooklyn.

And then the strangeness set in: playing opening day in a minor league park on the West Coast, and then three days later moving down and opening the season in Los Angeles in a football stadium – the Coliseum – improvised for baseball, with a crowd that had a strange silence about it. They didn't know us. It was new. It *was* a big league game . . . and it wasn't . . . sort of a facsimile.

I pitched opening day in LA, and the crowd . . . you weren't sure who they were rooting for. There was just kind of a blasé feeling, because there was not an identity yet with the Dodgers. It was a wild game against the Giants, and Clem Labine relieved me, as he had oftentimes, and nailed it down in the ninth.

No, the players had a real tough adjustment. Then, within the players, there was kind of a split group. In this sense: You take Furillo and Snider and Hodges, Reese, Erskine, Newcombe – Campy had already been hurt, so he didn't make the trip – we were the old guard, and we had to go to the West Coast with our best years, basically, behind us and now say, "Well, we've got to re-prove ourselves." We were on the downside of our years in baseball. I didn't have a lot left, and I had a lot of arm trouble on top of it. Then there was Podres, who was just coming into his own; Drysdale, who'd been a productive pitcher in Brooklyn as a rookie, a young pitcher; Koufax hadn't found himself yet; nobody'd ever heard of Maury Wills, Frank Howard, Larry Sherry. Those were guys in the minors. That was a difficult time . . . for me, especially.

I remember going to a doctor in New York with a friend of mine because I had this funny feeling in my heart. So he examined me and said, "Well, organically, you're in great shape. Your heart's strong. You've got some stress in your life – some kind – that's probably causing this palpitation in your heart.

"When you get rid of whatever that stress is, you'll probably get rid of that."

When I walked into Buzzi Bavasi's office, June 15, 1959 – I struggled all season and they kept encouraging me to stay – when I walked in and voluntarily retired, because I was just ineffective, the palpitation quit. And I haven't had one since.

It was a smart move on my part. I was not productive, my arm wasn't sound. Roger Craig replaced me and won eleven games the balance of the season. Maury Wills was brought up from the minors. He had a great finish. Frank Howard came in, Larry Sherry, Norm Larker – names that weren't even on the roster in the beginning of the season. Won the pennant in '59 by tying Milwaukee and beating them in a playoff, then beat the White Sox in the World Series. This is the '59 World Series ring. I was privileged to receive a ring. I stayed on as a coach, but I wasn't eligible to pitch in the Series. I stayed on for the balance of the year and retired, officially, after the World Series in '59.

And that was when the old guard and the new guard began to change. Hodges stayed on, had a good Series in '59. Snider stayed on, eventually was traded to, of all people, the Giants – the Mets first. I loved Duke's line in his book. He said that when he put the Giants uniform on and looked down at that orange and black where it had been Dodger blue and white, he said he couldn't believe it was him standing in that uniform. He said, "We hated the Giants so much, in that orange and black, that we didn't even like Halloween."

But Newcombe was traded to Cincinnati – I think that's when his stress started – and then to Japan, where he tried to hang on. I think that's when his alcohol problem surfaced. Reese retired as an active player and became a coach in '59. Furillo's legs finally went, and Carl was released and had a very bitter feeling about the release. He went to the press with his feelings, and there was an open battle. Carl left baseball rather bitter.

He eventually came back and worked at the fantasy camps for the Dodgers. It tempered his feelings some. But Carl was a strong-willed person, and I'm not sure he ever felt real forgiveness for the Dodgers releasing him in midseason. But he did temper his feeling and he was a good instructor in the fantasy camps.

The players just really admired Furillo. Carl was a workman-type ballplayer. He came to work when he came to the ballpark. Nothing frivolous. When he put on the uniform he went out to work, whatever the number of hours, and he worked. And he was intolerant of guys who goofed off and played halfhearted and didn't take care of themselves off the field. He didn't have any time for those guys.

We used to have a meeting in which we'd divide up the World Series shares. Anybody who was there for a partial year had to be voted on by the guys who were there all year. Furillo was tough – I *mean* tough – in those meetings. He'd say, "This guy didn't put out. You gonna give him that much? That's crazy. I don't vote for that."

Carl would keep it real straight because he felt that you owed a hundred-percent effort when you went out there to play. And if you were hurt a little? Ah, so what. I mean, if the bone wasn't sticking out then you ought to be in the lineup. Carl was a hard-nosed player and a consistent player.

Burt Shotten was like that . . . from the old school. You didn't pamper a rookie. You gotta realize that in those years there were no pitching coaches. Pitchers didn't have any pitchers to talk to except the guys on the staff. The "pitching coach" was a catcher, an infielder, or an outfielder. That's the way it was. Very few times did you ever see a pitcher on a coaching staff. So coaches could not relate to what really went on on the mound. Or how your arm felt. They'd only look at you, when you said your arm was sore, and say, "Well, it's not swollen. It's not discolored. I don't see any bones sticking out. Must be in your head! So you better go out and throw some more." That was the treatment.

So, when I went to Mr. Shotten with my muscle tear – which I felt like a sharp knife – I was pitching a shutout against the Phillies. He looked at me and said, very surprised, "Well, son, I can't take you out you're pitching a *shutout*. You stay right in there. If you get in a little trouble we'll come help you."

I finished the game and I did a lot of damage. And then I pitched another game four days later, and even though I could throw, I had a lot of discomfort. Real sharp pain. But I beat the Phillies again. I had them shut out until the eighth and beat them 8–1. But I did a lot of damage in those two or three games. Today the owners would not permit that because they'd have a property that's worth a lot of money, and they'd say, "Wait, get him out of there! Get him a rehab program going. Bring him back sound. Don't hurt him." But that wasn't the way it was in '48, '49, '50.

In a sense, I probably got more out of myself than I might have otherwise. I was always sorry I got hurt, but I don't *ever* want to lean on that and say, "Oh, I'd have been better if I hadn't got hurt." I just had this anxiety all the time about whether my arm was gonna respond or not. But, maybe it pushed me harder.

. . .

I pitched with a great team. My good fortune was that I didn't have to pitch against them. You know, that was one blessing for me: I didn't have to face Robinson and Hodges and Snider and those guys. And pitching *for* them we always got some runs.

I was always a little disappointed: my ERA was pretty high. It jumped up there the later years, when I was hanging on those last two or three years. But it was tough pitching in Ebbets Field. You'd usually give up some runs there. Tough to pitch a shutout in Ebbets Field.

But I pitched my best games there, in spite of that. Both no-hitters were at Ebbets Field. I did win a Series game in Yankee Stadium – eleven innings – but the other Series game I won was in Ebbets Field. So the pitchers would basically say to themselves: "Hold them one more inning. One more inning, we're gonna get some runs." And we just almost always did. So it was an advantage, in a way, for a pitcher to pitch in Ebbets Field, from wins and losses. It was not an advantage from earned run average. But I don't ever remember what my earned run average was. I always remembered how many did you win. Cause in the last analysis, that's what counts.

. . .

No, I wouldn't trade it. I'd like to do it over again. But I don't think I'd want to do it a lot differently.

You know, that was a rich experience to play with Jackie. Fine man, an intelligent man, great athlete, doing a very historic thing. Watching him, being a friend of his.

Campy! Oh what a story that is. How he's handled this paralysis thirty-five years from the neck down. Great athlete. To watch Roy handle that. Be with him, hear him talk, hear his sweet nature. No bitterness. No regrets. He'd say, "Ah, Ersk, there's just a few things I can't do anymore." He can't do *anything* anymore, except what people do for him: get him up, dress him, feed him, the whole business. Lives on a respirator now a lot. And Roy's got tremendous courage. He's just never let life whip him.

There were a lot of great strengths on that team. Hodges had that great quiet self-control. And Reese, in his gentlemanly way, was a tough cookie. He was a tough competitor and a hard-nosed ballplayer. Reese would play hurt a lot. He'd have a turned ankle, or a pulled muscle, or a bad strawberry . . . the guys'd say: "Pee Wee, we got an *eight*-game lead, why don't you take a couple of days off?"

Pee Wee would say, "Hey, one time when Durocher was playin' regular for the Dodgers and I'm just a kid on the bench . . . Leo had a headache and he asked out of the lineup. They put me in and Leo never got back.

"See these young guys waiting to jump in my job? No way."

He liked playing for Durocher. A lot of guys didn't. Leo was kind of a front-runner. If you're the darling of the team right now, Leo's all over you. If you're having a bad day, he's also all over you . . . the other way. But I think Pee Wee admired Leo, admired his tenacity. And even though Reese's personality was far different than Leo's, I think Pee Wee had that kind of tenacity. And he had a business sense for baseball. I mean, he wanted to do the thing that was right at the moment, and he didn't want any excuses. And as captain, he was able, actually, to be tough in an understanding way. I know that's how he helped Jackie.

But in a sense, Pee Wee had a cinch job as captain, because you could call Campanella a captain: he was a *general* on the field. Hodges was such an astute baseball guy; he'd steal signs and he'd strategize on the infield for defense. So he was a captain. Jackie! Good night, Jackie! His competitive spirit and his intellect all came into play . . . well, he was a captain. We had a whole infield full of captains. So to stand on the mound and look around at that team and say, "These guys are on my side . . ." I tell you, that's why I love baseball. I mean, I loved it then because we all saw every game as a money game.

Duke Snider and I were on our way home in '55, and we got stopped on the Pennsylvania Turnpike by a state trooper.

He said, "You guys were going seventy in a sixty-mile zone."

"Oh? We didn't know," we said.

He says, "Well, here's a warning ticket. And by the way, I lost money on you guys again this year."

"You *lost?*" I said. "We *won* the Series this year. What do you mean you lost?"

"Well, I bet on you in '49, '52, '53. I said nuts to 'em, I'm bettin' on the Yankees."

I told Duke later, "There, Duke, you just met a born loser. He bet on the Yankees the only time they lost."

It was a special time, and I think it's a mystery to me that in 1993 that era and that team has had such strong carryover. It's just great, but it's hard to explain how and why it's lasted.

I've been in banking, now, most of the years I've been out of base-ball. And one of the parallels I see in banking and baseball is that legislation has changed, making us do it a different way. That happened in baseball, it's happened in banking.

Lifestyles have changed, but people expect the product about the same as they always did. The same product. In banking, we still have checking, savings, loans. Basic products, but we deliver them in a *much* different way than we used to. Well, baseball – because of technology changes, lifestyle changes – delivers the product. A curve ball is thrown just like it used to be. You still hit the ball to the opposite field the same way you used to. You still field a ground ball with your head down and moving toward the ball. The fundamentals are still there. The product's very much the same.

But the delivery systems have changed how people are asking for it and want to get it. So night baseball, during the World Series? That's when the crowd can see it . . . more people can see it . . . the consumer. But you lose some things in the process. You trade off. And one of them that you trade off is World Series time.

When I was a kid in school, the teacher would have a break in the class and turn the radio on. You'd listen to this magic voice describing baseball in the *World Series*, which was Americana through and through. That's lost.

But you've got videotapes now, and you got kids that can play video games about baseball. I pitch in a video game, the 1953 Dodgers against the 1970 Reds, and I won! You've got a different delivery of the same thing. So you trade off some of the things. But I don't know of anybody's going to the well anymore and hauling up fresh well water.

My dad . . . the greatest technology in the world was when they put the conversion burner in the old coal furnace, and instead of going down and shaking down the grate and adding the coal and coughing with the dust and taking out the ashes, he walked over to this little dial on the wall and turned it and you could hear, in the old house where we lived, *Ha-room*! The old conversion burner kicked in and gas shot head up through the system.

To my dad, who's been dead many years, that was greater than hitting the moon with a rocket and people.

Technology change.

Well, we've had all those things happen. And yet, we still eat bread and butter. We sleep on a mattress. But all those delivery systems make life different. Baseball cannot avoid being different in that sense, because it's a different era. But I think there's a misconception of the current ballplayer.

Because the money got big, I think there's almost a resentment among some fans that this guy's playing the game for the wrong reasons. Sure the money's different, but baseball is show business. We don't think anything of Randy Travis making several million on a gold record, but if a guy leads the league and he gets this huge contract it just doesn't seem to *fit* the way we think of the athlete. But there are so many solid, right-thinking, genuine, young men playing major league baseball today. Family men who care about right values and want to put something back. That gets overlooked.

And I'm disappointed that the fan thinks less of the current player than he might think of the old-timer. We had guys that were goof-offs. We had guys that dissipated at night, that didn't take care of themselves, that didn't like the team they played on, that didn't like the manager, that "jaked it" – as we used to say – in the outfield, didn't put out. We had guys like that. Prima donnas that thought they were too good to bunt. Yeah, we had a few guys like that.

So it's kind of a misread to think that everybody in the old days played for the love of the game and would've given their life for a run and that the current players don't feel any sense of gratitude to the fan or to the game. That's a misread.

The only one that *doesn't* think that Roger Clemens isn't worth $1,500 a pitch is his mother. His mother thinks it's wonderful . . . and that'd be true with any mother.

I'll tell you this, I proudly display in my office my lifetime membership card to the Association of Professional Ballplayers of America. I'm very proud of that. And above it is my lifetime pass to major league games. In my day you had to play ten years in the big leagues to get that. Now it's eight, I think . . . if they still issue them.

I don't even know if they do. They should.

Dave Philley

September 30, 1994, Paris, Texas

Dave Philley played outfield and first base from 1941 to 1962, excluding minor league and military service from 1942 to 1945. In addition to playing seven and one-half seasons with the White Sox, Philley played for the Philadelphia Athletics, the Indians, Orioles, Tigers, Red Sox, and the Philadelphia Phillies and San Francisco Giants. A member of the 1954 American League pennant-winning Indians, Philley hit .270 in eighteen seasons, .299 as a pinch hitter.

Determination. Born with it. There was *nothing* whatsoever that was going to stand in my way from becoming a ballplayer. Nothing. My dad was in the grocery business here in Paris, Texas. He told me when I was about fifteen, "Hope you make a ballplayer, you're not good for much of anything else."

When I signed with Shreveport, the manager I played semipro for here in Paris said, "Oh, he'll be back in a month."

I got news for you: I wasn't. What it took: I knew I had some ability. I could throw and I could run, I knew that. And I knew I was going to work hard enough to put some of that together.

Shreveport signed me as a catcher. Homer Peel, the old Giants outfielder, was my manager there. "The way you run," he said, "we want to make an outfielder out of you."

You wouldn't believe it, but I could run. Last time I run the one-hundred-yard dash, back behind the fire department at the county meet, I ran a 9.7. I drew a wet track; it rained the night before. The best I could do was 9.6. Bob Dillinger over in St. Louis was the only one could outrun me in the American League for years and years.

There's two types of determination, as far as I'm concerned. There's determination in becoming a decent sportsman as far as benefiting your particular livelihood. Turn that around to see how the fans react, that's a different story.

I didn't know there was anybody in there. I never heard them, I never heard a word they said when I walked up to the plate. Guy could shoot a thirty-thirty behind me, I'd never jump. When you concentrate enough on the ballgame, you never hear those people.

You can't play the game without fans, no question about that. But a lot of fans think the ballplayers are out there putting on a show for them.

I've heard a number of people say, "Why do you want to fight on a ballfield?"

I say, "You don't understand that. They're not out there fighting just to fight, they're out there to beat one another. If something happens to deter that, here we go."

I've had second basemen and shortstops say, "I'd rather see anybody in baseball on first base than you." Because they know they're going to get knocked on their can down there. I'm not going to hurt anybody, if I can help it. Not at all. But I'll do my best to break up the double play. And if you got nine guys that are determined enough, look out, now, look out.

I didn't do things for reputation. Every ball I hit I hustled on. I'll show you an example. We're in New York, the old Yankee Stadium, before they did anything to it. They played me deep because I could hit it hard up the alleys. If they played me shallow I'd have an inside-the-park home run and they knew that, so they had to get back there.

Anyway, Joe DiMaggio was playing me deep center field, and I hit a ground ball past the pitcher between the second baseman and second base. I really dug, and I knew how to run bases. And I went into second base without much of a play. Double. It's a ground ball past the pitcher. I wasn't doing it to show anybody up. I did it to try to win a ballgame. That's the only way I knew to play the game.

Another thing I did one time. Hitting from the left side, I dragged the ball periodically. It wasn't to get a base hit 100 percent of the time – even though I could get one – but to keep the infield honest. If you didn't bunt the ball, drag the ball, they'd go back on the grass out there and you could *not* hit one past them.

Well, I could go towards the pitcher with the first step and I could beat him or anybody to first base because I got the first step going. So, they had to play me honest. And it got to the point where they thought: "This joker might bunt. We got to cheat a little on him." Well, Eddie Robinson was playing pretty close to the bag and I got too much of it, little hump-back line drive right over his head. I was the only guy in baseball that dragged a double, didn't let up till I got over into second base.

It's just what you were made of. Didn't try to show nobody up, never *did* try to. I just went out there to beat you. I didn't care how it came to happen, I came to beat you.

Here's my opinion. I might be wrong, but there's no human being living that played the game who took it more seriously than I did.

I saw numbers and numbers and numbers of guys go to spring training eight, ten, twelve, up to fifteen pounds heavy. Got to lose it. Now you become weak and you get injured if you're not careful. Well, my theory was if you're making a living out of your body, keep it as near 100 percent condition as you can. I did that year-round.

I played my last year in Boston, and I was an oddball as far as they were concerned. I didn't go out and cruise and night-life all night long. They couldn't understand that. I said, "In the first place, I don't believe in it. Number two, I'm making a living with my body, which I've done all my life, and I don't abuse it and don't aim to abuse it." Drink that firewater, it rusts your insides.

It's all been because of determination. That's the only reason I lack a few days as a player for twenty years, because of determination.

I'm not patting myself on the back. I was just an average ballplayer, but I was above average in defense and running bases. I know I was, I don't care what the records show. But defense and other phases, I was above average, and I'm not bragging. I led the league two years in assists for outfielders. I led the league two years in double plays for outfielders. I led the league two years in total bases.

I could run the bases in 13.8 seconds. You put some of those flyers on the bases and see if they could run them in 13.8. The shortest distance between two points is a straight line, and there's no deviation from it whatsoever. I ran the bases under that philosophy. You run out of base-line just before you get to first base and you hit it in your instep. Now you're going a straight line to the next base. Then before you get there you do the same thing, and then the same thing. You run halfway out on that grass out there and you can have the same speed I did and I could beat you to second base by at least three strides.

That's a part of winning. That's what you have to do. We taught that.

You cannot win without defense. In baseball it takes defense and pitching. One makes the other one. My philosophy: give three outs an inning, you're going to win; give four and five, no possible way you're going to win.

Errors are a part of the game, they happen. But determination will eliminate a lot of them. The mental mistakes and the dogging mistakes are the ones I'm talking about, where you didn't do the job you could've done. In other words, that's the one that'll beat you. *They're* not part of the game, they're mental situations.

All right, the example in Philadelphia, the Athletics. Bobby Shantz wins twenty-four games one year. And they said, "He ought to win." Played better ball behind him than any pitcher who walks on the field. Who caused it? Bobby Shantz.

You just think about this. Pitcher: ball one, two, three, four; ball one, two, three . . . behind on every hitter. Infielders and outfielders relax; now they hit one and you're not ready to go. Bobby Shantz is always around the plate. You *know* it's going to be hit to you, now you're ready to go, now you make those plays. He *causes* it. He causes the defense.

One makes the other, no doubt about it.

I thought I knew something when I got to the major leagues, but I didn't. It took me two days to learn I knew nothing. So I woke up in a hurry, and I went around the league to learn something. I said to myself, "I've got to find me an outfielder I think does things right. I've got to really observe him." And Joe DiMaggio was it.

People think I'm crazy, but I know this for a fact: Joe DiMaggio is the best ballplayer I ever saw. You can talk to sportswriters today and they say that Dominic was the better outfielder. They're full of garbage. Dominic made everything look hard. Joe made everything look easy. He played the outfield mathematically. Shortest distance between two points is a straight line, and that's the way he played it.

He caught all ground balls on his throwing side, to his right. You couldn't run on him, because he got all balls to his throwing side and came up throwing, right on a dime. And all fly balls would hit him in his throwing shoulder and he'd let it go.

Clemente was about the second-best ballplayer I ever saw. After DiMaggio. Al Kaline was next. I'm talking about people that did it all, for what it was worth. Not to put on a show, but for what it was worth to win a ballgame. Those guys did it all, I'll guarantee you. You put Kaline in New York and *man*, the publicity he would have got. He'd get it *all*.

. ▪ .

I hit .303 in Philadelphia in 1953. I was the eighth hitter in the league, and according to guys who kept records, I had eighty-eight line drives caught, and I could have led the league that year because I hit the ball hard all year.

Anyway, Connie Mack said, "You deserve a *good* raise, but we can't give it."

The first thing they did was they put in the paper that they had offered me a $6,000 raise and I wanted ten. When I read this–the raise had never been mentioned by Philadelphia at that time–I called the United Press and said, "I'm not looking for publicity, I'm mad." I told them what the story was, and as soon as I hung up I called the Associated Press. I was pretty bitter. Come to find out there was a whole sports page on that, ridiculing the Macks. But you know how sportswriters are, they added a little here and a little there.

Anyway, Philadelphia called me on the phone and said, "We don't appreciate you ridiculing us like that."

I said, "And I don't appreciate you lying, either. I had never mentioned what I wanted as a raise. And you said you offered me six and I wanted ten. That's a bold-faced lie and you know it is."

Well, if I call you a liar I'm ready to fight you. But anyway, I told them, "I'll tell you what I want–I want a $9,000 raise."

They said, "We can't pay you."

I said, "Somebody is."

I got talking to Hank Greenberg at Cleveland. He called me on the phone and he said, "We got a chance to trade for you."

I said, "You know what the story is and you know what I want."

He said, "All right."

I said, "Wait a minute. There's a little catch to it. I'm coming over there to win the pennant. You have a good ballclub there, but they're just going through the motions. I'll put fire enough in them so we win the pennant. I want a penny a head for attendance over a million."

Oh, he jumped at that, but he made the trade. I made $3,300 extra on that penny-a-head, and we won the pennant. Set a record of 111 wins.

After we got going, that Cleveland club was the most competitive I ever played on. You knew you were going to win. I'll show you an example.

New York came into Cleveland one night and Reynolds is pitching. You couldn't score eight runs off of Allie Reynolds in a week. Bob Lemon is going for us. Two outstanding pitchers.

Well, they get seven runs in the first inning off Lemon. That didn't phase that Cleveland club. That didn't phase them, I don't care how many runs you're down. In our part of the inning, Reynolds walked one or two and somebody blooped one here and there, and now it's 7–2. So he gets the bases jammed and Stengel jerks him right out of there, puts Bob Kuzava in.

For several years Stengel seen me hit from one side a couple of times and he'd forget I was a switch-hitter. He never knew the names of opposing players, but there wasn't but two switch-hitters in the league at that time, and he's going to get Kuzava to pitch to me. I just got over on the other side of the plate.

Well, to make a long story short, I knew he was throwing the curve-ball, so I waited on the curveball and hit it out of the ballpark, a line drive. Bases loaded. That made it 7–6. We scored two more runs and beat them 8–7. That's all the scoring was done, fifteen runs in the first inning.

That's what that club was all about. A lead, less than two outs in the ninth didn't mean nothing to them. Without a doubt.

They had a philosophy that I believed in. If you got a good ballclub, split with the top clubs, stomp these bottom clubs' brains out. Beat the heck out of them. Against Washington that year we won something like nineteen out of twenty-two ballgames. Those bottom clubs? Man, you talk about wearing them out.

Little things won ballgames. I was playing right field over there in

Cleveland and Doby had leg troubles. Play awhile, out two or three days. So I asked him one day, I said, "Larry, want to get rid of those leg problems? Get you some of those lower parts of thermal underwear and wear them when it's cold. Keep 'em on."

He did that and he wore them through July. He thought it was the greatest thing that ever happened. No more leg problems. Then in the outfield I told him, "There's a line out here between you and me. On that side is you, on this side is me."

Boy, he *ate* that up. And he went to work and had the best year he ever had. Lot of psychology involved. Once you see a guy get with it here and there, then the first thing you know, it's determination and here we go! That's what happened over there. Guarantee it.

But we just went through the motions in the World Series. The over-confidence of the first two games and then we started pressing after that. That's what happened.

And I'll tell you something else. The Giants were calling every pitch in New York. It didn't take me but a little while to figure this out. I told them about that; they laughed at me. I said, "What's that guy in the center field clubhouse doing?"

I said, "There's a window down there. If you watch them guys sitting in the bullpen; if they have their legs crossed on one pitch and don't on another, you'll find out something."

They didn't believe it. Of course that was the first game and Lemon got beat 5–2 in ten innings. But they wouldn't listen. And I *knew* it was happening.

But things happen on the field and people don't want to believe it, even though they're 100 percent true.

■   ■   ■

I had to work at hitting. I wasn't blessed with 100 percent ability as a hitter. I just had to get it, that's all.

That's one thing, I was a better hitter the latter part of my career because of up here – thinking. You start observing that joker on the mound every inning and it's quite an asset.

The latter part of my career I was playing different positions. Be in a hundred or so ballgames, mostly fill in, and then in between times I'd pinch-hit. I said, "Well, if you're going to pinch-hit you got to learn something about it."

That pinch-hitting streak I had in '58–'59? Didn't mean a thing to me because I didn't know anything about it until I had six in a row.

One sportswriter said to me, "You know how many pinch hits you have in a row?"

I said, "No."

He said, "Six. You know what the record is?"

I said, "No, I have no idea."

He said, "Seven."

Eddie Sawyer was managing the Phillies, and he knew about it too. He sent me up to hit in Pittsburgh and they brought Elroy Face in as a relief man with two on. He threw what they call split-fingers, forkball to us. I could call it. I took two pitches and hit the third into the upper deck for a home run. That tied the record.

Next day a guy named Benny Daniels pitched and they were trying to walk me. I fouled off one pitch. I still don't know how I reached it, one-handed, about two feet off the plate. Next one was about to hit me in the knee and I hit for a double. That broke the record.

Then Lew Burdette was pitching in Milwaukee, and I hit his spitter for a double to left center.

Finally, in Cincinnati, I think it was Art Fowler pitching, and I hit a curve ball with the bases loaded. Gus Bell was playing right field – on the goat walk, they called it in Cincinnati. The wind was blowing back and then he dropped his hands, gave up on it. All of a sudden he thought he might have a chance; he reached up and it stuck right in his web. That would've been ten in a row.

When I went over to the National League I kept a log on pitchers. I'd mark down fastballs and curveballs and balls and strikes, particularly if that joker was in a jam. And I'd see, well, he only got one out of three curveballs over, there's no use worrying about his curveball. Well, if he got most of his curveballs over, you'd have to hit the curveball. So you go up there and you look for the curveball. And they wonder, "How in the world could you look for a curveball on the first pitch?" Observation's what caused all that.

Not guessin' is lookin'. You look, observe. And there's another thing involved: It's amazing how many pitchers give their pitches away.

I went over to Philly a couple of years. They traded for Dark, and he says, "How many pitchers you got?"

I said, "Twenty-seven."

He said, "Man, I've been in this league fourteen years and I only got fourteen. You only been here two years and got twenty-seven."

Occasionally there would be a pitcher you could only call one pitch on, but that's all you would need, that one pitch. Like Burdette. I could only call his spitter. When our careers were over he wanted to know, "How'd you hit me like you did?"

I said, "Well, it was the spitter, if you remember."

He said, "How'd you think I did it?"

I said, "You only wet one finger."

Well, that really amazed him. He said, "Where do you think I got it?"

I said, "You spit in your hand. When you got your hand to your cap you spit right then." That amazed him again. I said, "There's another way you can tell. If you reached at the resin bag with two fingers up it was loaded. If the two fingers were down it wasn't."

Like Clem Labine was with Brooklyn. Duke Snider said, "How can you hit him like you do?"

I said, "I know every pitch that's coming. They can't fool you with nothing."

Playing the Dodgers in Philadelphia one night, I hit a triple, a double, and a single, and a line drive right at somebody when he did get me out. He asked me later on, when it was all over, how I knew.

I told him, "I called them all myself right at the plate. Nobody else called them for me. I called every pitch you threw, at the plate."

That's done by observation. Those guys that you play with that say, "What do you got on this pitcher today?" they don't remember. It never left my mind. When I saw a pitcher, I knew what he did.

Like Wally Post. When he come over to Philadelphia from Cincinnati, he said, "How can you hit that Spahn like you do?"

I said, "You can, too, if you do what I tell you.

"Get on top of the plate. First thing he's going to do is throw in tight, try to get you away from it. He deliberately gets two balls, no strikes on you and gets that screwball out there. If you get up close to the plate that joker's down the middle now."

First time we're up in Milwaukee he hit a triple, right center. Then he scored, and now he's in the dugout looking around, "Where's Grumpy? Where's Grumpy?" They called me Grumpy. "He did exactly like you said he would. Tried to get me back away from the plate."

I said, "Got the screwball down the middle, right?"

I'll tell you something. It got to the point where Spahn would try to learn something from me. One day I hit four balls off him like a bullet. Next day he says, "Man, you had quite a day yesterday."

I said, "Well, I was just up there swinging."

He said, "You hit some good pitches, too."

I said, "Well, I thought a couple of 'em were bad balls." And I turned and walked away. He tried to learn something and I knew it, and he wasn't getting nothing out of me.

Hal Newhouser over in Detroit was the same way. I could hit him like I owned him, and he had good stuff. The only thing I could figure out about him – those type of guys – because I *know* they're tough, I *know* I got to bear down so hard that instead of concentrating on hitting the ball hard I concentrated on just hitting the ball. I got three doubles and a single off him one day, four for four.

Next day he comes to me, says, "Boy you had quite a day yesterday."

Told him just like I told Spahn, "Up there swingin'."

"Hit some good pitches, too."

"Well, I thought some were bad balls." And I turned on *him* and walked away.

He got to where he'd flop his arms around and try to throw me a change-up. First time he did it, I hit it right past his ear.

Another one, fellow over in Pittsburgh named Bob Friend. A good pitcher, but I had him buffaloed. Over in Philadelphia one day and they got us beat. Harry Anderson hit before me. I think he was hitting fourth and I was hitting fifth at that time. He hit a ground ball to Dick Stuart at first base. Should have been the last out, but Stuart booted it. I followed Anderson, and Friend threw a curveball, and I hit it out of the ballpark to beat him.

He had a good sinking fastball. After another hit or two off him later on, he started to throw harder. But he'd hurt himself and the ball straightened out, and instead of the ball doing its natural stuff he just did you a favor.

He got on first base once and he said to me, "I know there's a way, and sooner or later I'm finding it out." But he never did.

I don't know what it is, but the soft guys gave me more trouble than anybody. Ball looks like a balloon coming up there and I'm trying to hit it hard. Go back to the bench talking to yourself. Like Eddie Lopat was. He didn't throw hard enough to mash your finger, but you go back to the bench talking to yourself.

Here's the deal: he didn't have a pattern. Whitey Ford had a pattern. Ford had a lot better stuff than Lopat had, but he had a pattern and you could *hit* him. If you had a man on a base that could hurt him, you got the curveball. If there's nobody on and you can't hurt him, you got the fastball. Lopat? You don't *figure* him out. He had a little dinky screwball, wasn't much of one. Little slider, little breaking ball: take a little off, add a little. No pattern whatsoever could you ever figure out. And it looks so big coming up there . . . I always said this: If I take it, it gets just enough of the plate; if I swing, that joker is just enough *off* the plate. And it's always that situation. And that herky-jerky-like motion, too.

What the story was, see, I didn't learn these things until the later part of my career. The first part of it I was just up there swinging, if you want to know the truth about it.

What started all this was Rudy York, the last year he played. To me, he was one of the smartest guys who ever played the game, as far as knowledge of baseball is concerned. But he didn't know the first thing about teaching it, *none* whatsoever. He started me stealing pitches. He was the greatest I've ever seen.

Rudy was a looker. He had a philosophy: if he didn't get what he was looking for on three pitches, he took it back and put it in the rack. He *never* swung if he didn't get what he was looking for.

He taught me all those things, how to steal pitches and whatnot. Some you couldn't call, but he showed me how to call them and how to relay them to him. And I'd do that, and I'd never foul him up, see.

I was a younger guy on the club, and one night he said, "Come with me."

I didn't know where, I thought we were going to eat or something. Well, he took me into – I don't know *what* it was – doggonedest joint you ever saw. Honky-tonk joint. I think it was in Philadelphia. I looked around there a little bit later – he got to mingling and things – and I sneaked out of there. The heck with this.

Come to find out, the manager was there. Next day he said, "I don't want to see you with York anymore."

I said, "You don't have to worry about that. That joker asked me to go with him. When I seen what that place was all about, back to the hotel I went."

Smart baseball man. But because ballplayers didn't do what he did or expected them to do, it frustrated him. That's the reason he couldn't teach. If he told someone to do something, he thought he ought to do it right now like it *oughta* be done. It don't work that way, and he'd get frustrated and couldn't teach.

■   ■   ■

Another thing, every club I was with I could hit 3 and 0 under situations. We were in New York one day when I was with Cleveland. We were getting beat about 4–3. About the eighth inning. Two on and two out. Count is 3 and 0. I look up, no take sign. I says, "Well, you got to get you a pitch you can handle and lay the bat on it." They threw one down there and I hit that joker so far back in the seats you wouldn't believe. Beat them 6–4.

When I was managing I would test players, young players. I'd get in a situation, 3 and 0, and see what he'd do. If he swings at just anything, take it away from him.

I had a guy named Todd Hunter, played for me in Dallas. Shortstop, a young kid. One day, bases loaded, 3 and 0 on him, I said, "I'm testing this kid right now." He looked at me: no take sign? Man, you could tell he couldn't believe his eyes. He got a pitch he could handle and hit a double, cleared the sacks. On the throw in he came to third base. I said, "Todd Hunter, I shake you up a little bit?"

"Man, you *sure* did!"

Well, he could hit it. But the next guy? They bounce one up there and he'll swing at it. You've got to take it away from him. Not every guy can hit the 3 and 0 pitch. Some can. Here's my theory: you get what you're looking for, or you don't swing.

Baseball is instinct. You have to work on instinct.

That's what a manager is all about, as far as I'm concerned. You think a manager is going to steal ten ballgames over a year? No. Game is won and lost on the field. Keeping the frame of mind of ballplayers with determination enough to win. That's what managing is all about.

Paul Richards was like that. He knew what ballplayers would and would not do under certain situations. One time he told Whitey Herzog to hit for the pitcher. So Herzog's in the on-deck circle and the hitter up doubled. He called Herzog back.

"Philley, get a bat."

He knows exactly what I'll do, and he knows exactly what Herzog'll do. Herzog'll hit the ball someplace but won't advance that run to third base so a fly ball will score him. He knows I'll pull the ball. If I don't get a base hit, I'm still going to move him over. Okay, what it is, I'm going to get a pitch I can pull; I'm not going to hit the ball to the left side of the infield. So, the second baseman, he dove at the ball and he threw me out – I hit it hard – but the runner went to third base. Next guy hit a fly ball. That's it!

Here's another philosophy I had when I was managing: there is no excuse whatsoever for any pitcher to get out on that hill and walk four, five, six guys a day, none whatsoever. Lack of concentration is what it's all about.

I was managing a kid one time and I said, "Were you that wild when you were down the bullpen warming up?"

He said, "No."

"Know why?"

"No."

I said, "I do. Catcher's squatting down there with nobody around. He can even move the glove around and you can hit it. He's still back there, might not be the same one but he's still back there. You get a signal from him and you don't even see him; you're throwing to an imaginary strike zone. If you can't hit him as big as he is back there, I'll get somebody who will!"

Next thing you know, bang, bang, bang. Fans thinking, "Wonder what the hell he said to him?"

This all started in the big leagues with a guy in Philadelphia named Sam Zoldak, left-handed pitcher. He said, "I can't throw to this hitter the way he stands at the plate."

Like I said, I broke in as a catcher and never really got away from it. I said, "Wait a minute, Sam. I don't care if that joker stands on his head up there at that plate. If you throw at who you're supposed to be throwing – to that catcher back there – I don't care where he stands."

I don't know whether it did any good to him or not, but that's what it's all about.

When I was with the Red Sox we had Gene Conley, the hatchet man for the Boston Celtics basketball team, about six foot nine. He'd win eight, ten games a year, lose that many. Had a good arm. I said, "Gene, I thought of something in bed last night. You got a good arm, you ought to be a winning pitcher. The only reason you're not is because you don't throw the ball where you want to."

I said, "I got a theory," and I called our catcher, Jim Pagliaroni, over to listen to this. I'm just a player, but I said, "You agree with a pitch that you'll throw, now you give Pagliaroni a signal where you'll throw it." Well, he started doing that and he started to think that was, literally, the greatest thing that ever happened to him. He won fifteen ballgames that year.

It's the art of concentration. Pitcher will tell you, "Oh, that's aiming the ball." But Warren Spahn – I didn't like him because he thought he was better than everybody else – but I heard sportswriters interviewing him one time in Philadelphia: "Do you throw to the hitter or the catcher?" I just happened to be walking by.

He said, "I see the hitter when he walks to the plate, to know who he is. That's the last time I ever see him."

That's what it's all about, that's what I was talking about. Concentration.

Lots of psychology in managing. One guy you pat on the back, the other you dig. You've got to learn the difference.

Had a pitcher named Johnson. He made a statement – everything that goes on on a ballclub, if you listen you find out what's going on. Anyway, he made the statement one time: "If I win about two more games, I'm gone from here. Up."

Well, this game he started he walked the first two hitters and had two balls and no strikes on the next hitter, and I walked out there and I said, "What are you doing in this game?"

"Making a living."

"With what you're doing?" I said, "You haven't got a gut in your body. You've got a yellow streak down your back a foot wide."

And I really gave it to him. I *tried* to make him mad, and I did. It was hard to keep from laughing. Catcher was out there listening.

To make a long story short, he got that hitter out and pitched a two-hit shutout. After the game, the catcher come up to me and said, "Maybe you should tell these other guys they don't have any guts."

The first year I was managing I had "No Neck" Williams, Walt Williams. Bill Wight brought him out there.

He said, "I don't know about this guy."

I said, "We'll work him out."

Worked him out and I said, "Bill, I need an outfielder. I believe we'll sign him."

He said, "Well, will it cost us money?"

I said, "No, I don't think so."

I asked him, "You want to play this game?"

"Yes."

"How bad?"

"Real bad."

I said, "Well, we can't give you any bonus money, just a halfway decent salary."

"Oh, that's all right."

So we signed him. Well, it wasn't a month's time I knew he was a big league prospect. Had as good an instinct as any human being you ever saw. Did things on the spur of the moment without having to think about it.

But he was one of those guys you couldn't get on. Players couldn't get on him, agitate him, because he'd pull his shell over himself. Soon as I got to know him, I just walked by him. I wouldn't stop and talk to him. I'd just say, "Walt, you're doing quite a job, keep it up."

He'd eat that up and, boy, there he goes.

Make one mad, pat the other on the back. Got to know the difference, too.

I'll tell you another thing. I'm with Detroit, and we're playing at Cleveland and Jack Tighe's the manager. Charlie Maxwell's playing left field, Kaline's playing right field. I'm playing first base. The tying run's on second base in the ninth. Colavito's the hitter. Tighe changes pitchers; sent Billy Hitchcock, the coach, out to do it.

I thought of this and I went over to the bench. Went all the way across the field; our dugout's off third base. Got Jack off to the side. Said, "Jack, there's two outs, what do you think about this: move Kaline to left field, put Maxwell in right. Colavito's a pull hitter. If he gets a base hit Kaline will throw that runner out, Maxwell won't."

"Good idea, go do it."

Now *that's* the mistake he made. He should've told one of the coaches to do that. But everybody in the cotton-pickin' ballpark sees me go from first base to the dugout, and then I got to go out there to Kaline and have him switch with Maxwell. As a player, I was embarrassed. Anyway, the guy popped up, that's it.

Next day, a radio guy come up. Well, here's trouble.

"What's the story on that?"

"No story whatsoever. I only saw a chance to win a ballgame."

That's all I was interested in – beat somebody, and I saw a chance.

Anyway, wasn't about a month or two after that another thing happened. We were playing the White Sox. Al Lopez was managing them. Earl Torgeson was pinch-hitting for the pitcher. Minnie Minoso had got hit in the jaw in his time up, and he died at third base.

Now the White Sox bring a pitcher in and the coach told McKinley, the umpire, "That's your pitcher." He wrote him down ninth.

When the coach got back to the dugout, I found out, he told Lopez that Minoso was bleeding inside the jaw. Lopez sent Torgeson out to left field. I looked up and saw Torgeson going to left. I went over to Jack and I said, "Jack, protest."

He said, "Why?"

"Torgeson's out of the ballgame. He's out of the ballgame when that pitcher is entered out there, and I saw McKinley write him down ninth."

He said, "That's right."

Anyway, he protests. The ump announced the protest.

Well, it rained and here come the umpires. Charlie Berry was at second base; he's the senior umpire. We got into it.

He said the pitcher hadn't been announced.

I said to McKinley, "Mac, had that pitcher been announced?"

"Yes, he had!"

Charlie said, "Oh, no! No, he hadn't."

I said, "Then you're a cotton-pickin' liar! I got witnesses right here, and that guy says he was announced and *that* guy is *out* of the ballgame."

He didn't like that worth a hoot. Well, to make a long story short, we won the ballgame and the protest didn't have to go through.

. . .

My dad was a semipro ballplayer, pitched and played shortstop. My older brother played two years of pro ball in the Sooner State League up there in Oklahoma, then one year here in Paris. My younger brother, I took him to Shreveport with me the second year I was down there. He was pitching down there for about a month. He could throw the ball by a lot of those Texas League hitters, then he come up with a sore arm. But he didn't have enough determination. It was work to him.

Me? Never did it seem like work to me. Never one minute of my eighteen-year career did it ever occur to me that this is work. This is fun to me. I'm getting paid for the fun.

Now, when I got through in the fall, I was tired. If I'd done exactly what I wanted to do, I'd've isolated myself somewhere where I saw no human being for one month. No telephone, no nothing. Now, when that month is over I can't wait for spring training to start again. Can't *wait*. It ought to be tomorrow, in other words.

That's what it's all about.

First part of my career, I took the game *off* the field. My wife, when I got home, wouldn't dare say a word to me. I'd jump down her throat if I had a bad day. I woke up to the fact one day that you can't change it. Leave it on the field. Tomorrow's another day. And I was a better player because I did that.

Like Comiskey – the son; he and his sister took over the ballclub after the old man died – told me one time. He said, "You'd be a heck of a ballplayer if you smiled once in a while."

I said, "Wait a minute, Chuck, there's nothing funny to me on that baseball field.

"I'm supposed to smile if some joker gets me out four times in a row? Nothing funny about that to me."

They knew I came to play. That's what it was all about. No false hustle about me, like Rose was. Something of his was a little bit false hustle, because he'd run to first base on a base-on-balls. Nothing false about me: I hustled to beat you. That's what it's all about, guarantee you.

DAVE
PHILLEY

Kind of like Lopez told the sportswriters over there in Philadelphia about me. Said, "I didn't know this guy could beat you so many ways."

I never went looking for trouble. I just had nerve enough not to be run over.

Vic Power

March 18–19, 1994, San Juan, Puerto Rico

Vic Power played every position but pitcher and catcher from 1954 to 1965 with the Philadelphia and Kansas City Athletics, the Indians, Twins, Angels, and the Philadelphia Phillies. A .284 lifetime hitter, Power hit .300 or better three times. In twelve major league seasons, he won seven Gold Gloves as a first baseman. His .994 lifetime fielding average ranks seventh among first basemen of all time.

After I retired, Bill Veeck said to me, "Vic, when you introduced your one-hand catch, they said you were a showboat. Now everyone is doing it."

I noticed one thing early in my career, you've got to be different. In major league baseball, you check, Ted Williams, Stan Musial, Mickey Mantle, Willie Mays, they all had a style. Like Willie Mays had that basket catch, I felt I should have something different.

Another thing: catching the ball with one hand makes it easier.

In Puerto Rico, when I was around nine years old, in the town where I grew up, in Arecibo, they had a guy named Carreon. He never played pro, just amateur baseball. I liked his finesse, the way he moved around the bag, and I tried to copy him. That was my inspiration.

Red Barber told me one time, "Vic, please, I'm gonna tell everybody on the radio today that you're gonna catch the ball today with two hands." So I promised him. And the moment I got a chance, I caught a fly ball – with two hands.

In Minnesota one time, Jack Kralick was pitching a no-hitter. The last out was a fly ball behind first base. I went after the ball and I caught it with one hand. People are still telling me, "Oh, baby, you drop that ball you're dead." That was my style. And I was sure I could get it.

The older guys, they hated that style. They wanted to kill me. They called me showboat, they called me clown. But they didn't call me that in front of me. They called it from the dugout. That shows they have some respect for me.

I enjoyed first base. It's a position where there is always action. Plus, it was a good public relations position. You get to see all the guys going around there – Mickey Mantle, Ted Williams, Yogi Berra – and you get to talk to them.

To be able to play in the big leagues, you can't be too soft. It's a tough game. And at first base you *have* to be aggressive, but you have to have some other talent, too. For example, I played first base in the major leagues at only five feet, eleven and one-half. In the big leagues there were some big guys at first base, like Walter Dropo. Big guys: six feet two, six feet three. But I had the flexibility to move around.

I noticed, too, it's easy for the left-handed first basemen to make the double play: they don't have to turn around. As a right-handed first baseman, I have to anticipate. So I can catch the ball one hand, already moving, and now I can throw and make that double play much easier.

That's the kind of baseball I teach kids. What I tell them is that every player has his own style. Don't copy them, but if you find a style that will make it easier for you, go ahead and do it. The secret is, practice.

Another thing, I knew the players and how to play them. I knew every player in the league and I moved with every one of them. Somebody said that maybe I was one of the most intelligent players to play the game. Because I was there all the time. When Bobby Richardson was batting, maybe I'd play deep to fool him, and the moment the pitcher was making the delivery, Bobby is not gonna see me because I'm moving with the delivery. When he bunts I'm right there on top of him. Sometimes that can be the difference in a game.

To be able to judge Vic Power as a player, you've got to see him. I say that because a lot of people say that Gil Hodges has better numbers. But Gil Hodges didn't have the range I had. I caught balls that somebody else would not have come close to. And Gil Hodges played on better teams. Gil Hodges was a nice man, but like I say, you've got to see Vic Power to judge him.

I think the secret is you've got to be proud of your position. I was proud to play first base. If you're proud, you're going to perform much better.

Harry Craft, Leo Durocher . . . I would say at least 60 percent of those guys didn't like my style of playing first base. They used to call me showboat all the time. I had a manager named Jimmy Dykes in Cleveland. I told Jimmy one time, "Everybody's getting mad because I play that position with one hand. What I'm gonna do is start catching with two hands because that's what people want."

And Jimmy Dykes told me, "*Never* argue with success. You're doing all right with one hand, you keep doing it with one hand."

Later on, when a sportswriter from Detroit called me a showboat and asked why I caught the ball with one hand, I told him, "Whoever invented this game, if he wished the guy to catch with two hands he would have made two gloves. But he only made one, and I catch with one."

▪ ▪ ▪

I wanted to be a doctor or a lawyer. When I was thirteen years old my father died. He worked in the sugar cane mills, where they make the sugar. One day he got a little cut on his finger and they told him to get a shot for tetanus. But he was a very strong man, a tough man, and he didn't want to get the shot. He died two weeks later. He never played baseball, and he didn't want me to play baseball. Maybe it sounds cruel, but I think that if he didn't die I would not have played baseball.

I couldn't go to school. We didn't have enough money. I had to find a job so I could support my mother and five brothers and sisters. They told me they'd pay me for playing baseball. At age sixteen I signed pro with a salary of $250 a month, and that was enough to support my family and to buy my mother a house. The next year they gave me $500, and three years later I was playing in the states. I went to Canada, and from Canada the Yankees signed me.

Quincy Trouppe took me to Canada. He liked me. He was like a father to me. He came to Puerto Rico to play in 1947. I was a pro already.

We were lucky to have all those colored players here in Puerto Rico because they taught us a lot of things. I played against Lorenzo Davis, Willard Brown, Johnny Davis. Maybe 80 percent of the big Negro stars who played in the states played in Puerto Rico, and I played against them. Beautiful ballplayers. Tough guys. I learned my game from them. The first time I saw a switch-hitter was Junior Gilliam.

One time I got a base hit, and when I got to first base the first baseman, an older guy, said, "Excuse me, I'm gonna clean the bag." I got off the bag and he tagged me out, baby. I was so ashamed.

The manager was so mad at me. He said, "Why did you get off the bag?"

I said, "But the old man told me, 'Excuse me . . .' He was so polite." I never will forget that experience, but that was good because that made me a tougher player. I was, maybe, seventeen years old. You think that when an older guy asks, you have to respect him. He tagged me out, baby.

Quincy Trouppe wanted to take me to the Negro league in the states. A lot of people told me not to play there because it was tough, riding on buses five and six days. And they told me about segregation. I didn't know too much about segregation.

But he talked with people with the Chicago American Giants and I was ready to go to Chicago to play in the colored league. Then something happened.

You remember most of the big league players like Danny Gardella, Sal Maglie, Max Lanier, Roy Zimmerman . . . all those guys who went to play in Mexico? They came back and made a new league in Canada, the Provincial League. They invited Quincy Trouppe, and Quincy Trouppe took me to Drummondville, a little town about an hour east of Montreal.

I played outfield for the first time in Drummondville because Roy Zimmerman, the old first baseman for the Giants, was playing first base. I played right field that year, and I was the batting champion.

I liked Drummondville. I learned how to speak French. I enjoyed the Canadian people. They were beautiful. We had no trouble with race in Canada. Everyone was the same. I had two fights in that league, and both of the fights were with white players but nothing race-related.

The next year I went back to that league. Quincy Trouppe became manager after six or seven games, and our team won the championship. My first pro championship. And Quincy hit a home run to win it.

After my father died, God sent Quincy Trouppe so he could be my new father. He was maybe thirty-five, forty years old. When we went to Canada, he taught me everything: I learned English from him; I learned how to dress. We lived together. We rented a house with another Puerto Rican, Roberto Vargas. He pitched for Milwaukee for maybe a month in 1955. Quincy cooked – the first time I ate pancakes, Quincy Trouppe cooked dinner for me – and Vargas washed dishes. I cleaned the house. It was responsibility I never had.

My hobby all my life has been photography. I learned that from Quincy. Music. I got acquainted with Count Basie and Duke Ellington, all the great jazz musicians, because of Quincy Trouppe. He never got mad. We went together all the time. He took care of our contracts. He did everything. He was a teacher, a father. That was the type of man he was. Beautiful.

I remember when we won the Provincial League championship – we played here in Mayaguez – they made him mayor of the city for a week. I was still in high school. I took a week off and we rode around the island taking pictures.

When Quincy Trouppe went to the big leagues with the Cleveland Indians in 1952, he was too old. But he was a very intelligent catcher, and he was a strong hitter with a lot of power. I guess he was the best catcher of that era here in Puerto Rico. Later, of course, we had Roy Campanella. But Quincy Trouppe was a *good* catcher.

■   ■   ■

The Yankees scout Tom Greenwade scouted me when I was with Drummondville. He sent in a report that I was a good runner and a good hitter. He said I had a good arm but was a poor fielder.

He saw me in the All-Star game in that league, and I remember I got a bad hop and I made an error on first base. I won seven Gold Gloves in the major leagues as a fielder, and Tom sent in that report. (That's why I tell the scouts now: "Hey, you have to follow these guys. He may have a bad day. You have to follow him.")

Greenwade was a nice old man who had a good reputation because he signed Mickey Mantle. Nice personality. I didn't get to know him too well, but I knew he was following me. Actually, he didn't sign me, because the Provincial League was an independent league. What the Yankees did was, they bought my contract. They paid $7,500, but I didn't care: I didn't know who the Yankees were. But when a sportswriter in Canada asked how much money they gave me, I went to the general manager and I told him, "Listen, unless you give me some money, I won't play with the Yankees."

Well, he was very nervous. He left and came back with some money. I thought I was a rich man. Later on I found out it was six, seven, eight Canadian dollars for one American. It was only $500.

I signed a contract to play in Kansas City, but later the Yankees decided to send me to Syracuse, New York. I didn't know why. I didn't ask and the Yankees never told me. The only difference I noticed in Syracuse from Drummondville was that they had a lot of older players. I was around nineteen or twenty years old. I played in Syracuse in 1951, and the next year I played in Kansas City.

But when I went to Kansas City, I noticed another difference. In Kansas City, at the beginning, I was living a double personality: a big star in the field, but the moment the game ends, well, I cannot go to the hotel where the white guys were living. I had to go to the colored section. I could not go to certain restaurants. If they had some picnic or party, they didn't invite me. They saw me as different. The minute the game was over, I'd see the guys going back, but nobody's inviting me anywhere.

But they never told me why. They never explained to me what racism was. All they said was that they had to find a place for us colored guys to stay, and that place was in the colored section. We didn't get to see the other guys, the white guys, except in the ballpark.

One time I went to a restaurant and the waitress tells me, "Sorry, we don't serve Negroes."

Well, my English wasn't too good, but I told her, "I don't want to eat Negroes. I just want rice and beans." She looked at me kind of funny as if to say, "Hey, this guy's dumb, he doesn't even know what I'm talking about." But I knew what she meant.

I used my common sense. You don't have to be intelligent. I used to walk down the street and I'd see some places, and if I saw some colored people inside then I would go in. If they don't have colored people there, then I don't get close to the place. Later on, after President Kennedy signed that law, I thought, "Well, I'm going to the same restaurant, and if they don't serve me I'm going to call the Kennedy office and complain."

I still have an accent now, but I had a heavier accent then. I went to the same restaurant and sat down. And this time they served me. I ordered a steak, but the girl forgot to give me a spoon, knife, and fork. My accent was so bad that when I said I want a fork she thought I said, "I want to *fuck*." And they showed me out again, and I didn't know why.

In Kansas City the police used to stop me all the time. I'm driving twenty miles an hour and they stop me and they ask me, "What are you doing in that car?"

I say, "It's my car."

They say, "Where do you work?"

"I work in Kansas City."

"Who are you?"

"I'm Vic Power, the first baseman."

"Oh! Routine investigation." And they let me go.

But they did it so many times that I got mad, and I went to an office at city hall and I put in a complaint. They called the police department, and the police said they stopped me because there were so many cars being stolen in Kansas City that they thought my car was one of the stolen ones.

I told the police, "I don't look like a thief. You look more like a thief than me." And that's when I started feeling what racism was. Because being a Puerto Rican, we don't see the difference between white and black.

In 1965 there was a poll and I was named the best-dressed big league player. I didn't look like a thief. I always had on a coat and tie, but I got stopped anyway. Routine investigation.

There was a newspaper in Kansas City, the *Call*. The editor wrote a little story. He was driving by the ballpark and he saw about a hundred policemen. There was a big fight between a husband and a wife. The husband was trying to kill the wife and she was screaming. The editor was wondering why all these policemen were just standing there doing nothing, and then he realized, "Oh, yes, they're waiting for Vic Power to get out of the ballpark so they can make a routine investigation."

The police didn't like that. The chief of police called me: "We're having trouble with the *Call*."

They stopped my wife one time. They wanted to know what race she was. I said, "She's a Puerto Rican. It's not a race."

But he didn't want me to talk to him. He wanted her to talk to him. But she didn't speak English. I tried to tell him that she's Puerto Rican, not American.

She was wearing a blond wig. I didn't know, maybe if they thought she was a white American it was against the law and maybe they'd put me in jail.

One time they arrested me for jaywalking. I went to court and the judge asked me how I plea, guilty or innocent? I told the judge that I was innocent.

He said, "Explain why."

I said, "I'm a Puerto Rican, and in Puerto Rico black and white go to school together, in Puerto Rico black and white dance together, in Puerto Rico black and white get married. When I came here to the states, I saw something different.

"I was walking in the street, and when I tried to go in a restaurant they had a big sign that said For White Only. I keep walking, try to go in a bar, and the bar had a sign saying For White Only. I keep walking, I try to get in a movie house, and there's a sign in the movie house saying For White Only.

"I keep walking and I go to the end of the block, and I noticed that when the green light came on the white people around me crossed the street. Then I stopped. I was afraid to go. When the red light came on I crossed, because I thought the red light was for colored only."

The judge said, "I'm going to let you go, but remember, the red light is for colored *and* for white, for everybody."

You know, I didn't get excited about segregation. I was an independent guy, but I had to put it out of my system. I followed Jackie Robinson's career, but I didn't know him. Remember, he went to the majors in '47, and I went to the states in '49. I liked his personality. He was a different guy, an intelligent guy. But I think he died bitter. That was my inspiration all the time I played in the major leagues – Jackie Robinson.

I never had a hero except for Jackie – and Joe Louis. They were my heroes. Joe Louis's comeback against Max Schmelling, that was something special. And Jackie, to live with that situation, and to become one of the better ballplayers . . . Oh, baby.

I did some things that he used to do. When I played second base I used to make some moves like tag the bag, jump in the air, and throw. Well, like you say, that's self-defense because some of those guys liked to come and to cut me.

■   ■   ■

The Yankees kept me three years in the minor leagues. At the beginning the sportswriters used to ask me, "Why don't the Yankees call you up?" I didn't know and I didn't even care that much. But what happened was that the Yankees weren't ready to have a colored player on the big club. Later on, as a joke, I said, "Well, what happened is they sent me to the minor leagues to see if I would turn white, so they can call me up. But I wasn't lucky."

I was the only colored guy with the Yankees in 1951 in Syracuse, the only colored guy in the organization. Later on, in '52 when I went to Kansas City, they brought Elston Howard up. He was in the army and he became my roommate.

The Yankees got mad because the sportswriters started questioning why they didn't call me up. In 1951 in Syracuse I hit .295. In '52 I hit .339, and in '53 I hit .349, the batting champion in the American Association. The sportswriters were giving the Yankees some trouble. And the Yankees had a lot of excuses, like, "When we call up a colored guy, he has to be a decent guy." Well, I guess I wasn't decent. They said, "Vic hasn't proved yet that he can hit major league pitching."

I said, "I've never seen major league pitching. When I see some, I'll tell you."

Later on they said, "We don't know where to play him." And I used to play all positions.

Well, finally, they called Bill Skowron up. Before that, the Yankees psychology was that a first baseman was supposed to be a big, left-handed hitter and white. And I wasn't that big, I was right-handed, and I was black; but I knew I could play some other position. I played every position but pitcher and catcher in the major leagues, but the Yankees didn't know what to do with me. The people from Harlem picketed at Yankee Stadium.

A lot of people told me that Stengel complained when the Yankees didn't call me up. I read an article where Casey said that he would like to have nine showboats like Vic Power. I think it was very tough for the Yankees. I know that maybe the Yankees lost a lot of sleep thinking what to do with Vic Power. They had a lot of excuses.

Okay, one time I was in the Yankee clubhouse in spring training. They had a sign in the bathroom For White Only. The only question I asked was, "Where does a colored guy urinate?" They didn't like that. I wasn't supposed to question. I wanted to go, but I couldn't because the sign said For White Only. And they said I was outspoken.

Finally they traded me to Philadelphia for Harry Byrd, Eddie Robinson, and a couple of other guys. I went to Philadelphia in 1954, my first year in the major leagues. In '55 the Athletics moved to Kansas City and I spent four years there. From Kansas City I went to Cleveland. I spent four years with Cleveland. Cleveland traded me to Minnesota. Minnesota traded me to California. And then they retired me in 1965.

One time when I was with Kansas City, we played an exhibition game at Fort Myers, Florida. After the game the bus stopped at a gas station so that we could go to the bathroom. I was the only Negro on the bus, all the other guys were white. I followed the other players to the bathroom, and this old man, the gas station attendant, told me I couldn't go in.

I said, "Why?"

He said, "Because no black bastard can go in there."

I didn't know what to do and I thought, well, maybe I would go behind the bus. But the old man was watching me and I was afraid. Finally I saw a Coca-Cola machine and I thought, "Well, I'm going to get a Coke and pour it out and urinate in the bottle." But I was afraid to pour it out because the attendant was still watching me. So I started drinking the Coke.

When the bus started up, I got on it with the bottle of Coke, and the old man followed me and told me to give him the bottle. I said, "Listen, I paid for that."

He said, "No, you gotta give me the bottle!"

I said, "Okay, I'll give you a quarter for the bottle."

"No," he said, "I want the bottle."

I said, "Take the bottle, you old son of a bitch."

Well, he took the bottle and ran inside to the telephone. The bus started and we left. After a few minutes a sheriff's car came with the siren on and stopped the bus. The old man and the sheriff were in it, and the old man said, "That black bastard, in there!" The sheriff told me that I was under arrest.

"Why?"

Now, some of the guys, white guys, said to the sheriff, "Can we pay a fine or something?"

He went out to the gas station attendant and they talked. He came back again and he said, "You gotta pay a fine of $500."

I didn't have all that money with me, so we collected money from some of the guys on the bus. (I paid them back later.) We collected $500 and gave it to them, and we left. When we got back to West Palm Beach, I went to see a colored lawyer so he could represent me in case I had to go to court in that little town, Lake Okeechobee.

The lawyer told me, "Vic, in that town no Negro has ever won a case." We jumped the bail, and that bottle of Coke cost me $500.

That was a bad experience, but you know what? That's life. That didn't make me hate the Americans as a whole. There are bad people everywhere.

.   .   .

I liked Cleveland. I played with two nice guys, very religious guys, and they tried to take care of me all the time. Rocky Colavito and Herb Score. They would worry about me. On Sunday: "Hey, Vic, you got to go to church." On Friday they reminded me to eat fish, not meat. You know, they cared a little bit about me, and I liked that.

I liked it because some of the others, like in Kansas City, didn't like me. I don't say they were prejudiced. Maybe they were jealous because I was the best hitter, the best player. And that happens in baseball. But then when I went to Cleveland, Rocky, Herb Score, Ray Narleski, they were nice guys. And I liked Jimmy Dykes as a manager.

Frank Lane fined me one time in spring training in Tucson. I went to bed early, but I wasn't tired and I couldn't sleep. I was reading in the paper that there was an eclipse of the moon. So I got up about two o'clock in the morning and I was standing out in front of the hotel looking at the sky when Frank Lane came in.

"What are you doing here," he said.

I said, "I'm looking at the eclipse."

You should have seen the headline in the paper the next day: Vic Power Claims He Was Watching Eclipse at 3:00 in the Morning. I swear to God, I was watching the eclipse. But he fined me.

I liked Frank Lane. My biggest salary was from Frank Lane: $38,000. I liked him, but he'd get mad when we lost. I remember one time he went into the clubhouse and took all the bats from the rack and threw them in the garbage can and said, "I don't know why I bought these bats, you don't use them."

When I signed one of my contracts, Frank Lane told me that if I hit .300 at the end of the season he'd give me a car. I finished at .298. Oh, baby, I was so mad. And Frank Lane called me to the office and he told me, "Listen, Vic, sometimes you didn't hustle enough: if you hustled more, you could have hit .300. Sometimes you didn't sleep enough: if you went to bed earlier, you could have hit .300."

Oh baby, he got me nearly crying. But after he finished, you know what he did? He threw the keys to me. He gave me the car anyhow.

I went home to my wife and told her the same thing. "Listen, sometimes you didn't cook for me. Sometimes I had to take care of the kids at four o'clock in the morning when you were sleeping. If you could have done more, I could have hit .300." She was about to cry when I threw the keys to her. Then she got dressed and we went for a ride, baby.

It was a Pontiac station wagon, white with red inside. Oh, baby, I enjoyed that station wagon. I brought it back to Puerto Rico. Trader Frank? He was a pro, baby.

Later on, they traded me to California. I liked it over there, but it was a tough club. They had Jim Piersall. They had Bo Belinski. They had Dean Chance. They had Jim Fregosi. That was a wild team. The manager was a nice guy, Bill Rigney. Gene Autry was a nice guy. It was a lot of fun but, baby, there was no discipline. They did everything they wanted. Nobody cared.

I played with some characters. Like Tony Oliva. He was the greatest natural hitter I've ever seen. He didn't care who was pitching.

In 1962 Minnesota brought me over to stabilize the infield. It was a young infield. That year Zoilo Versalles was the shortstop. He made thirty-seven errors, and I saved him forty-seven bad throws to first base.

Well, I was living in Minnesota. It's cold up there during the winter, and I had to get up every morning to shovel snow to take my car out of the garage to drive my kids to school. I was tired of it.

I was reading in a psychology book that in life man takes advantage of other men to get ahead. Okay, I thought, let me see if this works.

Now I'm sitting in my house with Tony. I said, "Tony, you know what I read? I was reading Ted Williams's book, and Ted said that the secret to his success was shoveling snow.

"Ted Williams was the greatest hitter – the most power, the most intelligent, the last guy to hit .400. And he said his secret is shoveling snow."

The next day Tony was at my house with a shovel. I was inside laughing, and he was outside shoveling snow. Then came October, the end of the season, and Tony Oliva was the batting champion. He said, "Vic, you were right."

And now look what happened: Kirby Puckett became the batting champion. I think he's been telling Puckett to shovel snow.

Do you remember Harry Simpson? Suitcase Simpson? He was a black ballplayer who played in Kansas City. He was mad at me because he didn't want me to talk to the white guys. But he never explained why.

My best friend in Kansas City was Cletis Boyer. Cletis looked for me, and I looked for Cletis. We were together all the time, and Simpson didn't like it. Cletis was a nice young guy from Missouri. Maybe he was seventeen. Simpson called me an Uncle Tom.

I knew what an Uncle Tom was, but I didn't want to fight with Simpson. When he called me an Uncle Tom, I said, "Hey, what position does he play?"

He thought I was so dumb that I didn't even know what an Uncle Tom was. But I didn't want to fight him. I knew how he felt, because I knew what segregation was. And most of the black players were changed because of it. I wasn't, because I was Puerto Rican and knew that everybody here in Puerto Rico, white and black, we live together. The real embarrassment is two black guys fighting on the same club. I knew where I was standing all the time. But I knew the tension some of those guys felt.

■　■　■

I have a little story about Roger Maris. Roger, for some reason – I never knew and now I'll never know – didn't like the trade. I was traded from Kansas City to Cleveland for him, and I think he didn't like it. He was so bitter with me, he wouldn't say hello to me.

I was playing second base with Cleveland one time, and he came in hard on me and nicked me with his spikes in my ribs. I told him, "The next time you do that you're in trouble."

He said, "I'll do it whenever I want."

I said to myself, "I'll be ready."

Well, the next time he slides so hard that he went all the way past the bag. He grabbed back with his hand and his head was there. I got the ball, jumped through, and threw the ball to first base. And now I'm coming down with my spikes on. But you know, Puerto Rican people, we're nice people. When I was coming down I saw his head and what I did was I opened my legs and his head was between my spikes. If I kept my legs closed I could have taken his eye out. But I think he got the lesson. He didn't slide hard against me after that. I didn't want to cut his face. If I'd done that maybe he wouldn't have broken Babe Ruth's record.

A lot of people said I had a bad temper. I didn't have a bad temper: it was self-defense. I had to fight sometimes. You have to defend yourself.

Like I say, most of those guys didn't like my style of play but they respected my style of play. The dugout in Boston is very close to first base. Jimmy Piersall is the hitter.

He hit a line drive to first base. I took it easy in one hand. As we're throwing the ball around the infield, I heard a voice say, "You black son of a bitch." Well, my common sense said that the only guy that could have said it was Jimmy Piersall, the last hitter.

I walked in front of the Boston dugout and I asked, "Who called me a black son of a bitch?" I knew nobody was going to say they said it. Nobody answered.

I wasn't afraid of anybody – I think that made me a better player – and I said to Piersall, "Did you say it?" And he threw up his arms and walked into the clubhouse. He didn't want a confrontation with me. Oh, I'm mad! I want Jim Piersall to get on first base, baby.

Bobby Shantz is pitching, a little left-hander. We're winning, I think 9–2. Around the seventh inning, Jim Piersall got a walk. I got my man next to me.

I walked to the mound: "Bobby, you have to throw over to first base."

Bobby said, "Vic, we're winning, 9–2."

I said, "Yes but you *have* to throw to me at first base."

Bobby was my friend. In one year we picked about fifteen guys off first base. Me and Bobby. My cue to him was, "Bobby, two out, I'm gonna play back." When the runner heard that, he would take a big lead, and the moment he did I was right behind him and we picked him off.

Bobby said, "Okay, Vic, I'll throw over."

Well, he threw to me and I got that throw and I hit Jim Piersall right in his neck with the glove and the ball. He got so excited: "You don't have to hit me that hard!"

I dropped my glove and I said, "I'll hit you that hard and I'm gonna kill you, you son of a bitch."

Then the umpire got in the middle, and Piersall said, "You don't want to kill me, I've got a big family."

I looked at him and we started laughing, the umpire and everybody. That's the Jim Piersall I knew. Later on they traded him to California, baby, and every day I was with him. I like him and he likes me.

When I was in the major leagues, I usually roomed alone. I roomed with Hector Lopez in Kansas City. When I was in Cleveland, I had Minnie Minoso, but usually I was alone.

Minoso was my best roomie – he was never in the room. He had so many girlfriends he didn't get to the room.

Minnie was a very proud guy. When the team lost, Minnie got mad. If he didn't get a hit, he'd get sick. He believed in voodoo. When he went o for 4 he'd wear his uniform in the shower so he could drown the spirits.

We were playing in Yankee Stadium and we were losing maybe 10–1, the last inning. The first hitter was Woody Held, and he made an out. The next batter was Tito Francona, and he got on base. Now Minoso's hitting, and I'm supposed to be the next hitter.

Casey brings in Ryne Duren and I didn't want to face him.

So I'm in the on-deck circle hoping that Minoso hits into a double play. And Minnie hit a ground ball to shortstop: double play and the game's finished. Well, I didn't want to keep it to myself; I had to tell Minnie.

"Minnie, I'm sorry, I was praying for you to hit into a double play."

He got so mad at me he wanted to kill me. I told him, "I just didn't want to face Ryne Duren." Oh, he was a proud ballplayer, baby.

Late in the game at Yankee Stadium there are long shadows. You can't see. One time, late in a game, Casey brought in Duren to pitch. Duren is warming up and he's wild, and the ball's going in the stands. I was the next hitter.

Finally: Play ball. I'm standing there and Duren is looking for Yogi's sign. Finally he asks for time and takes a handkerchief and starts cleaning his glasses right in front of me. And the next pitch was right behind me.

I was so nervous I just fell down. All the Yankees were laughing. I got so mad I grabbed my bat and I asked for time, and I walked in front of the Yankee dugout and I told Casey, "Listen, old man, if that guy hits me don't think I'm going to fight with him, I'm gonna fight with you!"

Casey was around seventy years old and he was just laughing. But I was so nervous I had to get it out of my system. Then I laughed because I knew I wasn't gonna fight with a seventy-year-old man. But Casey liked me. And the other guys liked me, Skowron, Yogi.

One time Yogi was on first base and I fooled him. The count was two and two. I called to the pitcher, "Hey, three and two and two out, forget about the guy on first base." And Yogi started running. But the pitch was a ball; now he's walking to second base. I was shouting at the catcher, "Throw the ball! Throw the ball!" But he didn't throw: he thought it was three and two, too. I think that was Yogi's only stolen base in his career.

Yogi, he drove me crazy. Every time I came up to hit, Yogi started asking me questions: "Vic, how's your family?" By the time I finished answering him I had lost my concentration and I would strike out.

The manager would always say to me when I was batting, "God-dammit Vic, don't talk to Yogi!"

I liked playing in Yankee Stadium because of Babe Ruth, Lou Gehrig, and all those guys. You feel like you're one of those guys. And Yankee fans—they're different.

One time I was playing center field and Bill Skowron was on third base. Mickey Mantle hit a long fly to center field and I caught the ball. Skowron took off for home, and I threw all the way in the air and we caught him. Double play.

When I came running in from center field, the fans gave me a standing ovation. I'm supposed to be the enemy. Here in Puerto Rico the fans feel that if you're from the other club we got to kill you. Here, when they say kill the umpire they really mean it.

Sportswriters used to ask why I hit so good against the Yankees: "Because you're still mad at them?"

I answered, "No, it's because I feel so proud just to think that Babe Ruth, Lou Gehrig were standing where I'm standing now."

Plus there are a lot of Puerto Rican people in New York and they used to come to the ballgames. I had a sister who lived in the Bronx—she still lives there—and every time I went to Yankee Stadium I stayed with her and her family.

■   ■   ■

My real name is Victor Pellot. When my mother went to school here in Puerto Rico, she had my grandfather's name, Pove. But her teacher told her that was wrong and changed *v* to *w* and added an *r*.

When I went to the states, they didn't know how to pronounce Pellot. So they cut the Victor, as in Vic, and they called me Power, Vic Power.

I met an American about a month ago in one of the hotels here and he asked me a funny question. I had a Detroit hat on, and he was from Detroit.

He said, "Hey, you from Detroit?"

I said, "No, I'm from Puerto Rico."

We started talking and I told him I played baseball in the big leagues. He asked my name and I told him, Pellot. But he didn't know who Victor Pellot was. Then when I told him Vic Power he said, "Oh, Vic Power, I always thought you were American."

That was the confusion. Every time the Americans come to Puerto Rico looking for Vic Power, they can't find me. And when the Puerto

Rican people went to the states looking for me, they couldn't find me either.

I'm the first Puerto Rican to win a Gold Glove. (In my first three years they didn't have Gold Gloves, so that means that in seven of my next nine years, when they gave Gold Gloves I got one.) Some of the Spanish papers in New York, when they listed the Latin American players that won the Gold Gloves they didn't list me because they figured that Vic Power is American.

I'm the first Puerto Rican to play in the All-Star Game, 1955. I'm the first Puerto Rican to play in the American League.

After I retired I wanted to stay in the states, but my mother got sick with cancer. So I came back to Puerto Rico, and I noticed that most of the kids here played the game by instinct, but they didn't know the fundamentals. They didn't know the rules and they didn't stay in shape.

So I conducted baseball clinics. About 20 percent of the guys who work with the kids now in Puerto Rico have come out of my program. I've been doing that since I retired.

We've been lucky. Maybe two hundred kids from the program now have college scholarships in the states. Whenever I'm in the states I recommend some of the guys to colleges. Especially infielders and catchers. They're lucky, they get an education.

I scouted for the Angels for about fifteen years. I didn't tell them anything unless they asked me. The philosophy of most of the major league baseball clubs was, send a scout to Puerto Rico to get some Roberto Clementes. It's not that easy.

I was a little frustrated with the California Angels organization because 90 percent of the guys I recommended they didn't take. They sent a cross-checker and he didn't like them. They didn't like Juan Gonzalez, they didn't like Carlos Baerga, Ruben Sierra, the Alomar brothers.

I said, "Listen, they're Puerto Rican. It will take them longer to develop and to get strong."

It was frustrating. But I've been lucky, about 20 percent of the guys I worked with have made it to the big leagues.

■   ■   ■

Somebody told me that since 1886 until 1994 only 13,000 players played in the major leagues. And I'm one of them. Just think of that. I'm proud of being a major league player.

One of my greatest experiences: my first year with Philadelphia, Connie Mack was still the owner of the club. He used to sit in the corner when he was the manager, with that funny hat and all dressed up. Somebody took a picture of me with him. That's history.

You have to know the history of this ballgame. You have to know who Connie Mack was and Ty Cobb and Doubleday. You have to know what Cooperstown is. I say that because Carlos Baerga came to me so excited and said, "Hey, I saw a picture of you in the front office in Cleveland. I didn't know you used to play in Cleveland."

To be able to go to the moon you have to study and think. And some of those guys didn't check and care. Some of these younger kids now, they asked me if I knew Clemente. And when I say I managed him, they say, "What?"

I remember some scouts from California – they sent them to me. We were riding in the car and they were talking about hitting. I didn't say anything and they kept on talking about hitting. About a half an hour later they said, "How come you don't say anything?" When I told them I won four batting championships, in Puerto Rico and in the minor leagues, they didn't talk any more about hitting.

I had the experience of playing with the greatest player of the game, Willie Mays. I saw Connie Mack there. I played with the greatest hitter of the game, Ted Williams.

I met Ty Cobb in Cooperstown in 1955. He was a very rich man. He'd just bought some stock in the Coca-Cola Company. When they introduced me to him he asked me, "How much are you hitting?" That was my second year in the big leagues. I told him, .319. I was so proud. I was right behind Al Kaline in hitting. To my surprise, Ty Cobb asked me, "Are you in a slump?"

I thought, what's the matter with this old man? Later on I checked his record. Baby, I knew what he meant. He was a .400 hitter and I was so proud of .319.

Around three years ago I was in Disney World. The day I was coming back to Puerto Rico I was in the airport and I saw this big guy. Baby, you can't forget this body, everything! He went to the drugstore and I followed him and we shook hands. He kept looking at me: "Who you are? Who you are?"

I told him, "I'm Vic Power."

He embraced me and he started crying. It was Ted Williams. That's recognition. There's no segregation there, it's the feeling of a guy that knew I played against him, even though I was the enemy. I get goose bumps just to think I fought for the batting championship twice against Ted Williams.

I get letters from young kids who say, "Well, I never saw you play, but my daddy talks about you all the time." They're so proud when they write to me about their fathers seeing me play and telling them that I was one of the best guys of the fifties.

Life has taught me so many things. Finally, my theory is that life is like it's supposed to be. And like I used to tell Rocky Colavito and Billy Martin: "If I am reincarnated I want to be a ballplayer. But an Italian ballplayer."

Joe DiMaggio . . . all those guys . . . they get all the publicity.

Del Crandall

June 20–21, 1994, Baltimore, Maryland

Del Crandall caught from 1949 to 1966, excluding his military service in 1951 and 1952. After thirteen years with the Boston and Milwaukee Braves, he caught for the San Francisco Giants, the Pirates, and the Indians. A .254 lifetime hitter, he played on two pennant-winning Braves teams, including the 1957 World Championship club. Crandall's .989 lifetime fielding average ranks fifteenth among catchers on the all-time list.

I got thrown out of my first home game in Boston.

The Braves had flown my folks from California to Boston to watch me play. I guess we were going to be there for a couple of weeks, a long home stand. Jocko Conlon was the umpire and he had called a couple of pitches which I thought were strikes. So I asked him about one of them.

I said, "Jocko, I think that pitch was a strike."

And he said, "I don't care what you think."

I said, "Jocko, I can't *tell* you what I think?"

Well, he took his mask off and got around in front of me and brushed off home plate and said, "No busher is gonna come up here and tell me how to umpire."

I said, "Well, you can stick that 'busher' right up your ass!"

And he threw me right out of the ballgame. Of course! My parents had just sat down. It was the first inning. The first time Jocko and I had been together. I can still see the looks on their faces, my mother and dad, and here I go. There was no scene. I mean, I didn't raise a fuss and Jocko didn't really raise a fuss. He just, all of a sudden, threw me out because of what I said.

As I'm walking toward the dugout I see my mother's face. She had her mouth open and her eyes were wide as she watched me go back down into the dugout. And I was gone.

Looking back on it, it was really something. But that was the kind of brashness or cockiness that I possessed, and might have been a bad quality had it not been suppressed to a degree after I got to the big leagues.

In those days, as a rookie you were really supposed to just stay in your place and not do anything like that. You were just supposed to be there. When your name was in the lineup, you were supposed to play. You weren't supposed to say anything about hitting. You just were there. You weren't supposed to have any say in anything, really. You had to earn the right to do that, but I don't think I understood that. Right from the beginning.

In fact, we left Walker Cooper and Bob Elliott in the clubhouse in 1950 one day because I went out and told the bus driver that everyone was gone. Cooper and Elliott had done something that *I* didn't like, before that. So I just said, "Everybody's gone." And we left.

I'm not proud of those things, but I think that was an indication of the type of competitiveness that I did have on the ballfield.

. . .

I signed out of high school. Couldn't wait. In fact, we couldn't sign a contract because our area had an American Legion team and you couldn't sign until the American Legion World Series, which I think was on September first or second. Anyway, I signed the very next day.

My mother told me that at age five I told her I was going to be a baseball player. What do you know about anything at age five? But she said that's all I wanted to be. So I think my mother and my dad and my sisters just took it for granted that I was going to be a ballplayer.

Whether you get to the big leagues or not is a matter of luck, and a lot of other things: A lot of help along the way by an awful lot of people, when you're trying to grow up and learn whatever it takes to play the game properly. Along the way I had so many people that were instrumental in terms of what I amounted to.

Had a guy by the name of Pep Lemon that was kind of a second father because I was in the park so much in Fullerton, California. He gave me every opportunity to play. I caught a major league pitcher when I was sixteen years old – Hal Gregg, you might remember the name. He was from southern California and he would come down and play Sunday baseball. And he said, "You can do it."

I was very, very small when I went into high school. I was under five feet. But then I just started to spurt. In fact, the way that I started catching was I went to Maple School, which was on the so-called wrong side of the tracks. There were quite a few Mexican kids in Fullerton at the time, and they developed a lot quicker and they were faster. I was kind of a chubby kid, and I can remember standing in line in fifth grade, when the coach, Art Johnson, carried the catcher's glove and the mask all the way down the line. I was at the very end of the line, and I could see all these other kids, very good athletes, saying, No, I want to play center field or I want to play shortstop or I want to pitch or I want to play second. He went practically through everybody.

This was the first opportunity I had had – because I was a rather timid kid – to do something that those bigger, stronger, faster athletes did not want to do. And I said, "I can catch!"

I think that's really what spurred me through to try to excel, was that fact. Because physically I wasn't the type that was athletic looking, not by any stretch of the imagination. I used to love to get hit because you could see the seams from the ball in my arms, and it wouldn't bother me. I wouldn't flinch. But as time went on I slimmed down and started to be able to run and throw, and I could do some things defensively.

Never could hit until my first year in pro ball. Then Dutch Hoffman, who was my manager at that time, came along about two months in to the season, and said, "This is what I want you to do every day."

I was hitting about .170 at the time, and Dutch had me hit pepper every single day! Holding the bat this way, throwing the head of the bat at the ball, over and over and over. And when that season was over I'd had a real good year. This was at Leavenworth, my first year of pro ball. That was Class C baseball.

Then the next year, at Evansville, I just couldn't do anything wrong. It seemed like everything I hit was off the tip of a glove, and I was hitting for power. And that's when I went to the big leagues.

But Dutch Hoffman, if he hadn't come into my life who knows what would have happened. I was fortunate that he made a suggestion and it worked. But how many suggestions did he have? He was the bus driver, he was the trainer, he was the manager, and he was worried about playing as much as he wanted to play, because he was a playing manager.

In fact, he put me in the outfield for a couple of games because he was a catcher and he wanted to catch. It was in Topeka, Kansas, and somebody hit a ball to me and I came in to make the play, but it was one of those rising line drives and the next thing I knew I had to run back to the wall to pick it up.

I was eighteen years old and I told him – and this was just an indication of my brashness, I would expect – after the game, "I don't want to play the outfield anymore."

He said, "What do you mean?"

I said, "Well, they sent me here to catch, and I want to catch. I don't want to play the outfield anymore."

"But just once in a while? Because I like to play."

I said, "Well, then you play first base. Because I'm not going to play the outfield anymore."

And I didn't. There's a *lot* of people to be thankful for.

I'm not sure I was ready to play on the major league level. But I think I could do a lot of things on the Class B level, in the Three I League, with Evansville. I could throw, I could run, I was having a tremendous year.

The Braves had just won the pennant and got in the World Series in '48. But apparently things weren't going too well for them, and Billy Southworth, the manager, came to Evansville to watch me play and I had a very good night. So they decided to get rid of some of the older players and bring up the young player. I'm not sure they knew how young I was. But it was just timing – having a good year at the right time and the right place. So I got a chance to go up and catch fairly regularly in '49.

When I got called up by the Braves from Evansville I called home, and when my mother answered the phone I said, "I'm going to Boston." She said, "What for?"

I had just turned nineteen in March and went to the big leagues in June. It was very, very quick. When I came up, Johnny Antonelli and I became instant friends. We were the same age. We shared a big room together right near the ballpark. So we roomed together at home and we roomed together on the road. We still see each other. I guess we're still the youngest battery ever. We were both nineteen.

When they brought me up in '49, I became the regular catcher. Bill Salkeld was there, but Phil Masi, the regular catcher, was traded to Pittsburgh June 15, the same day they brought me up. I think I caught almost as many games in '49 as I did in '50. They got Walker Cooper sometime in May of '50, and he did a lot of the catching from then on.

It was a team of veterans. We had Earl Torgeson, Bob Elliott, Marv Rickert, and Jeff Heath. Alvin Dark and Eddie Stanky were on the club in 1949, before they were traded. Then Willard Marshall came over, Buddy Kerr, Sid Gordon. I don't know that I was an outcast – that's a strong word – but I know there was definitely a big gap between veterans who were there – and who had had some success – and the young guy trying to *find* a little success.

There was a big, a big gap in communication with the older players. They expected a certain attitude, a certain respect from the young guys, and yet they did not seem to have any obligation to return that in any way.

I'm not trying to say that it was a terrible situation; I'm not trying to paint that kind of picture. But it just seems like a rookie was definitely a rookie, a young player was definitely a young player. And the older players felt like they were in a little different league than the young guys. And they'd earned it.

I think the veterans' attitudes had a very big influence on me later. I was not going to be like that. I think most of the rookies – I hope all of them – I played with later felt as though they were a part of the club when they were trying to make it in spring training, part of the club as the season went on.

For one thing, I had to handle young pitchers. That was my job. It was not like going out and not being involved with the young guys. I *was* involved with the young guys. They were part of the staff, they were trying to make the staff. Consequently, I think my attitude toward all rookies might have been changed to some degree by the fact that I was forced to do what I could for young pitchers.

The baseball at Boston was different. When I came up I had played baseball under Bob Coleman, who was a big supporter of mine. I only played for him just that half-year in Evansville, but we did some things on a minor league level that we didn't do on a big league level, that was not part of the way they played in the big leagues. I mean, I threw the ball all over the ballpark—I'd pick guys off second, off third, off first. That was how our club played in Evansville.

Well, when I got to the big leagues I did give it a try, but I found out that the players who played those positions weren't nearly as enthusiastic as I was about doing that kind of thing. Consequently, I did stop throwing, and that was a big, big change for me. The manager in B ball encouraged that kind of play; the manager in the major leagues did *not* encourage that kind of play. You have to adapt to whatever style the manager plays.

The pitching was so much different, of course. I didn't hit many home runs when I came to the big leagues. I think I had four each year, half of '49 and all of '50. So that was a big shock. But I think, just defensively, the way the game was played, that the managers were so different that I kind of had to suppress the type of play from what was expected in Class B ball.

I look back and I probably was not ready, from an *overall* standpoint, to assume that regular catcher's job. At the time I didn't know it. Then I went into the service for two years, which gave me a chance to mature and get stronger.

■   ■   ■

In Boston, we were low on the totem pole. It was a Red Sox town, I don't think there was any secret to that. But when you're nineteen and you come to the big leagues, I'm not sure you're too aware of too much that goes on around you. You're just so awed by the fact that you're in the major leagues. For me, all those other things didn't really matter much: the fact that the Braves didn't draw like they should; the talk that it was a Red Sox town and how there weren't many Braves fans. For me, those things didn't mean much. They really weren't significant because just playing major league baseball was the greatest thing that ever happened to me at that stage of my life.

When I was in the service in '52, they drew something like 267,000 for the entire season. So it got worse as far as coming out to watch the Braves play.

Then we moved to Milwaukee, which was just a very, very special place to play. We broke the National League attendance record our first year there. I think the Dodgers had it. We drew over one million for five consecutive years. The surrounding states – let alone Wisconsin – but Iowa, Minnesota . . . There were so many fans from those other states that it was just tremendous.

And the way the local people treated us, it was unbelievable. We got bread and meat and milk and dry cleaning from local merchants. Two of our kids were part of an advertising campaign by Golden Guernsey Dairy, because they just loved cottage cheese and milk. They had their pictures taken eating cottage cheese. I had a Dodge on loan from Wally Rank, a Dodge dealer, just about every year I was there. And Wally became such a good friend that a lot of us wound up buying cars from him. Bud Selig did a little of that then; I think he was in the Ford business.

From 1953 through 1959 we had some great teams, we really did. We almost won in '56, but we weren't ready. I'm not sure that you can put into words what it takes to win for the first time. But I think, probably, it's a matter of confidence, that all of a sudden now you're sure that you can win; up until then you're not sure. And I think that's where we were in '56. We were just not sure that we could win. Consequently we didn't.

Of course, the Dodgers played outstanding the last four ballgames and they made it difficult for us to win. Matter of fact, they wouldn't let us win. But there were four years there when we were really as good as anybody.

Prior to '56, Charlie Grimm was probably the best manager that we could have had at that stage of our development. He pretty much let us play. He didn't have a lot of rules, he didn't have a lot of plays, he didn't do an awful lot on the ballfield. But what he did have was a bunch of ballplayers that had the right attitude about playing the game of baseball. If it weren't for that I don't know what would have happened to us.

At that point, we didn't need an awful lot. All we needed to do was play and gain experience. Because most of us had the right approach to the game. We didn't need rules, we didn't need plays, we didn't need a lot of things. We just needed to develop and learn on the field, not having a lot of people confusing us. Which can happen at times.

So Charlie Grimm let us play. Consequently, we were able to learn how to play. We were able to learn the things necessary to win ballgames. And again, we were fortunate. You talk about Adcock and Logan and Mathews and Aaron. And the pitching staff – Spahn and Burdette and Buhl and Don McMahon. Those guys knew what their approach to trying to be better needed to be. We didn't need *guidance*.

All we needed was experience, and we got it under Charlie. He was very good for all of us.

Now, Fred Haney, when he came in '56, wasn't anybody who was trying to gain a reputation as a great baseball mind. But he had some things he wanted us to do, and he was probably a little more structured and wanted discipline a little bit more. But he wasn't overbearing.

I think it was our overall approach to the game, day in and day out, that made us. I mean, when you have the talent of Aaron – the best hitter, in my book, who ever lived – and you have the leadership of Mathews . . . I don't think there's any question that Eddie Mathews was our leader. He didn't say much, but he was a leader because of the personality he had, because of his approach to the game, because of his toughness, because of just the way he put pressure on the other club. Offensively and defensively, he was unquestionably our leader. And then you have Logan, who rarely made a mistake. And you have Joe Adcock, who could beat you with one swing and was as good as anybody with his foot on the base – he could stretch! And Billy Bruton could run 'em down in the outfield. We had Wes Covington, who had tremendous years offensively: RBIs per at bats, RBIs to hits. He was really a strong hitter for us. Then we got Red Schoendienst; that made us a real good club, because he could really play. I think Andy Pafko was there at that time. Gene Conley did some pitching for us.

It was a fun club. It was a club that, in the clubhouse, knew how to take a ribbing, knew how to hand it out *and* how to take it. There didn't seem to be any real animosity in the clubhouse. You'd have your say and then it was over. It was a special club from that standpoint.

I remember getting Bobby Thomson in '54, the year that Aaron came up, and he had no idea how to react to what we did in the clubhouse. No idea. The way we kidded each other, the way we picked on each other. Bobby wasn't used to that. Apparently, where he came from the Giants didn't have that kind of thing. I'm sure they had fun, but it wasn't the same. I remember Bobby getting *really* upset at that. In fact, he tried to stuff Spahnie into the whirlpool one day.

Bobby was trying to recuperate from the broken ankle he got in spring training and he was lying on the training table. He was getting taped and whatever else he used to do with the ankle. And Spahnie used to come in and agitate him, pour water on his back, whatever.

Bobby kept telling him to stop: "Don't mess around now." Then he got up from the table. If he'd been the type of guy that wanted to hit somebody he'd have hit Spahn. Instead, he picked him up and stuffed him in the whirlpool. Full of water.

But that wasn't good enough. A few days later, Spahnie came back and Bobby was on the table again. And Spahnie started messing with him and Bobby said, "Don't do that, Spahnie!" So when Bobby started to get up Spahn went and *jumped* in the whirlpool.

It was fun. We had good guys that liked to agitate, but they could also take it.

.   .   .

Beating the Yankees in '57 confirmed that we were a pretty good ballclub. Because the Yankees had one of their great clubs. But even before that, I think one of our big drives was to beat the Dodgers. They beat up on us pretty badly.

First of all, they played in a ballpark, early – Ebbets Field – that was very, very favorable to the kind of hitters they had. It was a very short ballpark and the wind blew out to left field all the time. I think all of us felt that if we could play in *that* field we could do even better as far as the bat was concerned. Whether there was any truth in it or not I don't know. But we used to always marvel at Ebbets Field, how fortunate they were to play in that ballpark. Not their pitchers, who had to pitch in that ballpark, but their hitters: Campanella, Hodges, Snider, Furillo.

The Dodgers were an experienced ballclub. They had Reese and Furillo, Robinson, Campanella, Erskine, Billy Cox, Duke Snider . . . you could go on and on. These were guys who, to us, when we moved to Milwaukee, were veteran players. So when we finally caught up with them, *we* started to become veteran ballplayers, and their players started getting old, which changed their ability to compete. They were beginning to run out of time and we were just getting to a peak. If we had been at the same stage when the Dodgers were at their peak – as far as our experience was concerned – there's no telling what would have happened. I mean, it would have been a real battle, because I think the ballclubs, talent-wise, were pretty similar.

Following the '56 season, when we finished one game behind the Dodgers, I think there was a different attitude. I'm not sure you can articulate it, but at the same time I think we just walked a little taller, a little more confidently during the course of the year. Then, as the year went on, we found out how well we could do, and we just continued to gain confidence. First of all, I think all of us had a pretty good idea of how good we were individually. And then, collectively, I felt that we could compete, and we could. It just turned out that we were able to apply pressure to the opposition and we were able to win.

For me, being in the '57 World Series was overwhelming. I mean, I was actually sick. That night, before we played our first game in Yankee Stadium, we were in New York and I was sick. I had the runs and I felt like I was going to throw up. I told Fran, my wife, who was in New York with me, "This is a great time to get sick."

She said, "You don't really know what's wrong? You're just uptight. You're probably just nervous. This is the biggest thing that's ever happened to you in your baseball life, something that you've been looking forward to forever. You'll be okay in the morning."

And I was. But when we started the ballgame – Spahnie started it for us, Lew didn't pitch till the second game – I could envision the people in the stands seeing my knees shake. I was really that nervous. My entire body was shaking, and that's no exaggeration.

I mean, this was the first time I'd seen Yankee Stadium. We'd worked out in it the day before, but . . . I mean, this was the old stadium being the way it used to be. You walked out into center field and saw those monuments. It was an immense place to try to hit in. And all the history, everything surrounding the World Series. Literally, all through Warren Spahn's warm-ups until the bottom of the first inning, I continued to shake.

Spahn always threw a screwball for his last pitch, when I would throw the ball to second base. Well, it was in the dirt, and when I came up with it I came up throwing. I threw the ball to second base, and the nervousness went away just like that. I suppose because I caught the ball and my mind was on the ball, and when I threw it to second base, right then it was all reduced to just another ballgame.

But just imagine, here's my mother telling me I wanted to be a baseball player since I was five years old. And then all of a sudden you get a chance to sign a professional contract. And then you hit so poorly you wonder what your future is going to be when you first get into pro ball. And then you get that out of the way and you go into your second year in pro ball and all of a sudden you're in the big leagues. And then finally you say, Well, now I want to *stay* in the big leagues.

And then you say, Well, I'd like to be an All-Star. And you're able to do that. Then, all of a sudden, here's the biggest thing to happen to you, the World Series, and I guess emotionally it just built up to a point where, going into that Series, I was a mess.

I don't know what the other players went through, but I know for me, personally, it was a matter of just trying to settle down and put it in a proper place, which I was able to do.

The seventh game really wasn't very eventful. Burdette was leading. I don't remember exactly when we scored, but we had a 4–0 lead for what seemed like a long time. I hit a home run in the eighth inning, and it looked like it was going to be a 5–0 ballgame, that that home run wasn't going to be significant at all. Then they loaded the bases in the bottom of the ninth and Moose Skowron was the hitter, a tremendous clutch hitter.

Sitting back there, I knew Lew had to get the third out some way. And I thought, well that home run is a pretty big run right now, because if he hits the ball out of the ballpark we still have a one-run lead and we have two out. But he hit the bouncer down the third base line and Mathews backhanded it and went to the bag.

I didn't know how anything could top winning the pennant. We did it at home, in Milwaukee, against the club that was in second place, St. Louis. And I didn't know how anything could be more exciting than that. You play 154 games and here you are at the end and you win it. That's a long time to spend with a group of guys who have the same idea of wanting to win. And it happens.

But then we won the World Series, and there's no comparison. I mean, now you're not only the best in your league, you have accomplished the ultimate in our game, to win the World Series. It was a tremendous thrill.

And I think one of the things that goes along with this is that you look around the room at some of the guys I'd been with for a long time: Aaron, Adcock, Logan, Mathews, Bruton, Covington, Spahn, Burdette, and Buhl. These were guys that you lived with for five and a half months, longer than that when you include spring training. And here you are, you're able to win this. It's really a close, close feeling. Maybe closer than you really are, but at that particular time it's really a feeling of closeness that I'm not sure many people really understand. Maybe if you're in the business of sports and you're on the field and you win your greatest prize – the World Series in our sport – maybe you have that same feeling. But I'm not sure that people understand how important a part *that* is in your overall athletic career. And I believe when you retire that's the one thing that you miss the most, the people. The guys in the clubhouse. And if you're not in uniform, you're really *not* one of the people in the clubhouse.

▪ ▪ ▪

Everybody likes to hit. I wasn't disciplined enough to be a good percentage hitter. I did have some power and I could hit the ball out of the park, and I could help the club at certain times during the course of the season. I think I did that quite a bit. But I really feel that if I would have been a little bit more interested in the offensive part and had been a little bit smarter, my average might have been quite a bit better.

I wouldn't take base on balls, and hitting eighth all the time you wanted to swing the bat. I wasn't smart enough to realize that taking a walk is usually much better than making an out. But I wasn't very smart, and that's just the way that I approached it. You look back and I guess you could have done a lot of things differently.

But defense, that was it. I was taught that the catcher was the defensive ballplayer of the club. Throw people out, block pitches in the dirt – that was what I did every day. If your ballclub won and you were the catcher, there was always some pride that you could take in the fact that you helped your ballclub win. If an outfielder or an infielder goes 0 for 4 and your ballclub wins, you feel good but what have you done? But if you're a catcher and you go 0 for 4, somewhere during that ballgame you get the feeling that you helped your pitcher.

I think that's the feeling that I liked the most. You're always involved in whatever happened. Every time the pitcher cocks his arms and throws the ball, *you* are involved. Nobody out there, except the pitcher, is involved every time the baseball is thrown. And outside of the pitcher, there's nobody that works as hard as the catcher, for that day; and the pitcher only works every four or five days.

Everybody else has to rely on circumstance to make a great play, to come up in the clutch and get that base hit. And the only two people who *don't* have to rely on that are the pitcher and the catcher. The potential is there every pitch.

Runner at third and the pitcher throws the ball in the dirt, you block it. Then the guy pops up to end the inning and maybe nobody notices it. But the pitcher knows what you did and the catcher knows what he did, and the manager might have an appreciation of what went on. So those are things that those two positions alone can experience, and nobody else really can.

A pitcher has the same feeling, I assume, that the catcher has when he has been successful. He has done a good job, he gets some real, personal gratification from it. A catcher, even though he doesn't get the win and maybe doesn't have the *same* elation that a pitcher does, still knows – if that's the big part of his game – he was a part of that. He can share in that elation.

And that's really why I liked catching so much. Here you're the only person that can see everybody on the field. Your center fielder can, to a degree, but he can't do anything about it. But here the catcher sees everybody, face on. Everybody is right there, so you can have an effect, just that one fact alone. If you know what your pitcher's doing and you know that this guy's not playing quite right, you have the right to move him. I did. Something you didn't like to do, but they accepted that and so you'd say, Well, I just don't think the defense is right. You have them move over, and sometimes it'll work out so that that little thing was enough to help the club.

Catchers don't do that much anymore, because I think to some degree fielders might think that the catcher is showing them up in some way, to move them. But that didn't seem to be the case with our ballclub. Whenever I wanted to move somebody I was able to do it, and people moved and nobody ever said anything. I don't think that was typical, even when I played. It was done, but it wasn't typical. It was an indication of the kind of players we had, of the kind of mental approach to the game – that this wasn't an attempt to make them look bad but to help our ballclub. And that's what we wanted to do.

I'm not saying I did it every game: sometimes I did it once or twice during a game; sometimes I didn't do it at all. But when it felt like I should do it I did. It just happened, that's all.

With the older pitchers, I thought that my responsibility was to be so familiar with their delivery that if they started to do something wrong then that's why I went out. I know Spahn, one of the things that he wouldn't do at times was to lift his leg up high. And when he didn't lift his leg up high it seemed that he messed up his command, because his delivery was different and he wasn't quite as sharp. And if I can see that I'll go out and say, "Hey, kick your leg up higher, it's not going up high enough." And when he did, that seemed to be his natural, fluid delivery, and that's when he did well.

I think anybody could catch Warren Spahn. He could execute so well. It was hard to call for a bad pitch with him because his control was so good. His delivery was very deceptive; it was hard for a hitter to pick up the ball. Joe Torre caught him just like that when he came to the big leagues from the minors, because Spahnie could execute so well. He could throw the ball low and outside blindfolded. When you wanted him to throw the ball inside, he could throw the ball inside. We got along extremely well from when I was nineteen and caught him for the first time.

Burdette, he and I probably got along as well as anybody. He used to start his windup before I'd give a sign. He'd *know* what I was going to put down.

With a lot of pitchers you just have instant rapport. Bob Buhl was a little bit different. He had some set things that he had in his mind, and I had some others. Del Rice caught him a lot, was kind of "his" catcher. They spent some time together off the field, and I didn't spend any time off the field with Buhl. I remember Buhl telling me, "I don't mind if you catch me; it's not that I don't want you to catch me. But this is what *they* want; Rice and I seem to be going good. I just don't want you to think that I don't want you catching me because that's just not true. In fact, I'd like to have your bat in the lineup."

But maybe not catching once every four or five days wasn't such a bad idea anyway. I didn't think so at the time.

Then you had the younger pitchers come along: Joey Jay, Carlton Willey, Bob Trowbridge, Bob Hendley, guys like that. So now you do feel that you have some other effect upon the pitcher. It's how you're able to evaluate their stuff, you're able to evaluate what they're able to get over the plate in given situations, not catch them into trouble, not ask them to do things that they couldn't do. That's where I think a catcher can help.

It becomes engrained. If the veterans were critical of the catcher, then the young guys would be hesitant about putting their future in this guy's hands. And I don't think that was our case at all.

With Juan Pizarro, I think in his case his potential was that he could throw the ball at ninety-five miles per hour. Well, that's not necessarily potential, that's somebody with a good fastball. To be able to pitch you have to be able to do other things, because you can throw the ball ninety-five miles an hour, and if you don't throw it in certain spots in certain times in the ballgame, you're going to lose. Guys'll hit you. And I don't think he developed that, when he had the good stuff. I don't think he developed that part of the game. It was just—throw the ball hard and then turn that little screwball over at times. But I don't think that he was consistent in getting the pitches where he needed to get them in times of trouble.

And that's what makes a good pitcher. They may give up home runs, but when the ballgame is on the line, they're able to consistently make good pitches, which puts the pressure on the hitter. You don't give too many real good pitches to hit. You get beat once in a while, but consistently you're going to win.

Pizarro was certainly built up to be better, and he had the fastball to be better. Like Rex Barney for many years. I mean, nobody threw harder than Rex Barney, but he couldn't win. He couldn't get anything over but his fastball, and when he got his fastball over it was right down the middle and people hit it.

It's one thing being wild and walking people. The other side of being wild is when you throw the ball in the hitting zone too much. That's wildness also. And they probably go hand in hand.

One on one, a pitching coach has always been a part of a pitcher's making progress. Every time they throw a ball in the bullpen, the pitching coach is right there. To learn to throw new pitches, the pitching coach is involved. The catcher comes into play when those things get good enough so that you can help a pitcher use that stuff properly and, as I said before, not catch him into trouble. That's where a catcher's role comes in.

I think there's a lot of emphasis on talking about what hitters *can't* hit. But my primary concern was the pitcher's stuff. I had to be concerned with his stuff and his capabilities. If they didn't match up well with the hitter, there wasn't much you could do about that. If you had a lowball pitcher and a lowball hitter, sometimes there wasn't much you could do except go out of the strike zone, low. They like to hit the low ball and they would chase low pitches once in a while. Same way with pitches up in the strike zone: high-ball hitters have a tendency to chase high pitches out of the strike zone.

So there were some things that you could do, but you couldn't change the basic stuff of the pitcher. His ability to make pitches and the stuff he had was more important to me than the weakness of the hitter.

Anybody who has been around long enough to get to the big leagues, and then spend a little time in the big leagues, understands that it's the pitcher of that day and the hitter that he's pitching to is how you have to call a ballgame. And once again, the most important thing is the pitcher's stuff.

I've always thought that Roy Campanella was a good catcher. I've always thought that I was a better catcher.

When you saw Campanella catch, you knew he was a good thrower. He worked hard behind the plate. He blocked balls pretty good. But the thing that separated Campanella from most any other catcher was his ability to swing the bat. He compiled some great statistics – home runs, RBIs, and batting average. And of course, he was the Most Valuable Player three times. So when you start talking about that kind of catcher, it's those kinds of offensive statistics that separate him from other people who could have been very, very good at their position. He just dwarfs you because of his ability to swing the bat. It was the sugar – the hitting aspect – that gets to be overwhelming.

When people talked about catchers, they talked about Jim Hegan in the American League and me in the National League. Defensively now. Because we played every day and we did those things defensively that helped our ballclub play well on the field. That's why when you get into conversations about yourself it's very, very hard. But when the question is asked and when you really want to get serious – I mean I poke fun at my career and that sort of thing – but I really felt – and of course that's for somebody else to judge – that I was the best defensive catcher in the National League. That's the way I felt.

I could always throw and I could always run, up until I got to be around twenty-seven years old, when catching started to catch up with me. And I could move behind the plate. And I hustled as much as anybody.

Those qualities I think were, in the beginning, attention getters. And I know eventually you have to do it on the field. But I think that people like to see those qualities. I know I do now, when I look at catchers. So I got a chance and did some things offensively so that I was able to play most every day. Because that's what really determines it, playing every day. Do you do well enough to be a part of the offense?

I thought that our pitchers had a lot of confidence in me. And I thought they relied on me a great deal, and that's an added incentive, too. If you know they're counting on you, then you *have* to give some thought to what you're doing. It's not just putting the fingers down, it's having some sort of idea as to the best way to help that pitcher that day. You can have this feeling yourself that you did it, but you can only hope that other people shared that. And from what I can understand, that was a feeling that they did count on me for.

I'm not sure you put this in the proper perspective until you're no longer the regular catcher. Then it starts to dawn on you that there is something to catching after all. That there are some instances during the course of a ballgame where you've made a decision that consistently seems to have helped that pitcher. And you look back and you say, "Well, there is some satisfaction in that." And I think, once again, that was shared by most of the pitchers I came in contact with. I don't think it's 100 percent because it never is in anything, but I think basically they had some appreciation for how I tried to do my job, both mentally and physically.

I really don't think there's any question about what's the hardest thing about catching. It's the every day going back there and taking the foul tips, because you get in streaks where it seems like every one hits you. It's the little nicks and little hand problems, not enough to get you out of there but it does bother you when you swing the bat.

That's another thing that I always took pride in – that I didn't come out because of those things. And I wasn't a big tough guy, by any stretch of the imagination. I must have a fairly decent tolerance of pain; I was able to play with those things.

It's the mental toughness that you really need behind the plate. I thought I was as mentally tough as anybody. I didn't feel like I ever got tired. It might have showed sometimes that I was tired, but I never felt mentally that I was tired. I never thought that I *should* rest. And I wanted to play. I *just* wanted to play, and I went through some tough hitting slumps.

I was one of those guys who would go into those 1-for-30 and 2-for-40 slumps. But I liked the defensive part of the game so well that not hitting didn't bother the defensive part of my game at all. So I think it's the mental toughness that catchers really need to have. Never get tired, just *don't* get tired – because it's usually mental anyway.

People who don't want to catch say they would never get behind the plate: "Foul tips hit you, you have to put that stuff on, and it gets to be ninety-two, ninety-five degrees. I wouldn't want any part of it." If they really knew how big the catcher's role is in a ballgame, they wouldn't think that.

I remember catching eight games in six days. Doubleheaders? Caught them all. I just wanted to catch. It was the only thing I wanted to do.

In the majors I didn't catch many doubleheaders. I caught some, but not as a rule. We didn't think about liking or disliking doubleheaders. It was just what we did. It would be just the same as trying to get players now to play doubleheaders. It's not what they do, so it's very objectionable to them.

You look back on it and you say it was tough. But at the time? You come in, you take a quick shower, you grab a piece of baloney and a piece of cheese, and you go out and get them again.

Mel Parnell

June 4–5, 1993, New Orleans, Louisiana

Mel Parnell pitched for the Boston Red Sox from 1947 to 1956. One of the most successful left-handers ever to pitch in Fenway Park, Parnell won 123 games, lost 75, and compiled a 3.50 earned run average in his ten major league seasons. From 1948 to 1953 he averaged eighteen wins a season. His twenty-five wins, twenty-seven complete games, 295.1 innings pitched, and 2.77 ERA were best in the American League in 1949. In 1956 Parnell no-hit the Chicago White Sox 4–0.

Baseball. It's a disease. It gets in your system and you can't get rid of it. I enjoyed it so much I'd like to be able to do it all over again. We had a lot of fun as kids. We had ballparks all around the city. Baseball was really *the* thing down here.

At the time we had the Cleveland Indians training here in New Orleans. We had the New York Giants up in Baton Rouge at LSU. Every weekend there was a series between the Giants and the Indians here at our ballpark. Cleveland had a pretty good ballclub. Of course, so did the Giants. Mel Ott, Bill Terry, guys like that. Good ones. Cleveland had the big first baseman, Hal Trosky.

And on Sunday there would be Bob Feller against Carl Hubbell. Every Sunday, we had an overflow crowd – they'd be on the *field*. It was the greatest exhibition in the world to watch. You'd see Feller out there grunting and groaning on every pitch that he threw, and old Hubbell taking it so easy, throwing that screwball up there. It was the difference between night and day, watching the two pitchers work. Complete opposites. It was great.

I saw Bob Feller the day he beaned Hank Leiber, who was a real good outfielder. His career was nothing after that. He hit Leiber and the ball bounced straight up in the air. They rolled the ambulance out and picked him up and took him away. Lucky he didn't die there. Man, it was a sad thing, I tell you. Made a lot of people leave the ballpark with an empty heart.

■   ■   ■

My father was a machinist for the Illinois Central Railroad. He was a top machinist, and he was in charge of what they called "the million-dollar train," the Panama Limited. It ran from New Orleans to Chicago. It would leave here in the afternoon at somewhere around four o'clock and get into Chicago the next morning at eight o'clock. It was a pretty good run.

That thing used to fly along the tracks. It was a real plush train, and that was his baby: make sure that thing was ready to get out of here on time.

The railroad wanted Dad to transfer up to Chicago and operate it from that end. He said, "No way!" He wasn't about to leave. I'm thankful that he didn't, because it certainly would have changed my life around, in baseball. I had my roots set here, as I was coming up.

He wouldn't travel with the train, but if they had a breakdown somewhere close to the city, then he'd take a crew out and analyze the problem and correct it. I was on it one time when that happened.

Yeah. It hit a mule, about twenty miles outside the city. It busted a valve on the engine and we had to wait for a crew to come out. Killed the mule right quick.

I was in the service at the time, going back to Memphis, Tennessee. I was stationed in Arkansas, just seventy-five miles from Memphis. That was the day that I was hoping I could have been in baseball, but naturally I had to answer the call.

I played in the service a lot. We had a pretty good team. We played a lot of the Southern Association teams at that time, and we beat them. We had two chaplains: one was a third baseman, one was a left fielder. Catholic chaplain was the third baseman, the Methodist chaplain was the left fielder. We won the Eastern Flying Training Command championship.

When I was transferred over to Maxwell Field, Alabama, the B-29 program, we had a *real* good ballclub. We had four ex–major league pitchers pitching on our ballclub. They wanted to send us to the semipro baseball tournament. We could have won it very easily because of our pitching strength. But just before our season ended, one of our last games, we had a team that came in from Medgar Field, Alabama, to play us, and one of their planes crashed on the runway at our base. Nine kids were killed. So instead of going to the semipro tournament we went around and played teams at various locations and donated the proceeds to the families of the guys who were killed.

■ ■ ■

Howie Pollet and I lived next door to each other. He went to Forte High School and I went to S. K. Peters High School. We played a lot of ball together. Howie's dad and my dad were very close. They used to oversee our playing quite a bit. We were thankful for that. It helped create our interest, too, as we were coming along, knowing that the fathers were there.

We had great high school baseball around here. We had a lot of pro ballplayers come out of the city. We just lost one the other day, fella by the name of Fats Dantonio, played with the Dodgers, played with Durocher. He just passed away.

We had three major leaguers come out of the same city block. All three were left-handed pitchers. Howie Pollet, myself, and a fella by the name of Larry LaSalle, who got up with Pittsburgh. He didn't stay long, but he got a tryout to the major leagues. He spent the first month of the season with Pittsburgh.

But that's a real rarity, three major league pitchers coming out of the same block, let alone left-handed pitchers. I don't think that any other city can boast of the same thing.

We had a lot of good ones. We had Zeke Bonura. Mel Ott, of course. I was with Mel Ott three days before he got killed.

Mel and I used to go over to a detention home and play with the kids. We'd put two teams together. He would play on one team and I would play on the other. I played first base. Softball. It was a lot of fun. We felt it was a good deed. We'd sit and talk with the kids.

Then, one day when he was on the Gulf Coast, he and his wife had just left a restaurant and had an automobile accident. Guy came over the centerline and hit them.

When his death was announced on the radio and TV, a lot of people – just hearing the first name Mel – thought it was me. My wife said the phone started ringing here at the house. I wasn't home. They heard the Mel part, but they didn't listen enough for the last name. Thank goodness it wasn't me. He was young in life.

I only pitched about five games in high school. We got a little short on pitching, and the coach asked me if I'd like to pitch, and I said, "Hey, I want to play, I'll play any position."

He said, "Okay, you'll be pitching our next game."

Which I did.

At the time they had scouts in the stands who had come in to see our left-fielder, a kid by the name of Red Levine, who was outstanding – a very good hitter and a kid with a lot of power. And it so happened that I struck out seventeen, and of course we got to talking.

Everybody thought I was gonna sign with the Cardinals, simply because I used to work out with the New Orleans baseball team, which was a Cardinals farm club at that time.

And Branch Rickey used to come down. Branch had us throwing batting practice – had another fella on our ballclub, a right-hander by the name of Ray Yocum – to the New Orleans team, double-A Southern League, and apparently liked what he saw, because he was after both of us.

He'd stand in back of the cage with his derby on and spats on and ask for the curveball or whatever pitch that he wanted to see us throw. He was getting a pretty good idea of what we could do and couldn't do.

Branch used to come out to the house and talk to my dad. I told Dad, "Don't make any commitments to him, because I don't want to sign with the Cardinals."

I'd heard too much about the Cardinals at that time. They were a chain gang then. You were a number rather than a name in that organization, they had so many ballplayers.

He'd come out to the house and he'd talk to my dad. I'd always sneak out of the house, go out through the back way. I didn't want to talk with him. I didn't want to be talked into the Cardinals.

We had seven members of our high school team sign to play pro baseball. Six of them signed with the Cards, and I was the only one that didn't. And truthfully, I was the only one that got to the majors. Rickey was Mr. Baseball then.

But Red Sox scout Eddie Montague came down, and Herb Pennock, and I got talking with them, and I liked what I heard. And of course, the name Parnell fit perfectly in Boston, being Irish. I liked the idea of the Red Sox. Of course, when I got to Boston and saw that short left field fence, I was wondering if I had made the right move or not.

.   .   .

Loved to hit. To me, it was the best part of the game. I hit seventh in the lineup when Lou Boudreau was the manager. I remember, I was the first one of the pitchers – Maury McDermott, Willard Nixon, and I – to hit seventh in the lineup. And when I first saw the lineup printed and I was in the seventh spot, I asked Boudreau if he'd made a mistake.

He said, "No, don't you want to hit seventh?"

I said, "Sure, see you later." And I ran outside and got my batting practice in. He used me, on occasion, to pinch-hit, which I enjoyed – coming up to the plate – but not against the guys I was facing. I was getting some tough cookies, guys like Feller, Bob Lemon, and Mike Garcia. Not the most opportune time to get up off the bench and walk to the plate.

I loved hitting. I took it serious, because I felt it meant a lot to me in a close ballgame. In a close ballgame it would keep me in the lineup. As long as I was in the lineup, I had a chance to get a win. Whereas if I couldn't swing the bat and got into a situation where maybe I'm a run behind, they'll take me out for a pinch hitter and eliminate a chance to get the win. So I got in my batting practice, consistently.

When I was coming up in the minors, 1942, at Canton, Ohio, I opened the season in right field. Some of our outfielders were hurt. I played pretty good on opening day. I got two hits and drove in a couple of runs. Boy, I was happy as a lark. Maybe I could play here every day.

Then word came down from the Red Sox: "Get that little skinny kid back on the mound! He's not an outfielder, he's a pitcher!"

That was the end of that. But to me, hitting is the joy of the game.

■　■　■

I loved Fenway Park, after I got acquainted with the setup there. It's not as bad a ballpark to pitch in as a lot of people think. Of course, you have to be careful with the pitches you make. The left field fence didn't bother me at all because I felt that I could protect myself. The thing that bothered me was the foul territory. There's very little foul territory at Fenway Park, and balls going into the seats just give guys another chance to take a shot at you.

Many of us made changes in our style because of that ballpark. I did, too.

Coming up in the Red Sox organization, I was a fastball pitcher. However, when I got to Fenway Park I figured I had to do more than just throw the fastball. So I went to the slider and sinker and worked more on my curveball. The fastball was a pitch you didn't want to give them to hit in Fenway Park. You wanted to keep that ball moving in on 'em all the way. I concentrated so much on the right-hander that I got a little too relaxed on the left-handed hitter.

When I first broke in up there, we were traveling by train when we went on a road trip. It was greater for us as baseball players than it is for the present-day player because I think we got more knowledgeable about the game. You can't go anywhere on a train, so what do you do? You sit there and discuss baseball, and you discuss situations and you discuss opposition. I think it made us better ballplayers. You had that closeness. It gave us a great opportunity to sit there and discuss guys who we had trouble with.

For the pitchers, we learned a lot from hitters. We learned what they were thinking when they got to the plate. Especially Williams. It was great getting into a discussion with Ted and talking hitting, because he gave you some viewpoints that a lot of other guys didn't.

I used to throw batting practice to Ted. In Boston. And I threw to him under game conditions. I wouldn't tell him what I was throwing, and that was the way he wanted it, as well. But he was improving himself at Fenway, because he saw very few left-handed pitchers at Fenway, and he figured that he would be keeping himself sharp against left-handers for when he got on the road.

And it helped me too, because I'm trying to figure out the best hitter in baseball, and anything I can find on him I can use against somebody else. Maury McDermott threw to him, as well. And I think Chuck Stobbs threw some to him, too.

■　■　■

I had some arm trouble at one time, and I was sent down to Johns Hopkins Hospital in Baltimore, and I talked to a doctor down there who made more sense than anybody I ever spoke to about arms and throwing a baseball. He told me the higher you delivered from, the more likely you were to have trouble, because you're compacting everything in your shoulder as you get up high. A submariner has less trouble, which is common sense.

Of course, I was one that threw from as high as I could get, and my reason for it was, the higher I could get – and throwing to the lower part of the strike zone – the ball's going out of the line of vision. The hitter's seeing the top of the ball and not the whole baseball. That's what I thought. That was my theory of pitching.

And I didn't toe the rubber like a lot of other pitchers. A lot of them would turn their foot sideways and pitch from the whole foot. I didn't. I went up on my toes on the rubber, to get a little more height. That was my feeling: the higher I could deliver from, the better it was for me. Then, in throwing the curveball or the sinker, it gave it a chance to get a little more breakage. We all have different theories, but that was the one that I had when I was pitching.

And I never pitched from the same identical spot on the rubber. The first inning I would start off in the middle of the rubber. Then I would ask my catcher in the middle of the first inning, "What is my ball doing?" So that I could know. For instance, if I was missing just outside the plate, I would move over a little more to the third base side of the rubber and bring the ball back to the plate. If I was missing on the inside, I'd go a little toward first base. I don't know how many guys do that today, but that's what I used to do. I used to quiz my catcher, Sammy White, all the time, and Birdie Tebbetts too.

■　■　■

Sammy White was a great catcher. He instilled a lot of confidence in a pitcher. He used to say, "Just throw it. If I can't catch it, I'll block it. It won't get past me." When a catcher tells you that, you've got confidence throwing a pitch anyplace you want, knowing that he's gonna get to it.

Frankie Hayes caught me in my first big league game. Against Washington. And I lost that ballgame 3–2, and he was partly responsible, with a passed ball. But it didn't matter to me, I wasn't gonna say anything to him.

Frankie didn't like rookies too much. I could understand that. He was friendly with the older veterans, and of course the rookie coming up and taking the veteran's spot . . . He kind of resented that and didn't particularly like the rookie.

But I had to room with him on our first road trip. When we broke camp, we went to Washington, D.C. He and I were roomies, and I'm lying there with one eye open and one eye closed. If he would have made a move toward me, I would have been gone. But he was a good catcher. Even in his later years he was real good. Then, later on, we made a trade and got Birdie for Hal Wagner.

We had Matt Batts, who I came up through the minor leagues with. Then we got Buddy Rosar, and we had Gus Niarhos and Del Wilber. Niarhos was a great little catcher. He was small in stature. He was just a little ball in back of the plate. He was somewhat like Tony Peña is. He got real low down on the ground and gave you a real good low target.

We had some good ones. But I liked Sammy. Sammy gave me a lot of confidence.

I'd say the catcher doesn't understand the pitcher's arm. A pitcher's arm is quite different than an arm used in any other position. And another thing, the catcher doesn't understand the feel of the ball, what a pitcher really has to acquaint himself with.

Lots of people think that because a catcher calls the pitch he's more knowledgeable or has a better grasp of the game, for what to use against a hitter. It's not so. The pitcher has a sense of feel, and if he gets a ball and the ball feels big in his hand, he may not want to throw that ball. He'll throw it back in. Although they're the same size, they feel different at times. A pitcher may get a high raised seam on a ball, which he could get a good grip for a breaking pitch. Catcher doesn't know that, manager doesn't know that. Nobody knows that but only that pitcher.

In many cases I shook my catcher off simply because I wanted to pitch my game, because I knew what I had in my hand. And I wanted to use it to my advantage.

And that's the thing I liked about Sammy White. Some catchers used to like to protect themselves. So, with a man on first base they call a fastball, simply because if that runner breaks, they want a pitch that's easier for them to handle. And the fastball would be easier to handle than, say, a curveball or a sinker.

I had an argument with one catcher over that. I don't want to mention his name, but we didn't get along too well after that, because of him protecting himself with a runner on first base. That fella's hurting me and hurting the ballclub.

Sammy and I'd work together. Sammy and I would talk in between innings.

I'd shake him off, but he had a good knowledge of what I could do, and that was very helpful for me. I'd shake him off on some pitches depending on the feel of the ball, and sometimes in "situation" pitches.

See, if a guy hits a home run off you, a lot of pitchers are afraid to throw that pitch to the hitter again. Not me, I want to start him off with that pitch, in many cases. I wanted him to see it again. Because he's not expecting it, for one thing. I want to let him know that I'm not gonna give in to him. In other words, you were lucky to hit one out of the ballpark.

But in many cases it wasn't luck. The guys were talented and they were capable of doing that. To me, the biggest misnomer in pitching is "making a mistake." Guy hits a home run, next day the pitcher "made a mistake." It's no mistake. Those guys are good hitters, that's why they're up there. If they couldn't do that, they wouldn't be there.

Lou Boudreau wanted to call pitches from the bench. I said, "Hell, there's no way that you can tell what's going on from the bench.

"I got the ball in my hand, I got the sense of feel, I know what I want to throw, I know whether I got a high raised seam on a ball. There's no way you can tell that on a bench, and I'm not gonna go with what you call on the bench.

"It's between Sammy White and me. We're going to decide what we'll use on these hitters."

And that's what we did.

Let me pitch my game. If I fail, it's my fault. If I win, give me the credit for winning.

∎ ∎ ∎

When I went on the mound, I didn't give a thought to that left field wall. I knew the pitches I wanted to make to hitters to keep them from hitting the ball hard off me. And I had very good luck in Fenway. I didn't have many home runs hit off me at Fenway Park. And I think the reason for it is, naturally, because I pitched inside.

We had some guys in our league . . . Vic Power, the first baseman . . . Opening day in Philadelphia and Vic Power was in the lineup. Of course, in our pregame meeting the word was, "Zip one in under his chin and he's yours the rest of the day."

So, hell, when he came up to the plate, that's what I did. When I turned the ball loose from my hand it looked like the ball was going right to his head. Naturally, I wasn't trying to hit him in the head, but it got close.

We had a little second baseman, Billy Consolo, who's now coaching at Detroit, and Billy let out a scream. When I heard the scream I just turned around and looked toward second. Billy came running in and said, "Man, we didn't play like this in high school, in California."

I said, "You're not in high school right now. You're playing for bread and butter." Billy still tells that story.

But after that, Power was yours.

We had another guy who was the same way, used to play second base for the White Sox, Cass Michaels. Cass didn't like to be thrown at. And eventually he got hit in the ear. Caused his death, I understand. Nice guy. A real nice guy. I think it was Marion Fricano who hit him.

But you don't try to hurt a guy. To me, pitching inside is winning baseball. Outside's for losing. I'd still do it. That was my strength, and I couldn't deviate from it, because if I did I was hurting myself. The other guy'd be eating and I wouldn't. So it was a case of having to do what you did best. That's the way I felt.

If a guy got hit, it was his fault for not getting out of the way. I hit one of my better friends, and the guy who was the president of the American League, Bobby Brown. Bobby was standing in close to the plate, and I hit Bobby in the hand and broke his hand. I felt bad about it, but it wasn't intentional. I was just trying to push him back from the plate a little bit.

But by doing that I probably won the pennant for the Yankees that year. They had Bobby alternating with Billy Johnson at third, and after Bobby had his hand broken, Johnson got into the lineup on a permanent basis, and he had one helluva year. Nobody could get him out.

We had a great rivalry with the Yankees. It was just a fantastic rivalry, really. We had a lot of fan interest in between Boston and New York, through Rhode Island and Connecticut. A lot of Yankee fans and a lot of Red Sox fans. Going through towns like New Haven, New London, and all through that area. When we'd go through a train station, it was loaded with people who just wanted to wave to us, just wanted to holler hi to us. We waved back.

The Yankees had a great ballclub, we had a great ballclub. They were probably a step quicker than we were on the field, and that, along with Joe Page, really made the difference.

The Yankees were pretty coy in their operation. They picked up Johnny Sain right at the end of his career. Johnny came in and gave them a couple of pretty good years. Picked up Johnny Mize – he gave them a couple of pretty good years. They were wise. They used these old guys to come in and settle down a ballclub, and it's no doubt it was an asset to some of the other guys on the ballclub.

Bobby Shantz, helluva little pitcher. He was good in a number of ways. He was a good little fielder, too. You couldn't get the ball past him.

Every time we faced the Yankees, Ellis Kinder and I knew who we'd be pitching against. It'd be Kinder and I for the Red Sox and Reynolds and Raschi for the Yankees.

And most of the time, I think, I got Reynolds, who was a helluva pitcher. Raschi was a completely different type pitcher than Allie Reynolds. Reynolds had great stuff. As a matter of fact, he threw a no-hitter against me one time.

Vic Raschi was a high-ball pitcher, a Robin Roberts type. His high fastball would rise and the hitter was constantly hitting underneath it, hitting it up in the air.

But with Reynolds, lot of time you just didn't hit it. He just had great stuff. He was a very good competitor. He was one of the best. He'd really challenge you all the way.

And Eddie Lopat. You could catch him with a Kleenex. You didn't need a glove. He'd get the ball where he wanted. You couldn't do much with it.

We were barnstorming one year. We were playing in Denver, playing a team Paul Richards got together, and Lopat pitched against them the first day and beat them. The next day, Richards told him, "Man, the crap you throw up to the plate, I don't know how you get anybody out."

Lopat said, "Get a bat and I'll get *you* out."

So Richards got up to the plate, and damn if he didn't strike him out. The guy had great location on his pitches.

I had good luck with the Yankees, simply because they were power hitters, guys who'd like to hit the ball out of the ballpark. And I just kept the ball in tight on them. Mantle, Bauer . . . even DiMaggio didn't give me that much trouble. But Yogi did.

Yogi could do it all. You'd throw the ball down the middle of the plate, and he'd swing at it and miss. You'd throw one up over his head and he'd hack it off the wall somewhere. He was a tough guy to pitch to. There was no set way to pitch him. I never could find out how to pitch him.

We had a good ballclub, but it just wasn't good enough to beat the Yankees there at the end. They were just a step ahead of us. And the trouble is, we developed the old Fenway stroke, and when we got on the road we were in trouble, because we just didn't reach some of the fences in the other ballparks.

The game was different then. Today, a guy gets around a hundred pitches, they jerk him out of a ballgame. But when we used to pitch, I know a lot of ballgames where we'd run 140 or 150 pitches. It didn't make any difference.

The year I won twenty-five, I had an elbow problem all through the season. The muscle was torn from the bone and the nerve was caught in between the bones. It gave me problems. I started thirty-three games and completed twenty-seven, which they don't do today. I wouldn't say the elbow was bad, but it bothered me. Eventually it got real bad and I had to have an operation.

In one series in 1949, when I won twenty-five games, I pitched on two days' rest. When they said pitch, you pitched. As long as you felt all right. And truthfully, I enjoyed it. I didn't feel that I needed all that rest. I didn't like it when you got into the real hot weather and they'd stretch it out and add another starter into your rotation. I like it when you have a four-man rotation. Every fourth day you pitch. You knew just what day you'd be pitching, so you could set yourself up for that day.

I liked that about Joe Cronin. If you pitched today, he'd tell you, "Okay, you pitch three days from now."

Now Joe McCarthy didn't do that. McCarthy used to put the ball under your cap in your locker. He said he didn't want you to go home at night and have that on your mind and maybe have a bad night sleeping, or whatever. But that never did bother me. You had a pretty good idea when you were gonna pitch. After a while it got to be routine, so you didn't let those things worry you.

McCarthy's wife told me that he used to sit down at night and lock himself in a room and try to figure out a combination against the opposition. He didn't change the pitching too much because we had certain guys that were starting. If he had to come in with a fifth man or a relief pitcher or something, he tried to get the guy that had better luck against the opposition they were playing at the time. Certain hitters, too, he would jockey around a little bit depending on who was pitching. I liked McCarthy. I thought he was a very good manager.

In 1948, in our playoff game against Cleveland, he never did tell us who was pitching the ballgame. And I, along with the whole ballclub, assumed that I'd be pitching.

The night before, my parents, who were up in Boston, and my wife ran me to bed at nine o'clock: "You'd better get to bed, you've got the biggest one of the season coming up tomorrow."

So I went to bed just to keep from hearing them telling me that.

I get to the ballpark the next day and I'm taking my good old time in the clubhouse, like pitchers always do before the game they're scheduled to pitch, because you don't have to get out till later to get your batting practice. McCarthy comes up behind me and puts his hand on my shoulder and says, "Son, I've changed my mind. The elements are against a left-hander. I'm gonna go with a right-hander."

So with that, he tells John Fitzpatrick, our clubhouse boy, to go out and get Denny Galehouse. Well, he brought Denny Galehouse into the clubhouse and told him he was pitching. Denny, he just turned colors. He was shocked.

So I got dressed. I ran out on the field for the completion of batting practice, and all the guys say, "What are you doing out here?"

I said, "I'm not pitching."

They said, "You've got to be kidding!"

I said, "I'm *not* kidding. Denny Galehouse is the pitcher today."

I kind of believe the switch had an effect on our ballclub. Because if not me, we had Earl Johnson, we had Jack Kramer. One of the three of us should have been the pitcher. I don't think they would have been as shocked if Johnson or Kramer had been mentioned. But Galehouse—in all fairness to Denny, he was a helluva pitcher—was at the end of his career. School was out for Denny at that time. McCarthy just took a gamble and it didn't work.

Two guys wrecked us in that ballgame—Ken Keltner and Boudreau. They kept bouncing that ball off that left field wall.

Some of the writers up in Boston wrote so many untrue stories about that game, saying that nobody wanted to pitch, which was ridiculous. They said that three or four of us refused to pitch, which was *real* ridiculous. Because if you pitch that game and you win it, that's more money in your pocket. Besides, a win meant more money in next year's contract. So it was a ridiculous statement to make.

■　■　■

Boston was a great baseball city. Very good. And of course, after the Braves left it got even better. You had the mixed element there between the Red Sox and Braves. A lot of the Braves fans became Red Sox fans.

As long as things were going good, they were beautiful. But they could get a little tough, and I think they were led that way by the press.

I don't know if you've ever heard of sportswriter Dave Eagan, the old colonel up in Boston. He wrote for the *Record American*. Well, this guy, he was a critic. Everybody was bad: Marciano was a lousy heavyweight – he only won fifty without getting beat; Casey Stengel was a bad manager – he won more pennants than anybody else; Williams was a lousy hitter.

I grabbed him one time about a story he wrote about me. I asked him, "Why'd you write that story?"

He said, "Well, don't believe what I write. I'm selling newspapers."

I said, "That's fine, I appreciate that, but don't sell them at my expense."

I asked Ed Costello – I don't know if you know Ed Costello or not; Ed was the sports editor for the *Boston Herald* – if he could loan me his column for a day, and he said, "Sure, take it for Sunday."

So I wrote a story about Dave Eagan, but I didn't mention his name. But anybody who read it knew who I was driving at. So Eagan came out to the ballpark and he told Ed Costello, "Well, your buddy's got me over the barrel, but wait till he has a bad day."

And when I had a bad day, he got even. But I had a chance to get a few things off my chest. I didn't appreciate some of the critical things he wrote about a bunch of us on the ballclub. It was a lot of untruths. Like he said, he was just selling newspapers.

But, people would read that stuff and they'd believe it. They didn't know otherwise. They thought it was all true fact that he was coming up with. This guy was a dreamer.

But it was a good city, a good baseball city. We always felt that we were playing in one of the better cities in baseball.

．　■　■

We had an umpire in our league, Bill McGowan, who was a real good umpire. He was always rated number one in the American League. But he was a little on the hard-nosed side.

We had a guy who was a great bench jockey, Ray Scarborough. And Scarborough was on him one night, really giving him a rough time. So McGowan comes over to the bench and he had a few words with Scarborough, and he threw his ball-strike indicator at Scarborough and it went underneath our dugout bench.

Just as soon as it went under the bench, Scarborough was down on all fours looking for that ball-strike indicator. And he got it!

McGowan asked for his ball-strike indicator and Scarborough said, "The hell with you, you're going to have to get it from the league president."

So he got it from the league president – with a two-week suspension. McGowan told Scarborough after that, "You better not pitch when I'm behind the plate."

Scarborough says, "Don't worry, I won't."

But Ray Scarborough was one of the best bench jockeys I've ever seen. He'd run guys berserk. Luke Easter, in particular.

Boudreau was our manager at the time, and Easter would ask Boudreau to run Scarborough out to the bullpen, because our dugout was too close to him at Fenway, right out there by first base.

Scarborough was great. They used to call him Pickle Nose, because he was a pickle salesman during the winter in Mt. Ida in North Carolina.

They had a guy in Philadelphia that was a ribbon salesman over at Gimbels. This guy used to sit in left field in old Shibe Park and he'd get on the ballplayers.

He used to get after Williams. Remember when Williams said that he wanted to be a fireman? He had something on every ballplayer. He used to give Vern Stephens a rough time, calling him the Mexican Jumping Bean – you remember when he jumped leagues and went down to Mexico. For some reason, he never did pick on me. But he had his pets that he'd get after all the time. Buddy Rosar wanted to be a cop; he'd give Buddy Rosar a rough time.

We used to get a kick out of him. The guy was hilarious. He must have read all the baseball magazines to try and get some scoop on every ballplayer so he could throw it up at them out at the ballpark.

He'd give Scarborough a real rough time with the pickle thing. When this guy opened his mouth from the left field bleachers – he's sitting in the upper deck, left field – it sounded like he was right there in the middle of the infield. The guy had a real voice!

Finally one day, Scarborough was walking around through Gimbels and he saw this guy selling ribbon. Scarborough used to give *him* a rough time after that.

. . .

I went over to Japan barnstorming with Lefty O'Doul in 1951. Lefty O'Doul was God over in Japan. He was the one that got baseball introduced to the Japanese. He went over there and started talking baseball and holding clinics and then started bringing teams. He used to bring some of the Pacific Coast League players with him, and then he went to the major league guys. He could've run for emperor over there and he would've won.

We played the Japanese thirty-five games. We won thirty-four and tied one. That was a great experience, something I'll never forget. They say we got the greatest reception in Japanese history at that time.

I recall the streets, the Ginza in Tokyo, which is similar to Broadway in New York, and all you could see was heads, people were jammed together. The crowds were so thick that the cars we were riding in couldn't get through. Burnt up clutches on the cars and everything. Finally they had to discontinue the parade because we couldn't move, there were so many people.

And all the people wanted to do was to touch us. We were American champions, as they called us. They were climbing all over the cars, just wanting to touch us.

We had the two DiMaggios, Dom and Joe. We had Ferris Fain. We had Bobby Shantz, Dino Restelli, Al Lyons, Eddie Lopat, Ken Lehman . . . We had a collection of pretty good talent.

We enjoyed it tremendously because of the love of the game shown by the Japanese. They were just terrific. We'd walk down the street in any of the cities in Japan, and the merchants would come out and grab us, bring us in the stores, and give us a gift. Called us American champions. I'll never forget it.

If it started raining, you didn't stop play. You just kept playing in the rain. They wouldn't leave. They were jam-packed into the stadium, and that was it. It was really a pleasure playing over there. And their talent was pretty good. It was surprising to us.

Of course, we helped them change their game somewhat. We were the first bunch to go over after Babe Ruth, which was some twenty years before. But they were still playing by their methods, which we helped them change.

They wouldn't argue with an umpire, because the umpire was appointed by the emperor. They wouldn't take a man out on the double play because they thought that was dirty baseball. But we said, "No, that isn't dirty baseball, that's part of the game." We got them to do that.

They'd make an error and they'd take themselves out of the ballgame. We said, "No, you don't do that. You're the best on the ballclub at that position. That's why you're out there, so if you make a mistake, that's excusable, as long as you're trying."

We'd hold clinics with them on the train rides going from city to city. We were helping them, and of course we enjoyed it. And they appreciated it, too, because it did improve their game quite a bit.

While we were over there, we got the opportunity to go into Korea.

General Westmoreland took six of us into Korea, and we visited troops up in the front lines. In Korea, we had Dom DiMaggio, Ferris Fain, Jackie Price, George Strickland . . . Offhand, I don't recall the other.

We had some pretty hair-raising experiences. Enjoyed that, too.

A lot of those kids up in the front lines, they didn't get to see anybody at all. Being athletically inclined, we were able to get up closer to the front lines than many of the other entertainers. We were able to climb the hills to get to them.

The area we were in was under attack one night. Scared the daylights out of us.

We had a South Korean guard guarding our tent. We were sleeping. First shot was fired, he took off. He was gone. We were on our own. So we just rolled our bunks over, right on top of us, and laid in the sand and waited until things quieted down. It was a great experience playing over there.

Now I go on trips and people say, "That's all you did when you were playing ball – travel." But it was altogether different then. It was work then. Now it's pleasure. To me, it's quite different. Now, for pleasure, you get out to see things.

When I was playing baseball or broadcasting, we used to concentrate on what we had to do at the ballpark. We couldn't get around town that much. As a matter of fact, as a ballplayer I never did get into the Empire State Building, as many times as I've been in New York. But I did it for pleasure. Took the cruise around the Statue of Liberty. Never did that when I was playing ball.

When I say we didn't have time, we had time but we had things to do. We were playing day games, too. By the time the game's over with and you get back in town to a restaurant, have something to eat, it's too late to do a lot of that. It's nightclubs and that's it.

Of course, nightclubs were taboo for us. You didn't frequent those, because rumors would always start. And you certainly didn't want that kind of stuff. It was a matter of bread and butter, and we concentrated on that, feeding our families.

I don't pass up an opportunity to go someplace where baseball players are involved. To me, what I enjoy most is seeing all the guys again. We sit around and rub shoulders and reminisce. Have a few laughs. I could do that every week.

The no-hitter is something you just never forget. Something that's always laying in your mind. Of course, I hear from a lot of people now that are rounding up various things on no-hit pitchers. Baseballs, pictures, drawings . . . the sort of stuff you get that people want you to sign.

And it makes you feel good to know that you're remembered. Somebody wants your signature on something.

I had ten more years in the majors than I thought I would have. When I first got there, I didn't know. I was hoping, but it seemed like it wasn't an easy thing to do.

Alex Grammas

February 24–25, 1994, Birmingham, Alabama

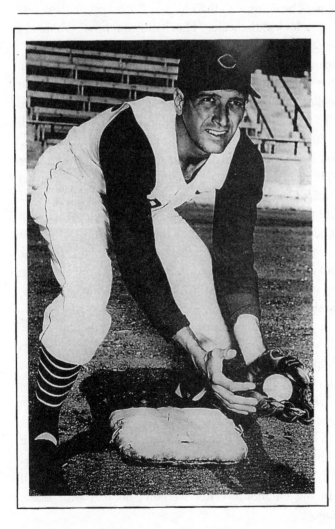

Alex Grammas played shortstop in the National League from 1954 to 1963 with the St. Louis Cardinals, Reds, and Cubs. A .247 lifetime hitter, Grammas managed the Milwaukee Brewers in 1976 and 1977 and spent twenty-five years coaching third base with the Pirates and the Reds.

I can remember that first day I went to spring training in '54 with the Cardinals. Eddie Stanky was our manager. Mr. Busch came down, either the first or second day, and Mr. Anheuser came in with him. And Stanky always had an assigned weight for each guy. I didn't have one assigned to me because this was my first year.

So Stanky waved at guys to get on the scale, and if they were two pounds over that'd be $100, $50 a pound. "That'll cost you fifty! That'll cost you a hundred and a half!" And I never will forget Mr. Anheuser – he was an old fellow, walking a little slow at the time – and Stanky saying, "Get up on the scale, Mr. Anheuser!"

I thought, what's he doing with this old guy? But he got up there and Stanky didn't even look at the scale: "That'll cost you fifty!" Oh man, I thought I'd die laughing.

By God, I learned a lot from Stanky. A lot of guys didn't like him, but he didn't bother me. As long as you went out and tried to do the best you could and didn't make the same mistake twice, you had nothing to worry about. There's nothing wrong with that in my book. They tell you once, that ought to be enough. He was a helluva man. I loved him.

I had a good rookie year. If Stanky had stayed there, I might have played more. He played me; he wasn't afraid to play me. St. Louis let him go in the middle of August of '55, something like that.

Stanky could see things that were going on on the field, whether it would be practice or whether it would be during the game. He'd just notice things. How the hell did he see *that*? But he did. He'd see little things that went on and he'd keep you involved: "What's on? Anything on? What's he giving? Is he giving a hit-and-run? What's on? Anything on? Take sign on?"

That's how he used to raise money for a big party at the end of the year, every year at the Chase Hotel: that costs you two dollars, this costs you a buck. Kept you in the ballgame. He'd walk up and down the bench and ask everybody. Gotta get someone. Gotta get that money. You *know* he's going to get somebody. He's got fifteen guys sitting there and at least eight of them don't know.

But I used to like to watch the coach anyway. I just got in the habit of looking at him when I was on the bench. See if he's hitting and running. See if he's stealing. Whatever. Now these guys spend half the time up in the clubhouse. They wouldn't do that with Eddie Stanky. No *chance*!

.   .   .

My father was Greek, born in the old country. My mother was Greek, too, but she was born here. I'd say he came to Birmingham around 1910 or so, right before World War I. Then, when Greece was at war with Bulgaria, he went back and joined the army. After the war was over he came back here, and he never went back to Greece until 1965. He and my mother were there for six months.

My wife and I went back in 1992 for three weeks. We went to her dad's hometown, saw the house where he was born. We went to my dad's village, outside of Sparta, and spent four nights in the house where he was born. We saw all the places we'd read about in our study of Greek history.

See, when we were kids we had to go to Greek school after we went to regular school. Regular school classes would start at 8:15, and as soon as school would get out at 3:00 we'd catch the streetcar across town to Greek school, right at the church. We'd be there from 3:30 to 6:00 every day. They taught everything: language, history, cultural activities. My wife and I have known each other all our lives.

I went in the service in 1944. I was going to Auburn at the time. I was in the Philippines most of the time. My brother was over here until about three or four months before the war ended, then they sent *him* to the Philippines. In fact, I saw him over there. Sure did. He was in the engineers. They'd have had it rough if we'd had to invade Japan.

Nine months later I came back home. We went to Japan for the occupation, probably in September, and I came home about July the following year. We were the first occupation troops there. I was in Fukuoka, on the southernmost island, the island of Kyushu. I've been to Japan three times since, and it's hard for me to believe, after what I saw there the first time, that they've done what they've done. I still can't believe it.

When I got back, my brother and I both went to Mississippi State to play baseball. We both had the GI Bill, but they gave us a scholarship in addition. My brother played shortstop or outfield and I played third base.

We both signed professionally out of Mississippi State in the White Sox organization. He went to Hot Springs in Class C ball. I went to Muskegon, Michigan, in Class A. We both had good years. The next year he went to Colorado Springs in A ball, and I went to Memphis in double-A. After that he gave it up. They wanted to send him back out to Colorado Springs the next year and he didn't want to do it. He'd just hit .335 out there.

Oh, he could hit. He could run better than me and he could throw. If he'd have stayed with it, he'd have made it. But he felt like he just didn't want to go back there another year. And this was after the war.

My dad wasn't all that fond of the idea of my playing ball. At the beginning, when I said I was gonna try professional baseball, I tried to assure him that I wouldn't just hang around, that if I didn't think I was making progress I'd quit. You can get a feel for how things are going, how people think about you in a game. But after a while, he was my biggest supporter.

I signed in 1949. I was twenty-three, and I didn't get to the major leagues until I was twenty-eight. So I was lucky to stay in the major leagues thirty-seven years, ten as a player. I managed in the minor leagues one year after I finished and then I came up. Harry Walker brought me on as one of his coaches at Pittsburgh. Stayed there five years. Then I went to Cincinnati for six years. Then I managed in Milwaukee two years and I went back to Cincinnati for one. Then I went to Atlanta for one and then to Detroit.

I played third base in college and third base my first year in the minors. I thought I could play third base as well as anybody, and still do. But they made a shortstop out of me.

I did a pretty good job at shortstop. I'm not saying I did a bad job. But I think I could have played third as well as anybody. I had good hands. Quick hands. Could come in on balls. Learning to play shortstop was a lot different.

They moved me my second year, when I went to Memphis. I played shortstop ever since, and I got to where I liked it. Al Todd, a former catcher, was my manager at Memphis my first year. He played with the Pittsburgh Pirates and the Phillies. Luke Appling came in the next year, and Luke traded me to Tulsa, where I played for Al Vincent.

You should know Al Vincent. He coached with Paul Richards for a few years. Al Vincent, really, was the guy that invented the big glove for knuckleballs. Paul Richards got credit, but Al Vincent is the guy that came up with the idea. He was with Richards in Baltimore.

Al helped me as much as any minor league manager I ever had. He was a good, sound baseball man. He helped my hitting and every phase of the game. He was a good student of the game.

He flattened my bat out a little bit. I was too much upright and I wasn't getting to the ball as well as I should. He had a theory about pulling the ball. I wasn't a pull hitter, but I tried it and it worked. Just as the pitcher is about to release the ball, he says, step in. Just a little bit. Step in, not back, but step in. What it does is open up your hips. If you step in it's like having an open stance in golf. Your hips are out of the way quicker and you can get to the ball inside faster.

My first three years in minor league ball, we never went out early for extra hitting or anything. But Al would take you out and work with you. And you feel better when you think somebody has confidence in you, that you're going to be somebody. It's a pretty good shot in the arm.

The first day I got to Tulsa, I went in Al Vincent's office and reported. I sat down and we talked for about five minutes. He said, "We got a pretty good ballclub here. But we needed you to make us better."

I thought, well, maybe this guy knows a little about me anyway, instead of just letting you put your uniform on and hiding you. He started working with me. He worked with Johnny Temple, too. I played with Johnny at Tulsa for two years. Johnny was a good hitter before he came to Tulsa, but working with Al paid off for him, too.

If somebody can reinforce your own feelings, then your chances are a lot better to do the job. Plus the fact that if he saw you doing something – maybe fielding a ground ball or not touching the bag right – he'd tell you, "This is the way you've got to do it." And he was right.

I remember making an unassisted double play, and he said, "Let me show you how to make that." Nobody ever showed me, but it made sense after he told me. And it was easy.

When you make an unassisted double play from shortstop – you're catching the ball and you're going to throw the ball to first – this first foot is going to hit the bag. But you stay behind the bag and throw as you hit the bag: Boom! As opposed to trying to come across it, because now you've got the bag for protection, for one thing, plus you're getting rid of the ball quicker.

See, these are little things that are easy to do, but they're things that have to be told to you sometimes. Al was the kind of guy that would notice things. Very similar to Stanky.

And Al was a tough manager. Tough manager never bothered me. In fact, I liked it better. I never wore my feelings on my sleeve. A guy gets in your face when you've done something wrong, what can you do? You just don't do it again, that's all I know. Only way I know to remedy it is don't do it again. (I don't think I was a tough manager. Maybe I should have been a little tougher.)

Then I went over to Kansas City, triple-A. We had a helluva ballclub: Elston Howard catching, Moose Skowron at first base, Jim Bridweser at second, Horace Smith – a pretty good ballplayer – at third. I played short. In the outfield we started with Bill Virdon, Vic Power, and Cliff Mapes for a while, then Bob Cerv. I think the next year about eight or nine guys off that team went to the major leagues and stayed. That's pretty unusual.

ALEX
GRAMMAS

———

152

We hit a bad streak one time. We were playing in Indianapolis and the manager said, "I don't want to catch anyone in the hotel before four in the morning. Go out and get drunk, whatever."

I think we won something like thirty-four out of the next thirty-eight games. We went to the Little World Series. We beat Toledo. Toledo had a good ballclub. Gene Conley was one of their pitchers. They had a fella named Glen Thompson, a right-handed pitcher who was probably as tall as Conley. A good pitcher. But we beat them in the playoffs and then played Montreal in the Little World Series. Tommy Lasorda pitched on that team, and they had Don Hoak and Rocky Nelson. They beat us.

Bob Cerv and Moose Skowron—I don't know whatever got into them, whatever possessed them—but one day they clamped their hands behind their necks and butted heads to see who'd give up first. They hit about three times and Moose hung him up. It was *awful*! Imagine hitting your forehead like that? Boomp, boomp, boomp. Moose? The tears were coming out of his eyes it hurt so much.

■　■　■

I'd say, as a general rule, baseball people are the most fun to be around. I don't know how I could have met nicer people. Very few of them are bad eggs. Very few. Some of them are characters, but they're nice guys.

We had one guy in St. Louis . . . We'd take three-week road trips, and this fella wouldn't even take a suitcase. His roommate caught him using his toothbrush. In those days they had steel beer cans—they were hard to bend—and this guy would put the initial dent on it against his head—boom!—then he'd take one hand and just crush it. They finally got rid of him. And the thing is he could have been a half-decent player.

Characters? I once saw Marv Throneberry miss first *and* second on the way to a triple. That's the truth. I was *there* with the Chicago Cubs at the Polo Grounds when he did it. Missed first *and* second on the way to a triple! The ball was way down there in the bullpen, which was nine miles away. That was the funniest thing I *ever* saw. If I'm not mistaken, we had scored four runs in the top of the first, and this triple would have tied the game. Can you believe that? First and second, that's almost impossible.

That was in the first game of a doubleheader. In the second game, I saw Lou Brock hit one in the center field seats, 460 feet.

And I'll tell you the type of guy Stan Musial was. If I was sitting by myself in the lobby of a hotel, he'd come over and say, "What are you doing?"

I'd say, "Nothing."

He'd say, "Come with me." And he'd take me to dinner. That type of guy.

Remember Happy Felton in Brooklyn? The star of the game would be on the Happy Felton Show. He'd give him $50. In those days $50 was something. Stan and I were walking back to the clubhouse one day after the game – he always had big days in Brooklyn; it just seemed like Ebbets Field was his ballpark – and Felton called him, and Stan said, "All right, I'll come tonight, but from now on take care of the other fellas."

Take care of the other fellas. I played with other clubs; I never heard anyone say that but him.

He was in the outfield when I came up, but he played first the next year. He couldn't throw too well – he'd hurt his arm – and he'd make that throw to second base and that ball would dip. That's a tough ball to handle when you have to get out of the way of a base runner, a ball sinking from a left-hander into the dirt. I used to kid him: "You got a sixty-foot arm!"

But he was a gentleman. Not only that, he was a baseball player! He could play it. And he could run. Stan was fast.

Pee Wee Reese, shoot, there's a guy who stole twenty-five, thirty bases, but he'd try to steal when you needed them. He could have stolen fifty or sixty bases – easy! – if he did it the way they do today, running all the time. And he hit that home run sometimes when you needed it. He was just a solid baseball player.

He was also good for the club. You could tell they relied on Pee Wee. You could *tell* it. He had that knack. He just drew the players to him. His own players. I don't know, but I guarantee you when Jackie Robinson went there Pee Wee had a lot to do with keeping things on an even keel on that club. You could see it from the other side of the field, the way they congregated around him.

I told him one time, "Pee Wee, you're my idol." I embarrassed him, I think. But he had something about him that was just magic. I don't know why he never wanted to manage. I guess he never did want to get into that rat race.

Ted Kluszewski. He was a gentle man. He had such good hands he could catch bare-handed.

Oh, and was he was a good hitter! I bet he didn't strike out thirty,

thirty-five times a year. He'd get the bat on the ball some way or another. He'd fist it in or do something. He used to tell me, "These guys today think it's a crime to get fisted. You get fisted, but at least you get base hits on them."

Ted helped our hitters in Cincinnati a lot when he was playing and when he was coaching over there. I coached with him over there for quite a few years. George Foster swore by Ted, yes sir!

I can remember Durocher. My first year with the Cardinals, Leo stayed on me from the dugout. Oh man, he really did. But I had a day against him in St. Louis one Sunday afternoon in a doubleheader. I think I had seven hits. He never said another word. He never got on me again. I give credit for that.

Solly Hemus was the St. Louis shortstop when I came up. Another good guy. I saw him do something I have *never* seen before or since. We were playing a game one night and we were behind. We needed base runners and he was leading off. And you *know* he's not going to swing the bat till he gets two strikes on him. That's a *cinch*. Because that's his *job*.

Anyway, the pitcher threw a strike to him, and he kind of straightened up and fouled that ball off. I looked – I wasn't quite sure what was happening. The count's one ball and two strikes and he takes the next pitch: ball two. Then he fouls off another.

"He's doing it on purpose!" I said. "I can't believe that!"

He must have fouled five or six balls like that. Just take them and turn them, pull them.

If I was trying to foul a ball intentionally, I'd try to foul it off the *opposite* way. But he'd just take it and turn his wrists over on the ball and just foul them. He ended up walking.

You just don't see things like that. I've *heard* of them happening. Luke Appling, they said, could hit foul balls all day long. But I never had seen it. I tell you one thing, I take my hat off to the guy. It's one thing to think about doing it and it's another thing to do it. Takes a *lot* of nerve. You've got to be awfully sure of yourself. But that's the reason Stanky loved him. This guy would do anything, get hit with a ball, anything, to help win a ballgame.

. . .

I could catch a ball. I never had any trouble catching it. Hitting it? That might have been a little bit of a different story.

When you make a play in the hole, you've got to get rid of it fast. Well, Vic Power and I were together on the Kansas City Blues, and I made a play in the hole one day. But he had a way of timing the throw to the bag so he'd be on the run as he caught it. Hell, I'm in the hole – I can't find the target: it's moving! – and I've got to throw it *over* the bag, and that's hard to do when you don't have much time.

When we got in off the field, I said, "Hey, Vic, I've got enough trouble over there in the hole without trying to hit a moving target." He said, "Okay, I'll be there for you." And he was.

The town I used to love to play in was Brooklyn. I just liked the atmosphere, and I always seemed to get base hits there. But I *loved* the Polo Grounds. The Polo Grounds had the best infield I ever played on. Eddie Stanky came up to me one year, the latter part of the season, and said, "I don't think you'd ever miss a ball in this ballpark."

I said, "You know something, I don't think I would either."

Fenway Park, the dirt was similar. You could step on it and all, but that wouldn't make big holes. It just seemed like it was never pitted up. That's the way you get a lot of bad hops. After the first inning, the ground gets chewed up and you can't smooth it out. But at the Polo Grounds you could do a little housework with your foot and it looked like it was just when the game started. It was an outstanding infield. I was confident with that infield.

Connie Mack Stadium, that was a tough one. That infield had a lot of loose dust on top. The ball hits the ground and that loose dust gives it a tendency to stay down. You don't know what kind of hop you're going to get. It was a *tough* infield to play. You really had to make sure you stayed down on a ball there, because if you didn't it would be between your legs.

Cincinnati had a good infield. The Polo Grounds was the best, but Crosley Field was next. And strangely enough, it was brothers that were the groundskeepers for each park. Brothers! They had the two best infields. So it's not by accident.

Nowadays they take more pains manicuring infields, and you can see it by the fielding records they set. You played shortstop in my day and you made twenty-five errors in a year and that wasn't bad. You make twenty-five errors now, you're horrible. You see Ripken and those guys, they make three errors in a year. That's unheard of at shortstop. Now, *he* can catch the ball, Ripken. Oh I *like* him! You bet I like him. Anybody who wants to play every day. Good, steady baseball player – I know that. And I know that when you hit the ball to him you're out, I know that.

We had Gene Alley at Pittsburgh when I was coaching there. He hated the St. Louis ballpark. As good a player as he was, he just could

not make himself field ground balls in St. Louis. He just couldn't.
I'd bet you even money that if it wasn't a high hop he'd miss it or
have trouble catching it. That infield at old Busch Stadium had him
psyched out.

I'll truthfully tell you, I never worried about infields. I *liked* some
better than others, but I never got a negative thought when I was on defense. I tried to figure out what the ball was doing when I was taking
ground balls during batting practice and infield practice. Like I was
telling you about Philadelphia, a lot of times during the summer they
wouldn't water the infield good enough, soak it good enough to hold
the dirt. By the end of the game in Philadelphia, in the summer, your
socks would be black.

I guess the only place I really hated was Bradenton, Florida, in the
spring. You couldn't get a decent hop. So I just shortened up, instead of
being back in my regular position, so I could get the ball quicker. It
wouldn't get a chance to bounce as much. I figured that way I'd head it
off at the pass.

But with Gene Alley, it was in his head. He always anticipated it was
gonna be a bad hop – which is not a bad way to feel – but at least you've
got to make it, be ready to come up with your hands in case it doesn't
take a bad hop. He got hit a couple of times in the arms on bad hops,
and I think it just psyched him out.

There's a lot of dead time in baseball, and that's a lot of time to worry
when things aren't going well. And that's what makes baseball so tough.

If somebody hits you a ball, every eye in the ballpark is watching
you. If you boot it, you've got a lot of time to think about it. It cost you
a run or it cost you two runs. Now your ballclub's behind and you're
thinking about it. And thinking about the things that go wrong can be
disastrous. You have to be able to live through those things and be able
to overcome them.

I didn't worry, no. I was concerned about what I did, sure, but I
didn't worry about it.

Bill Mazeroski never worried what infield he played on. No, no, no!
He didn't care where he played, he knew he was gonna catch it. He had
as good a pair of hands as any human that ever lived. He was amazing.
Double play? As good as anyone *ever* will make it. Some may make it as
good someday, but never any better. Can't!

I'd play catch with him. You've seen guys put their glove up and let
the ball hit the heel of their glove so they catch it in their bare hand?
You know what he did? I'd throw the ball hard, right there at his face,

and it would hit his glove, bounce into this hand as his hands were crossing. And you couldn't see it happen! If I did that, the ball would hit me right between the eyes. I'd say, "Do that again!" and he'd just laugh. I mean throw it hard! And the ball would be in his throwing hand. I mean, how did he do that? No way I try that, buddy. I just let it stick, then take it out. That's the only way I could do it.

• • •

I was more mature coming out of the war. When I was playing, I think I *did* help some players. I think I did, but I never got in anybody's way. And it wasn't just one way. I've had guys help me, too. But I think we talked more baseball. I don't know why I feel that way, but it seemed we were always talking about the game.

One time we were playing at Charleston, West Virginia. They got a pretty good size ballpark, deep left field, and Vic Power is trying to pull the ball. I took him over to the side and said, "Let me ask you something. We go to Minneapolis and you hit line drives off that wall in right field like Ping-Pong balls. Over here you look like you're trying to pull the ball out of the ballpark. Why do you do that? Why don't you try to hit the ball to right field?"

He said, "I'll do that for you, Grammas." The next time he comes to the plate, he hits a pea over that right-fielder's head.

He was an amazing man. The guy could hit! He'd get down in that crouch and you'd wonder how in the world he could hit. Sometimes you *swore* he threw the bat at the ball to hit it.

One year in Kansas City, Moose Skowron got off to a rough start. The year before he had a great year. But he just wasn't hitting the ball. I tried to talk to him: "Looks like you ought to go to a lighter bat." But he just wouldn't do it.

"Just try."

"Last year," he said, "I hit thirty home runs and knocked in one hundred or so runs."

One day we were taking batting practice in Kansas City – that was a pretty good size ballpark – and he broke his bat, and I gave him mine. Well he used about a 35-37; mine was a 34-31. He started rifling balls out of that ballpark, one after the other. He had a lighter bat. And he stuck with it. He brought his average from .220-something to .300-something before you could turn around. It's little things like that.

Listen, I was just fortunate to be around as long as I was. I wish I could've played more, but the main concern is to stay there first. You had to get five years to get on the pension. But you know what five years pension was when I played? Fifty dollars a month. Ten years would get you $100.

Then Harry Walker got me started coaching in Pittsburgh. You know, a man gives you a chance to do something, it's up to you to prove that you deserve it. Try to work like hell. Just because somebody says I want you to coach for me doesn't mean you'll be there forever. You know *he's* not gonna be there forever.

Then someone else has to see you and appreciate what they see you do, in order for you to stay in the game. You have to do that for years. You have to almost prove yourself every year. That's what pushes you, that's what keeps you going – the fact that you know that nothing's a given. I worked hard and it worked out.

I enjoyed coaching. I really did. Especially coaching third base. You know, I don't think anybody ever coached third base in the big leagues longer than me: twenty-five years.

I tell you one thing, I could search high, wide, and every other way and never find anything I'd enjoy more than what I did. Shoot, I always knew how lucky I was. No way I'd ever say anything about this game . . . nothing but good. Nothing. No chance! If guys don't realize how lucky they are to be playing this game at the major league level, then something's wrong with them.

Andy Carey

January 21, 1994, Newport Beach, California

Andy Carey played third base from 1952 to 1962. In addition to spending eight and a half seasons with the Yankees, he played for the Kansas City Athletics, the White Sox, and the Los Angeles Dodgers. A .260 lifetime hitter, Carey played on five Yankees pennant-winning teams, including the 1953, 1956, and 1958 World Championship clubs.

I've always been a very heavy eater. No one ever beat me. My very first spring training in Phoenix, Arizona, with the Yankees in 1951 – that was Joe DiMaggio's last year, so I had the chance to meet him and the guys who had been heroes, as far as I was concerned – I asked them, "How much can you eat here?"

The Yankees in those days signed for all their checks, so they told me, "It doesn't make any difference. You can eat whatever you want."

I had double-double of everything, and I'd run up bills of $45 to $50. Well, after about a week of this, the secretary of the club, Bill Corey, put the Yankees on meal money.

Here's this young brash rookie eating himself out of the league before he even gets into the damn thing. They didn't think too kindly of me. They were a little teed off. Here I'd changed the Yankees' thing, and I hadn't even been through spring training yet. I'd just signed. They always kid me about my appetite. They never talk about what I did on the baseball field, they always talk about my appetite.

   ■ ■ ■

I went to Alameda High School, graduated in '49, and went to Saint Mary's College on a full scholarship. Johnny Virges was the coach at the time. Then Saint Mary's dropped baseball and I elected to sign a pro contract. I don't think there was a team that *wasn't* interested in me. Joe Devine, Bill Brenzell with the Cardinals, Bernie Deviveras with Detroit. My dad, who was a lawyer, handled all the negotiations.

Devine signed me in 1951 – he was the Yankees' head scout – on a bonus. I think I was probably the second-biggest bonus player at the time. Jackie Jensen received $75,000 and I received $60,000.

I played triple-A my first year with the Kansas City Blues in the American Association. It was a big shock for me. I'd never been out of California. I'll never forget being in the infield this one time in Kansas City when lightning struck about a block away – they'd have these electrical storms that lit up the sky – and I was on the ground. I was a little embarrassed, but I looked up and there were a few other guys down on the ground too. But that scared the heck out of me.

George Selkirk was my first manager. Old Twinkle Toes. Took Babe Ruth's spot. And I'll never forget it. I was hitting about .240, something like that, triple-A, first year away from home, and I dropped a ball with the bases loaded. We lost the game. We went back home to Kansas City and Selkirk called me into his office – the guys were dressing then – and he chewed my ass out, unmercifully. I was crying. . . . He went after me for about an hour. "You big strong sonofabitch," he said. "You can't . . ."

I probably hadn't hit any home runs. "You're doing this, you're doing that . . ." He just went after my case – I probably deserved it – but I got so damn mad I think I went 18 for 22, and I got my average up. I hit well over .400 for about a month, I got so mad.

That's where Stengel picked up his thing about getting me mad. And I ended up the end of the season hitting .288. And then, when I went to spring training the next year, Selkirk said to me, "Go ahead, assert yourself. Let them know who you are."

So I went over there to spring training, St. Petersburg, and I was on third base and Rizzuto was at shortstop and Gil McDougald was on second base, so I drew a line between shortstop and third base and Rizzuto said, "What the hell . . . What are you doing there?" I said, "I want you to know: this is my side over here. You stay off my side. This is *my* territory!" This brash young kid, twenty years old telling Rizzuto like that. He never let me forget that one.

Rizzuto! He would go on road trips and he would come back with more gifts, free gifts, than any man I've ever seen in my life. Wherever he went, he received freebies. Rizzuto would come back with more gifts for Cora; she must have loved him when he went on a road trip. And, obviously, he had the worst arm in baseball. It was like, he'd get the ball and, bang, as soon as he had it, it was released. And it would be like a race against time for that slow arch – the arch of St. Louis, the McDonald's arches – to get that darn ball to first base. And it would always be bang-bang at first base. In fact, sometimes in his later years, when he would get a ball deep at shortstop, he would throw it to me at third base so I could throw the guy out, because there was no way he was going to get the guy out. But you could never get him caught in a rundown. He would be full speed at first step. He was absolutely amazing that way. He'd get caught down between second and first, between third base and home, and he would somehow get out of it. I mean they couldn't maneuver fast enough to do it. He was phenomenal that way. Good bunter. Good hitter.

. . .

Stengel wanted me to be a shortstop. And I said, "I'd rather be a good third baseman than a mediocre shortstop." I was a hard-headed kid – I don't think I'm as hard-headed now as I was then – but he wanted me to be a shortstop. Then when Billy Martin broke his leg in spring training, that gave me a chance to play third full-time. Billy had been at third.

I really didn't like playing shortstop, but Stengel always liked to move people around: Martin would play shortstop, third base; McDougald'd play there; he even had Skowron play third base sometimes.

"And Carey?" he'd say, "Where's Carey play? *Third* base!" He would get after my case. I think I was a scapegoat a lot of the time. If he wanted to get on some other guys, he would get on Carey, because he knew if he made me mad I'd play better. So he was always, constantly, getting me mad. You could ask anybody on the ballclub. And yet I think he appreciated me. I think he knew that I worked hard, and I was there for eight and a half years, so obviously I had to be doing something good. I would get mad, but I'd always forget it the next day.

Stengel knew what he was doing. He had a lot of talent, obviously, but he'd come from Oakland, where he won the Pacific Coast League championship. In fact that's where he found Billy. Billy was his boy. He was a fighter. And then he came into New York and did a helluva job, really. I thought he was an excellent manager. Of course he had the talent, too.

I mean we had guys on the bench who would have been playing first string with any other team. We had tremendous depth. And the Yankees were such that they had good offense, good defense in those days, and even when one of the stars would slump it would seem like somebody else would pick them up, get hot for a week or two weeks. They had well-rounded teams. Depth at all areas, and a great pitching coach in Jim Turner, who brought up some good talent.

What the heck, you have Mantle, you have Berra, Bauer, Skowron, Joe Collins, Johnny Mize, Jerry Coleman, Billy, Rizzuto, McDougald, Woodling, Slaughter. Reynolds, Raschi, Lopat were the big three. Hell, we were basically a dynasty. We really were. Wherever we went, it was a full house. Everybody came to see us get beat. You either loved us or hated us, and most of the people seemed like they hated us because they didn't like us to win so much.

I can remember the first World Series trip from Yankee Stadium over to Ebbets Field and being escorted by all the policemen and then getting into Brooklyn, where the fans would throw tomatoes at us and eggs. When we finally got to the ballpark the bus looked like a mixed fruit salad.

Break up the Yankees!

1953 was my very first full year. That's when they won five straight, '49 through '53. Bobby Brown was the third baseman at the time. Dr. Bobby Brown. He was like a big brother to me. I'll never forget. He said, "Kid, whatever you do, get a good reputation, then you can do whatever you want after that, but get that reputation first and it'll follow you – as long as you don't screw it up too much."

Take the Copacabana incident, for example. It was Billy's birthday. In fact, I was invited to that party with Bauer and Mantle and Whitey. I'd had a cold for about two or three days, and I said to myself, "No, sure as hell something'll go wrong and I'll get my name in the newspaper."

My roommate went to it, Bauer, and I remember him coming home and saying, "Oh, do I have some problems, Roomie." But they'd always blame Billy.

But the Yankees were pretty much role models. Suit and tie on the road, things of that sort. They *were* the top team. Here they'd won World Series titles in '49, '50, '51, '52, and '53. In fact, the '53 ring I have has the number 5 on it, for when they won their fifth straight. So I felt very fortunate being able to break in to a lineup that had won four straight championships. I platooned with Bobby Brown and then McDougald on and off at third base. McDougald was probably the most versatile guy. In fact, he was an All-Star at all three positions – third, short, and second base. I don't think he ever did get his due as far as recognition. He was a tremendous talent.

■ ■ ■

Stengel wanted me to hit to all fields, so I tried it. Consequently my average went from .302 to .257, and it was a very hard adjustment for me, but you try and do what they tell you to do. I was screwed up for about two or three years. I finally got back into it about two years later. I look back on it now and I was foolish to have changed, because if I hit that well being a pull hitter, why change? They kept hounding me, and when I went bad they said, "Well, see! You're trying to pull hit and you're not trying to hit to all fields." But I'd been a pull hitter all my life and I'd always hit .300. Hell, I went to triple-A in my first year of pro ball and hit .290 as a nineteen-year-old. I mean that's not too shabby.

I would love to have played in Boston. I came close to it a couple of times just before Frank Malzone came there. But for some reason the Yankees didn't want me to go over there. Probably because they thought I'd do too well against them, being a pull hitter. See, I was always a lowball hitter, and they always threw lowballs in Boston. That's probably one of the reasons I did so well there.

In fact, a funny story: We were playing in Fenway one day and Sammy White was the catcher – I forget who the pitcher was – but all of a sudden someone yells, "Time out."

This is like in the sixth or seventh inning, and we're behind about two or three runs.

"Time out!"

Martin comes out of the dugout and pulls me over. I look at him and say, "What do you want?"

"The old man wants you to hit a home run."

"What?"

"The old man wants you to hit a home run. Get a good pitch and hit a home run!"

Sammy White hears all of this.

Very next pitch, I hit a home run. In the screen at Fenway. I come around, I hit home plate, and I say, "Well, what are you gonna say? The old man says to do it, Sammy!" He's laughing. He couldn't believe it.

True story! True story—the called shot by Carey. It wasn't as significant as Babe Ruth's.

In Japan, after the season in 1955, I led the team in home runs with twelve. That was my honeymoon in '55. We had Johnny Kucks, Eddie Robinson, myself . . . all three of us had just been married after the season.

I led the team in home runs. I hit three home runs three times. I was getting dolls all over the place. Those Osaka dolls? I had them all over the place. Every game that we played was a packed house. I think we had one tie, 1–1, and I think the only reason that happened was that when Ford tried to pick a guy off of second base the ball hit him in the head and ricocheted out into center field and the guy scored. I think the game got called because of darkness, 1–1. But we beat them all the other times. We were in Japan, I think, for a month. We were in Hawaii for two weeks and then to Japan: Hiroshima, Sapporo, Osaka, all the major areas. My honeymoon. I had my honeymoon with the Yankees baseball team.

Then I came back and I started hitting these nice big outs in Yankee Stadium.

"Ohhh, nice goin' Carey," Stengel would say when I'd come back to the dugout. "Hey, that was a great four-hundred-foot fly ball! What happened Carey?"

"Well, they caught it."

And he'd say, "Well, you've got to go to all fields!"

But he'd forget that I was hitting maybe .300 while I was doing all that. As a pull hitter.

But they wanted me to do the other, and I ended up hitting .237 one year. Terrible. The only thing that kept me up there was my fielding. My fielding was always pretty good. Lucky I had the glove.

I was one of the pallbearers at Stengel's funeral. Afterward we had something of an Irish wake at his home. We had a few drinks and I remember going out in the backyard. He had avocado trees, and I was up there in a tree in my suit pitching avocados down to Buzzy Bavasi's wife and Red Paterson's wife, and I felt at the time, "The old man, he'll probably have a bolt of lightning come down and strike this limb." And when I started thinking about that I was out of that tree real fast. True story.

He was a writer's delight. With his crystal ball . . . In the meetings, I wish I'd have had one of those tiny little recorders you have now. They were the most classic, classic clubhouse meetings. I mean, he would rant and rave. A lot of times he'd give some guys names. It took me about a year to decipher who in the hell he was talking about half the time.

He'd say, "That damn left-hander." Talk about "that right-hander, that bearded son of a gun." He would never mention names. Or hell, I played with him five years and he introduces me to somebody as Max Carey. I said, "Casey, my name is *Andy* Carey. I've been with you five years! Remember me? Third baseman? Number six?"

I remember, when I first went up there, he came up to me when I had shaving lather all over my face and he said, "Kid, I want to talk to you." And I'm sitting there and listening and he goes on and on, and when he went away I didn't remember what the hell he said. He was talking about hitting or fielding or something. All the lather had evaporated from my face. I had to relather again.

But he did it. What, ten pennants in twelve years? Not too shabby.

• • •

I remember Larsen's perfect game in the '56 World Series. He pitched, what, ninety-seven pitches in nine innings. A perfect game! No one reached first base by any hook, crook, or whatever.

Larsen got bombed in the second game. I think he only lasted two innings, and for him to come back like that was sort of unusual, too.

Interesting, prior to the fifth game, the night before, my mom and dad were down in Times Square, and they had two newspaper headlines printed: one read "Larsen pitches no-hitter;" the other one, "Gooney-birds (we called Larsen, affectionately, Gooney-bird) pick Larsen to win fifth game."

Dad took them back to the Concourse Plaza Hotel and put the one that said Larsen pitches no-hitter on Larsen's door. Then he thought about it and said, "No, I might jinx him." And he went back, tore it up into little shreds – and my mom's still a witness – and flushed it down the toilet. But he did keep the one that said "Gooney-birds pick Larsen to win fifth game."

I still have that. I have the original.

Larsen had experimented with pitching from a no-windup, which was really developed by Bob Turley. He was very successful with it. You know, he'd just stand out there, look at the hitter and just pitch. And obviously it was very effective for Turley, so Larsen wanted to try it because he hadn't had too successful a year. He came into the Series using it after experimenting with it for maybe two or three weeks.

I can remember the game very distinctly. In the third or fourth inning, Jackie Robinson hit a smash to my left that I dove for. It ricocheted off of the tips of my fingers and went to McDougald at shortstop, and he threw Robinson out, bang-bang.

There was another play in the middle innings where Hodges hit a line drive to left center – it might have been a home run in Ebbets Field, or at least against the wall – but Mantle was playing back there far enough and backhanded it, a tremendous play.

And I think the other one that was fairly close was Hodges again. I believe that was in the seventh or eighth inning, a low liner I caught off my shoestrings to my left, but I threw it to first base just to make sure, in case the umpire thought I might have trapped it. Afterward I thought, "My God, what if I'd thrown that ball away!" You don't think of it at the time, but it sort of brings beads of sweat to your face.

On the bench? You know, ballplayers are superstitious, probably even more so in the old days than they are now. I think it was about the seventh inning and Mickey was sitting next to Larsen and Larsen says, "God, wouldn't that be great if I pitched a no-hitter!" And Mantle just looked at him and he walked away.

And I think that one of the guys was sitting in a certain place, and he wouldn't move. But I think the mood on the bench was that we knew what was happening, but not until the seventh, eighth, and ninth inning would you start thinking seriously about something like that. Then, when you're out in the field, you have to say to yourself, "The most important thing is that we win the game."

Something like this only becomes a phenomenal event after the fact, and the more you get into time and the decades that have passed since then do you realize how significant that game was. But at the particular time? "Great, I'm glad he made another $5,000 or $6,000." But you didn't really grasp how significant that was to baseball history.

Listen, Maglie pitched a helluva game that day. Two zip? Mantle hit a home run. I scored the other run, I got a single through the box off of Maglie, went to second on a bunt by Larsen, and Bauer drove me in from second base.

As always, Yogi said it best: "Well, that's the best game he's ever pitched."

．　．　．

They always remember you with the Yankees. Wherever you go, you were a Yankee. I think it was Johnny Lindell who said one time that "No matter what, it's a strange thing, I played with the Yankees and wherever I go I'm always a Yankee." And look at Reggie Jackson. Hall of Fame. A Yankee. He was only there a few years. . . . But they always remember him as a Yankee.

It was great to be a part of those great teams. We used to be on the Ed Sullivan Show. . . . I was on the Perry Como Show, singing "You Gotta Have Heart" just before the World Series. We went on the Arthur Murray Show one time, and I was one of the dancers. Moose Skowron was a dancer, and I think Whitey Ford was a dancer. I won the contest, and one of the writers said, "Yeah, Carey was the best of a bad lot." It was a lot of fun, looking back.

You get out here on the West Coast and people are not the baseball fans that they are back East. I go back East now–Florida, New York– and you'd think it was like I just quit playing ball. Yankee fans, they remember me. And like I said, I was paid to play the sub's part.

Hell, as old as I am, they still remember me. The card shows. They still idolize you. It's just amazing. It's just absolutely amazing to me.

Roy Sievers

June 3, 1993, St. Louis, Missouri

Roy Sievers played first base and the outfield from 1949 to 1965. In addition to playing seven and a half years with the Washington Senators and five with the St. Louis Browns, Sievers played with the White Sox and Phillies. The 1949 American League Rookie of the Year, Sievers hit 318 career home runs and compiled a .267 lifetime batting average. His forty-two home runs and 114 RBIs were best in the American League in 1957.

You never know what's gonna happen. It's all in here, inside of your heart, what's in the individual himself. It's sometimes the break that you get. A lot of players, if you get a break and you don't take advantage of it, you'll stay back in the minor leagues. But if you get a break and you take advantage of it, like I got, the first year with the Browns. . . .

I wasn't playing. I struck out the first two times up in the big leagues. I said, "Well, I'm going back to double-A. I'm going back to San Antonio. That's where I'll need more experience. I guess that's what they're gonna tell me."

Well, the third time up I doubled down the left field line, drove in two runs. Zack Taylor, the manager, comes in and says, "You're playing the doubleheader tomorrow."

Well, I went 7 for 8 in the doubleheader, and Whitey Platt didn't play anymore. I just got hot with the bat at the right time and I stayed in the lineup. And sometimes that's all it takes with a ballplayer.

You get an opportunity to play, and if you don't hit right away, if you don't do it right away, then the next thing you know you're going back down again. They'll send you back out. But if you get hot with the bat at the right time, or if you get hot pitching, you'll stay with the ballclub.

You've got to want to play. If you don't want to play this game, to me you ain't gonna play it too good. You've got to want to go out there every day and to bust your tail every day to do something.

■　■　■

My dad had a chance to go with Detroit when he was young. And his dad says, "Well, you're only going to make so much money a month there. It's gonna be kind of a hard life for you. You better think about working here and staying home."

My dad always thought that if he left, the corner he used to bum around on wouldn't be there when he came back. So he never did go, but he was quite an athlete, from what I gather talking to guys who played with him during his career in St. Louis, here.

He used to make twenty-five dollars a Sunday, pitching. Pretty good hitter, too. I guess that's where I acquired some of my ability as a hitter. Everybody I talked to said he could have made it, could have made it in the big leagues.

He worked in automobile appliances, iron and steel, down at Beck and Corbitt on Second and Branch streets downtown. He just played on a Saturday and a Sunday. Twenty-five dollars to pitch on a Sunday. That's how he made extra money.

He used to play with us all the time in the alley when we were grow-ing up. He played cartball, he played bottle caps, he played all that. He worked seven days a week. On Saturday and Sunday he used to watch the company, the building. Made extra money to help out. Seven days a week.

Probably the biggest thrill for me was for my family to watch me play. You know: their son made it to the major leagues. Boy, they just enjoyed it.

Knock on wood, I had real good days when my parents were there. I know I always made my mother feel good: "Well, that's my son. He's out there playing."

My dad, he didn't say too much, but I know that down deep inside he felt good about it. My mother'd come out to the ballpark here in St. Louis when they had Ladies' Day. And of course, my older broth-ers always ridiculed me: "Why didn't you do this? Why didn't you do that?"

Probably just trying to help me improve myself. They'd always be on my case. All the time. And my brother next to me is still the same way. He criticizes the ballplayers today – how much money they make and how they ought to tax them more.

And I say, "Hey, why don't you get out there and see what you can do. It's not easy. You go out there and face Feller three or four times and he's throwing the ball ninety-five to one hundred miles per hour and he's got the good curveball. And the fans get on you . . ."

My brother still enjoys it – at the old-timers' game once in a while. I still get a kick going to an old-timers' game, putting the uniform on. It's such a thrill to me. You can't describe it to the average person. It's just something that's in you. You just can't describe it.

Like when you go to New York, Yankee Stadium, and you see all those guys and there's 60,000 people in the stands. They introduce Roger Maris – when he was alive – then Yogi, then Whitey Ford. Then, of course, they always come out with number seven, Mickey Mantle. And then the big guy, number five, DiMaggio. And the whole place goes nuts. The goose bumps would go up and down my arm. There's just nothing like it.

∎　∎　∎

I started in Pine Bluff, Arkansas, in '47. In the minor leagues, we had two triple-A clubs, two double-A, two A, two B, two C, and two D clubs. When we went to spring training there was 450 guys there, and you got a number on your back. You might be number 405. Then, every morning you got up, you walked over and you had breakfast, and you look on the board: 405, you're playing on field number two today.

You have lunch and you go over to the board again: 405, you're play-ing on field number four this afternoon. Sometimes you'd have supper and you'd see: 405, you're playing in town tonight. In an exhibition game in the town of Pine Bluff, Arkansas.

I ended up playing in Hannibal, Missouri. Had a great year in Hannibal – hit thirty-eight home runs, drove in 144 runs, hit .317, then hit eight home runs in the playoffs. I think we played eight games, nine games in the playoffs. Had a great year! I said, "Man, this is easy."

Throughout the years, going back to some of the functions, I see some guys. They walk up to me and say, "Roy, you remember me?"

And I say, "Yeah, I remember your face."

And they say, "Well, I pitched against you in such-and-such a state. I remember the home run you hit off me. I can't believe you hit that ball that far."

I bet about eight guys in the last two or three years tell me that. I say, "I really appreciate you telling me that."

They say, "Oh, no! I'll tell you, you were some kind of hitter. I'm just glad I had the opportunity of playing against you."

That makes me feel good.

• • •

The first year with with the Browns I had a great year, '49. The next year they tried to have me go to right field more. It kind of screwed up my stance, and I ended up hitting .238 after hitting .306 the first year.

So I said right then and there, "I'm going back to my old way of hit-ting. I'm not going to step to right field."

Well, then I hurt my shoulder in the beginning of '51, and I thought maybe my career was over. But Bill Veeck had the club, and through constant work at the ballpark through the winter, my arm got stronger – I had a dislocated right shoulder – and I went out to spring training a month ahead of time.

My arm felt great. I felt good. Then our coach, Rogers Hornsby, hit a ball to my left – I was playing third base – and I picked the ball up and threw off balance and my arm came out again. Well, I thought this was it: "My career's gotta be over. Looks like I'm through."

Then Veeck says, "Go back to St. Louis."

I had just arrived. So I went back, had Dr. Prostein – he just died re-cently, ninety-nine years old – look at my shoulder, and he said, "Well, you probably have to have an operation."

They gave the results to Veeck, and Veeck said, "Well, *he's* not going to do it. We're going to go to Johns Hopkins, in Baltimore."

Veeck was a great man to play for. The owners wanted him out of baseball for some reason. I don't know why it was. I guess the way he was with publicity. The stunts he used to pull. But if you hit a home run or you got a key base hit in a situation, like against the Yankees, when you'd walk into the clubhouse the next day there'd be a little note on your locker: "Here, go get a $200 topcoat on Bill Veeck," or "Go get a $150 suit." Just something every day.

Somebody did something, why there was something in there for you. It was unbelievable. So you put out a little extra for people like that.

I loved Veeck anyway. I loved him and I loved Mary Francis, his wife. Just great people. It was just a pleasure and an honor to play for them.

I tell you one thing, he could do more things on that one leg than a lot of people could do on two. When he put that wooden leg on, he'd play handball. Oh yeah, I played handball with him at St. Louis University here. He'd go up a flight of stairs faster than anybody, he'd dance. . . . He just enjoyed life. And he was a great man for baseball.

Anyway, Dr. George Bennett performed the surgery on me about a month after spring training, and through work at the hospital and doing other exercises, I played in August or September that year. Not much, but I played. And through constant work, coming home, doing construction work – you know, pulling nails and lifting plywood and pouring concrete – my shoulder got stronger.

And then I played in '53 with the Browns. Played ninety-two games, hit .270, and drove in thirty-five runs. Then the Browns' franchise was sold to Baltimore, and Baltimore for some reason had some letter or something saying I couldn't throw no more . . . throw far.

Well, Jimmy Dykes said, "I think we ought to get rid of him. Get somebody else."

And that's when they traded me to Washington for Gil Coan. And to me, it probably turned out to be one of my biggest breaks in baseball.

■   ■   ■

I got over there and Bucky Harris had the ballclub, and he said, "You're going to play left field. I want you to be in the lineup and I want you to hit."

And that's the way it started. I broke their home run record for the first three or four years with Washington. Bucky, yeah! He said, "I want you in the middle part of the lineup – we know you can hit, and we want you in that part of the lineup to stabilize some of the other guys that we got now." The kids and that . . .

We had a pretty good year the first year I was there. I didn't hit much. I hit .232 – something like that – but I hit twenty-nine home runs. But then each year that went along, I started getting better.

I hit forty-two home runs in '57 and hit .301. I wasn't making much money at the time, so when Calvin Griffith says, "How much money do you want?" I said, "I'd like to get a 100 percent raise."

And he said, "What do you base it on?"

I said, "I hit forty-two home runs, drove in 114 runs. I beat Mantle, I beat Williams out. What else do you need, Calvin? I'm not making much money *now*."

He told me, "We can finish last with you, we can finish last without you. Make up your mind, cause you know you're not gonna go home and make that kind of money."

Well, it ended up I got about an 80 percent raise. So the following year, '58, I hit thirty-nine home runs and hit .295 and drove in 108 runs, and Calvin wanted to *cut* me $10,000.

I says, "*Calvin*, what do you base it on?"

He says, "You didn't win no titles."

I said, "You know what you can do with the titles!"

The titles didn't mean that much to me. Mantle beat me out again, with forty-two home runs that year.

If you made $20,000 with Washington, Calvin'd let you stay there for twenty years. But once you started getting higher or wanted more than that, you were gone. Calvin'd get rid of you. He wouldn't pay that big salary.

They were tough at that time. I played for probably two of the toughest guys, Bill DeWitt and Calvin Griffith. They were tough with the money. I know the first year with the Browns, when I had the good year, I walked in the office and they had both Bill and Charley DeWitt in there.

I said, "Hey, wait a minute, I'm only going to talk to one guy. Bill, you're the president. Charley, you'll have to leave."

He was the traveling secretary, so he left. So, Bill DeWitt said, "Well, what do you want?"

I said, "I want $20,000."

That's 1950.

And he says, "What do you mean, you want $20,000?"

I said, "Bill, look at this. I read in the paper, Connie Mack offered $200,000 to make a trade for me, and money. I read that in the papers, and don't deny it." And I said, "I want 10 percent of that."

So I ended up getting a $5,000 raise – no, I got a $4,000 raise. I went from $5,000 to $9,000. And I had the bad year and I went back down again, to $7,000.

Of course, cars back then were $1,500. You could buy a house for $7,000 or $8,000.

With the Browns and the Senators it was always tough, due to the fact that every time we had a fairly good ballplayer develop, even with the Browns, they had to sell him to make money to stay in the league. Sometimes they borrowed money from the league office to survive.

And Washington was kind of the same thing, too. Their farm system didn't have that many great ballplayers at the time.

The Athletics, they were like the Browns. They didn't have much, either. But it was always a good series when you played them. Shantz – Bobby Shantz – pitched, Lou Brissie pitched, Art Fowler . . . They had a good staff, man. It was tough. Gus Zernial played left field. Ferris Fain played first base. They had a good ballclub, but they always finished in the second division, too.

I played against Connie Mack for two years. He was unbelievable. He was ninety years old and he'd sit straight in that dugout with the old blue suit on with the high collar and the straw hat. And every once in a while he'd take his hat off and he'd move an outfielder. Ninety years old, still sittin' on the bench. Great man.

The Yankees were the top team of that time. In the '50s. Hell, they won ten out of twelve pennants. The top clubs were Detroit, the Yankees, White Sox, Cleveland. Any time you made a mistake against them good clubs, it cost you. It cost you a ballgame.

But what a ballclub the Cleveland Indians were. You walk in there, you face Feller, Wynn, Garcia, and Lemon – and Score came along later. You would walk in there for a week and go 0 for 20 real quick.

Back then, in the '50s, they had four hard throwers on every ballclub. And them guys went eight or nine innings every day, every time they pitched.

I used to love to face the good pitchers: Vic Raschi, Allie Reynolds, Whitey Ford. The Cleveland staff. Then the Detroit staff: you had Virgil Trucks, Dizzy Trout, and Hal Newhouser. Man, they were great staffs back then. And the White Sox had four hard throwers. The Red Sox had four good throwers. Parnell was a great left-handed pitcher up there.

In New York, the players used to tell me all the coaches would say, "Watch this guy hit."

And Stengel, too, "Watch this guy Sievers hit. This guy can hit."

There were rumors that I was going to go to the Yankees at one time. And Williams wanted me to go to the Red Sox. He tried, he said, for seven years to get Joe Cronin – who was Calvin Griffith's son-in-law – to make a deal with Washington to get me in Boston.

He said, "I guarantee you, Cronin, you get that kid up here in Boston and we're gonna win some pennants."

Never happened. Calvin would never get rid of me. I couldn't believe that. Boy, I'd love to have played in Fenway Park for eight or ten years.

Walt Dropo used to tell me, "You'd never hit up there."

I said, "What do you mean I'd never hit?"

He said, "You'd change your swing to hit the ball up in the net."

I said, "I would never change my swing."

He said, "You say that now, but I guarantee you."

What a way to end your career, up there. Whew!

Then I had good years in '57, '58, and '59 with Washington. And Calvin traded me in '59 to the White Sox. He got Don Mincher and Earl Battey, plus $150,000 that Veeck gave him for me.

When I joined the White Sox in spring of that year, 1960 in Sarasota, I walked up and shook hands with Mr. Lopez, and I said, "Al, it's great to be here, and I hope I can be of some kind of help to your ballclub."

And he said, "Well, I'm glad you *are* here, but I didn't want you. Mr. Veeck wanted you, and I don't know where I'm gonna play you."

Nellie Fox heard that and he said, "I can't believe that man said that to you."

And I said, "Well, I guess he's speaking the truth."

He probably didn't want me, because they had Ted Kluszewski, after '59 when they won the pennant. They had Earl Torgeson. I was in great shape, which is what teed me off. I was in great shape; I wanted to play.

I just bided my time, and then as it turned out, after a month of the season, Klu's only hitting like .180, and Lopez put me in, and I got hot with the bat. Klu never played again. I had two more years with the White Sox.

I read in the paper one time that Lopez didn't think I was the caliber of a first division player. He didn't think I had the ability of being a first division player. Well, as it turned out, after the two years I had with the

White Sox I went through my scrapbook and I read that he had changed his mind.

He said, "Sievers is a first division ballplayer. He's a good ballplayer and he's had two great years for me. I was a little wrong criticizing him at the beginning."

Which made me feel better. I wrote him a letter thanking him. I said, "I appreciate your kind words saying I was a first division ballplayer." Which I proved to myself that I was.

I always wanted to prove that, and I did with the White Sox and the Phillies. That made my career. That made me feel better.

When you finish last or seventh all the time, the batting statistics don't mean that much. For example, if I was on a pennant-winning ballclub and I did all those numbers in those years, well, my name would mean more in a lot of respects, and I'd get a lot of consideration for certain things, like maybe the Hall of Fame.

Of course, I never think about the Hall of Fame because with my credentials with the Browns and Washington, I was always seventh or eighth, and a lot of times they don't take the ballplayers from the second division ballclubs. So I never think about that.

. . .

But I didn't play ball to get into the Hall of Fame. No. I played because I loved to play. It's something that you can't describe to the average person. You get to the ballpark, there's something about it. You get your uniform on, you go out there, and especially you play better if there's a big crowd out there. I always played better if there was a big crowd. Sometimes you have to reach back and get a little extra to do it if you've got 3,500 people in the stands. But if you've got 40,000 people in the stands . . .

But it was my way of making a living. I knew I had to go out there every day and do my best to help the ballclub win. Regardless of what you did, you had to do something, because there was always somebody in the background waiting to take your job. We didn't win many games, but we always had a lot of fun playing.

We always played good against the top clubs. Like New York, Chicago, Detroit, Boston, Cleveland. We always went out there and busted our tail off a little harder to beat them guys. The pitchers couldn't wait to get to Washington or St. Louis because they knew they had a sure win in their pocket, and they always wanted the ball, to pitch.

With the Phillies, a couple of years over there with Gene Mauch . . . He had me in the middle part of the lineup to help stabilize their ballclub, and it turned out in '64 they had a shot to win it. Then they traded me in August – late August – because I had a bad leg.

The general manager, Quinn, says, "I want somebody to play every day. Get rid of Sievers."

I was the oldest guy. And to this day I told Mauch, "I'll play in September, my leg'll be all right, and I'll play in September."

He said, "I can't do much about it. Quinn wants to get rid of you."

So they sold me back to Washington. I went over to see Gil Hodges and said, "I have to have a week off, or two weeks, with my leg, and I'll be ready for you in September."

Well, I played in September and I hit five home runs, drove in about fifteen or eighteen runs, and hit .300. And I saw Mauch about three years after that and I said, "I told you, Mauch, I could play in September."

He said, "I knew that, but I couldn't convince Quinn."

They ended up getting Frank Thomas, and Thomas ended up breaking his thumb, so they had to get somebody else. And nobody wanted to pitch the last four or five games. I couldn't believe it. I was watching the paper every day back in Washington. The Phillies had a six-and-a-half-game lead with eleven games to play, and then they get down to the nitty gritty at the end and they lose. The Cardinals backed in. Cincinnati had the best club that year.

When we left spring training, we had it in our mind that we were gonna play as hard as we could and compete. Well, as it turned out, we started competing right away. Everything started to gel. And when you got into the seventh, eighth, or ninth inning and you needed a base hit, somebody'd come in and say, "Hey, let's get it goin'. Let's get rollin' here."

And if we were a little behind, it seemed like it worked. And Mauch would chew us out when something went wrong. They said that the last two weeks he didn't say hardly anything at all. He'd walk in his office and close the door, and that was it.

You know, he's been there a couple of times, and he's never got the big one. I know down deep inside it's got to hurt him, the way things have happened.

I was reading that paper every day and, oh, I couldn't believe it. "They're losing again," I said.

They lose 1–0 and Chico Ruiz steals home on them. Then nobody wanted to pitch. He was using Dennis Bennett, Chris Short, and Jim Bunning. He could've pitched Art Mahaffey and the other kid we had. Give these other guys a chance to rest. But it never happened.

I guess he wanted to win it in the worst way and win it the way he wanted to, and that was it. Had to be a shocker. Something you'll never forget as a player, and I know he'll never forget it as a manager.

∎ ∎ ∎

I wish that they would still leave the gloves on the field, like they did years ago. Very seldom did you see a ball hit the glove. It was a rare occasion if a ground ball or a line drive would hit a glove in the outfield. And very seldom would you see a ballplayer ever step on a glove in the outfield.

And you never had to worry about it. You never even thought about it.

One day, I put a snake – a rubber snake – in Phil Rizzuto's glove. We're all sitting on the bench, waiting. Phil came out of the dugout real quick and he got right to the glove and he started to go down and he must have jumped ten feet in the air. He was scared of bugs and snakes. Boy, he was hollerin' and screamin'. He wouldn't touch that glove for nothin'. He had Joe Collins come over from first base. And Collins tiptoed over and he starts stampin' on the glove, and we're laughin' like heck in the Browns' dugout. And then all of a sudden Rizzuto looked over at the Browns' dugout . . . and eeeeeah!

And another guy was scared of bugs: DiMaggio. Yeah, that's what I heard. He didn't like that stuff either.

I mean, that was part of the game.

∎ ∎ ∎

Years ago, we used to sit in the clubhouse, especially if we lost, we'd sit there, eight or ten guys on their stools, and you'd have a beer and you'd talk about what happened during the game. Or maybe, four or five of us would go out and get a bite to eat and talk about what went on during the game.

We used to have to take a train from St. Louis to New York in a day and a half. And the majority of the time we were on the last couple of cars when we pulled into the station. We had to carry our own bags back then, and those suitcases were heavy.

They always talk about jet lag. . . . If we took the train from St. Louis to California, it's two days, and half the time the air conditioning didn't work and you had to put the window up or the cinders would fly in off the track. Man, it was hot on them cars.

With the Browns . . . when we left California after spring training, when we were traveling to come back and open the season up, we'd usually stop in Phoenix, San Antonio, and a couple of other towns.

The Cubs and Pittsburgh, they'd go off and stay in a hotel, we'd have to stay on the cars, the sleeping cars, because the Browns didn't have money for the hotels. You think about that today.

They didn't want to spend the money so long as they had the Pullman cars. Yeah, we had to get off and walk into town – of course, we were close to town anyway – and go wherever we had to go. Eat breakfast. They'd take the baseball stuff and put it in the ballpark. Then after the ballgame you'd walk back, or take a cab back, to the Pullman car and go to bed. We didn't mind. We were young. We didn't think that much of it.

Great life, huh?

It *was* a great life. Had a great time. Got to meet a lot of great people. You meet movie stars, you meet, in Washington, Congressmen. I met Khrushchev when he come over here. I had lunch with four presidents of the United States. I had lunch with Kennedy, Johnson, Nixon, and Eisenhower.

Nixon – supposedly, I was his favorite ballplayer. My roommate, Jim Lemon, was Eisenhower's favorite ballplayer. You know, first day of the season, president comes out and throws the first ball. I never got a ball thrown by him, but I got Nixon's signature on a ball and I got Eisenhower's signature on a ball.

It was just a great way to make a living. Super. To this day, I really enjoyed it. You can't describe it to the average person.

Vern Law

January 22–23, 1993, Provo, Utah

Vern Law pitched for the Pittsburgh Pirates from 1950 to 1967, winning 162 games, losing 147, and compiling a 3.77 career earned-run average. In 1960, Law won twenty games, lost nine, and led the National League with eighteen complete games. In the 1960 World Series versus the Yankees, Law won two games, lost none, and was the starting pitcher in the unforgettable game seven. He is the father of Vance Law.

People ask me, "What game do you remember the most? Was it the World Series?"

And I say, "Heck, no. It's the ballgame I didn't even win." That's the one I remember the most.

It was against Milwaukee, it was in 1957. I wasn't even supposed to pitch this night. I was supposed to pitch the following night.

I went to the ballpark. I'd only had two days' rest, and our starting pitcher came in sick. His stomach was upset and he couldn't play, so Danny Murtaugh hollered out to me, "Hey, Deacon!"

I got the nickname Deacon because I didn't swear, didn't drink, went to church, and did quite a bit of speaking in other churches, youth groups and so forth. It's a term that's familiar to the people back East. In our faith, the Church of Jesus Christ of Latter-day Saints, we have, I guess, what you'd call a lay ministry. We are called, and we are set apart to do different jobs in the church, whether it's being a bishop or a counselor or high priest group leader, whatever. . . . We're called to different positions in the church and we serve . . . all of us give of our time, you know. It's not a paid ministry at all. Now, I was an elder at the time. . . . Well, they don't know what an elder is, but they do know what a deacon is, and so I guess I just came by that naturally.

Anyway, I said, "Yeah, what do you want, Skip?"

"Hey, can you pitch tonight?"

I answered, "Yeah."

He says, "Okay, come on in. Come on in."

You know, I was out running, getting my exercise, and getting ready for my game the next night.

So I went in. I started the game at 7:30, and at 12:59 I'm still pitching. I'd pitched eighteen innings of a nineteen-inning game. And I was getting them out . . . one, two, three.

He tried to take me out in the thirteenth inning. He asked me how I felt, and I said, "Skip, I'm fine. I'm getting them out. No problem. I feel good."

He said, "Okay, I'll let you stay in."

Again, the sixteenth inning: "Deacon," he said, "I better take you out."

I replied, "Skip, I pitched this long. Let me stay in to either win or lose it."

And he said, "Okay," and he let me stay in. Eighteenth inning – I pitched that – we're at home, and the score is still 2–2, and we get to where he can pinch-hit for me and he said, "Deacon, I've got to take you out. If you ruin your arm, they'll run me right out of town. You've pitched eighteen innings, I can't ask any more of you."

I said, "Well, it doesn't look like they're gonna score for me."

So, he took me out, and my reliever, Bob Friend, came in, and he pitched one inning, gave up a run. So we're getting beat 3–2. Well, we came back and scored two in our half of the nineteenth, and you know who got credit for the victory? Friend! I didn't even get E for effort. Lew Burdette was the starter for Milwaukee that night. It was Burdette who went up against Haddix when he pitched that twelve-inning perfect game. They had five different pitchers in for them.

But during the course of that game, I gave up nine hits, I struck out twelve, I walked two, and gave up two runs. Yet I didn't win the ballgame, but I think I probably got as much publicity for not winning as I would had I won it.

The amazing thing about it is, four days later I pitched thirteen innings before I won that one.

. . .

It's interesting, those things that you remember about the game. About individuals. You know I played against a lot of guys, a lot of *good* players, and I remember those guys. They're friends, now. They weren't then. You wanted to beat them.

That was one thing that was very hard for me: I couldn't get too friendly with the other team. I'd acknowledge them and say, "How're things going." But I never chased around with the opposition or got too well acquainted with them, because when the time in the ballgame came up where I had to pitch inside, I didn't want to hesitate.

There's actually only one time where I went after people in a ballgame, and that was because of Roberto. It was a fact, around the league, that if you threw at Roberto the first time up, he was no good the rest of the day, because that front foot of his was out and his rear end was out. For two weeks I saw him take some pitches up around his head. It was lucky that he didn't get killed, because some of them were close.

Well, this day we're in Philadelphia, and first time up, boy, did he get lowered. I mean the first pitch out. The hat went one way, the bat another, and him another. I mean it was that close. He escaped with his life on that particular pitch. He very weakly grounded out, and he came back and he started hollering and swearing. I don't know if you've ever heard a Spanish-speaking person try and swear in the English language, but it was *bad*! It was bad! It was terrible, and I said, "Roberto, hey, hold it, hold it! I'll take care of it. I'll take care of it, just be still."

Well, first guy up was Richie Ashburn. Threw right there, at his head; down he went; I got him out. Next guy, right there; got him out. Next guy right there . . . and the umpire calls time. He goes to their bench – he didn't come out to the mound – he went to our bench: "Another ball comes close to one of these guys, it's a five-hundred-dollar fine and a five-day suspension."

Well, from that time forth the pitchers' control got real good, and nobody threw at Roberto from that point after. It was all over. In the *league*!

And that was the only time that I really went after people. Not with the intent to hit them. If I wanted to hit them, I'd throw behind them. Because you throw at a guy's head, he's going to get out of the way – he's going to get mad, but he'll get out of the way. But you throw back there, in back of them, they freeze, they don't know which way to go. And you get them.

Like I say, I didn't want to hit anybody, but I wanted to deliver a message, too. And that was to leave Roberto alone. And they did. From that point on we had no more trouble.

Well, it happened another time with me, too.

I think this was around '58. I think we were still battling for the pennant, and we'd gone out to San Francisco to play. And Ruben Gomez was pitching. He had a habit of throwing at people – you probably remember Joe Adcock running him all the way up in the Polo Grounds, clear up into the clubhouse in center field. Matter of fact, Ruben hit me. Right on the mastoid bone.

But anyway, I was pitching this day, and he threw at a couple of our guys and he hit one or two of them, I don't remember how many, but he hit somebody. And we didn't retaliate. We turned our cheek and took it on the other side, I guess. At that time they had Marv Grissom, who would throw at his mother, they had Maglie – he'd buzz you – so there were guys on that staff who you had to hang a little loose with.

Anyway, we went on down, played the Dodgers and back home again, went to Houston, played a series and back home against the Giants. And I start off the series and opposite me is Ruben Gomez. Anyway, we had a good game going. It was about the seventh inning and we're still tied nothing to nothing, and we get up in our half of the seventh and Mazeroski hits one out of the park, but it was just foul. By this time Maz – he's at second base – comes back, picks up his helmet and bat, and steps up there, and the next pitch is right there – the ball went right underneath his hat. I mean he really got lowered. And I looked down the bench and Murtaugh is looking at me.

He says, "Deacon, come here. I'm not asking you to throw at this guy, I'm telling you. And if you don't, it's a one-hundred-dollar fine and I expect a one-hundred-dollar check on my desk after the game."

Well, as it happened, Gomez was the first hitter up the next inning. I think everybody in the ballpark knew. I think the umpires knew. Because immediately when he stepped up there, I threw a pitch right at his head, and down he went, and immediately the umpire starts walking out to the mound and Murtaugh joins him—he wanted to protect me and keep me in the ballgame. But before they get to the mound, Murtaugh turns around and hollers at Gomez, "You throw at one more of our guys, you're going to get one right there!"

Well, Gomez grabs his crotch. And Murtaugh saw red. He charged after him, and by this time we've got all the players on the field and we've got a free-for-all going. And out of the corner of my eye I see somebody flying through the air and he's got somebody pinned to the ground. So I go over there and see what's going on, and here's Willie Mays, he's got Cepeda pinned to the ground. Cepeda had gone to the bat rack and got the leaded bat and was out there with that leaded bat. Of course Mays, being a peacemaker, saw that and he pinned him; he held him right there. Had Cepeda used that bat, his career would probably have been cut very short, because they probably would have banned him from baseball. Mays probably saved his career for him.

Anyway, this whole thing was written up in the *Saturday Evening Post*, and you know where the guilty finger pointed? Right here. I'm the guy that started the whole thing.

Again, sometimes you're going to be shoved into a corner, and even though it's against your principles, against the way that you like to play the game, you're going to have to protect your own players. In a case like this, well, it was just something that had to happen.

But today—it really is true—you can't throw inside to hitters today. It was an accepted thing back then.

I don't know, maybe it would be difficult for me to play today, because I did use the inside of that plate an awful lot, and like I say, if you can't pitch inside, you're not going to win. Because if hitters know that everything will be away, away, away, it's a piece of cake for them.

•   •   •

Forbes Field was a good pitcher's park. For the fans it was good too, for the most part, because they were close down to the field, and they felt a part of it. They did have several bad seats because of the structure of it: people got seated behind poles once in a while and it was very difficult to see. But to play in, it was a good park, particularly from a pitcher's point of view. The dimensions were big and you could make a mistake, and if you had a good center fielder, which we had, he'd run down your mistakes for you. A lot of the guys loved to hit there because it spreads out, and you can hit the gaps better with line drives and take more extra bases.

And of course, you had the red brick wall with the ivy on it. And you had a park in back of the left field wall. It was a nice area. I'd go over to the ballpark and you knew the names of the groundskeepers, the people working the concessions stands. You knew them. You had a real relationship. A lot of the fans would come early; you had a relationship with them. That was just part of the game.

I could have had Honus Wagner's baseball cards, had his signatures on balls. Because he was on the bench. He was sitting on the bench as an honorary coach when I first got up there. If I could have perceived the future and what kind of price a signature from Honus Wagner on a card would mean, I would have been a wealthy man.

He was a very kindly gentleman. He would sit there and watch, and if I had a bad day or something, he'd pat me on the back and say, "Hey, you'll get them next time. There's always tomorrow in this game. You'll be fine. Just keep working hard."

He was never out of line with his remarks. He was just a very kind individual. About the seventh inning, why, he'd go in the clubhouse and have an Iron City beer, maybe more than one. There are a lot of stories about him stopping on the way home. He'd walk home after a ballgame and he would stop at all the bars. And of course everybody knew him. He had a lot of free drinks on the way home.

But he was just an honorary coach. And he'd be there, have his suit on, sit there on the bench with us. Of course, that was one of the rules, you know: if you were on the bench you had to be dressed. You know, in a uniform.

We had several there in the Pittsburgh area that were associated with the ballclub that were outstanding former players. Of course, George Sisler was there with the ballclub for a number of years as a special assistant and helped out a great deal with scouting and reports.

Nice people around Pittsburgh. For the first two or three years we lived right there in Oakland, in an Italian neighborhood. We also lived in a Jewish neighborhood. Then, after we had two or three children and needed a little bit more room, we lived out farther away. But we lived practically in every area in the Pittsburgh area: Mount Lebanon, North Park, South Park, Murraysville, all around.

• • •

It's true, I was scouted by Senator Welker, but this was before he was a senator. He saw me play out in Payette, Idaho, in a high school tournament. He was a lawyer at the time, but he was also a friend of Bing Crosby, who was one of the Pittsburgh vice-presidents. They had gone to school together at Gonzaga University in Spokane, Washington, and had remained friends over the years, had hunted pheasants, and had done a lot of things together. He was kind of a birddog scout.

The score was nothing to nothing going into the latter innings, and they were trying to get a man on base, so they sent up a midget to hit. The guy was about three feet tall, maybe three-and-a-half feet tall. And he had a baseball uniform and a small bat, and *my* gosh, I had never seen anything like that before. Anyway, my brother, who was my catcher, came out to me and said, "Vern, what're we going to do?"

I said, "Well, I guess he's a member of the team. He's got a uniform, and he's been announced. Just go back there, get on your knees and give me a low target, and I'll try and hit it."

Well, as it turned out I threw three straight strikes. Struck him out. Of course that even impressed the senator more. Then, I can't remember whether my brother got a base hit and I drove him in or if I got the base hit, a double, and then he drove me in. Anyway, we won the ballgame.

The senator was impressed. He called Bing Crosby and told him, "You better check this kid out."

So they sent out Babe Herman, who was then a scout. Of course, they couldn't sign me until after I graduated, but right after graduation day I had nine different organizations there wanting to sign me.

Each one of them would come in, and each one was coming in smoking a cigar. The scouts. And of course my dad was very staunch about no alcohol, no tobacco in the house. So he'd tell them, "You can come in, but that's got to stay outside." They didn't make too good of an impression with my parents.

Well, the last people, the Pirates, came in. No cigars. And they presented my mother with a box of chocolates and a bouquet of roses. Then, halfway during the conversation, the phone rings and on the other end of the line is Bing Crosby. And of course Bing Crosby was *the Man* back then, and of course my mother, she almost fainted. Well, they made a *very* good impression. And my parents decided that I should sign with the Pirates.

About ten years later–this is after the Dodgers had moved from Brooklyn to Los Angeles–I'm scheduled to pitch this day and into the clubhouse comes Bing Crosby, and we get to talking.

He said, "You remember your signing day at all?"

And I said, "Well, a little bit about it. I know I didn't get anything to sign."

Crosby said that Senator Welker, living out there, knew all about the Latter-day Saint people, commonly called the Mormons. "Probably what you don't know," he said, "is that they bought a box of cigars and passed them out to the scouts before they went in."

Anyway, as they say, I guess everything is fair in love and war. I had to chuckle at that. That was kind of a determining factor. The other guys didn't make too good of an impression.

. . .

Our whole family had been sports oriented. My dad had played a lot of semipro but never had any opportunity to do anything with it. Back then he had to make a living.

I think they were pleased. The only thing that they didn't like, of course, and I didn't like, as well, is Sunday baseball, because, you know, there are better things to do on Sunday than play baseball. But that's part of it. You know, you sign a contract and you abide by the contract. And sometimes my turn would come around on Sunday. Even though I didn't like to play baseball on Sunday, it was my job. You try to justify Sunday activities in the sense that, well, there are a lot of farmers, they have to get up and milk those cows on Sunday, they have to take care of their animals. That's their work, that's their livelihood. Lot of gas stations, lot of guys have to work that pump. And in my particular profession, it was baseball.

My dad was a machinist. He worked on the railroad early in his life and then during the war years, World War II, he worked on submarines. We moved to California. He worked at Mare Island at the submarine base. Then after the war was over, why, we moved back to Idaho, and he worked as a mechanic in an auto shop and truck shop.

I always had work during the off-season. But back when I signed it wasn't important that you have a college education. Back then there were a lot of jobs that required less skill and not as much knowledge and expertise as in this high-tech world today. There was always work.

I had a butter route – butter, cottage cheese, other kinds of cheese. Delivered to all the stores in the valley. I did that, and that paid quite well. And there were other things that held my interest, such as carpentry work, which I did quite a bit of and still do a lot of today. Anyway, there was always a lot of things that I could do. I was not just a one-dimensional person. I did have a lot of other interests.

It's a year-round job, now, it has to be. I mean, they may take a month, a month and a half, two months off. But then they get right back with it and get ready for the year, because they don't have as much time in spring training as we did, to get ready and take off the excess weight that you may have put on in the wintertime.

I ran mine off. I did a lot of hunting and fishing, and that sort of thing, in the off-season as well. And running up and down hills. I didn't have any trouble with that. Matter of fact, I would get ready for the spring by doing a lot of running and staying in shape. And I worked out inside. My brother would catch me. I was ready to go four or five innings when I got to spring training. A lot of guys didn't back then. I mean, they sat around the whole winter, drank beer, came to spring training twenty or thirty pounds overweight, and then they nearly died. After three days of spring training, you could walk down the street and you could tell who was the athlete and who wasn't. I mean they were so stiff and sore they could hardly walk.

．　．　．

You know, in 1960, when we won the World Series, there was hardly a night when I was home. I was out speaking, promoting baseball to different groups, and so on and so forth. We did that. Not just me, there were others doing the same thing on our ballclub. We did it for nothing. I'd say that more than 90 percent of the time we did it for nothing. Little Leagues and different organizations. Of course, I spoke at a lot of the churches, too. But still I was promoting baseball.

It was a crazy series, 1960. The Yankees were predicted to beat us four straight. And on paper we couldn't match them, because they had better players. But we also had twenty-five guys that wanted to win, and we did everything we could to win. We had guys that wouldn't quit. I mean, we'd get bombed one day and we'd come back and we'd beat 'em 3–2 or 5–4 the next day.

We just had a group of guys that meshed very well, that got along well together, that liked each other, and fought for each other. And we were fortunate to win it. Of course, like Geno Cimoli said, "The

Yankees broke all the records, but we won all the money." It wasn't very much, but what there was, we won. Our purse was $6,800.

They hadn't had a World's Champion there in Pittsburgh in thirty-something years. What was it, 1931, '32, or something like that? And here we are, thirty years later, facing the same organization.

That whole year was exceptional. We were winning games we had no business winning. I mean, we'd be down three runs in the ninth inning with two outs and a 3–2 count on the hitter, and we'd come back to win it. A guy might get a walk or a base hit or an error or something. And first thing you know, a guy would pop one out and we'd wind up winning the game. And that didn't happen just once. It happened about thirty-four times during that season, where we won the game from the seventh inning on. Which shows you the character of our ball-club. We had guys that would just get it up and grind it out. Don Hoak, I think, was probably as instrumental in the spirit of our ballclub as anybody. He was nicknamed the Tiger, and he played like one. He'd scratch and claw and he'd motivate the other guys on the ballclub. He'd get things going, and if he didn't get things going, why, he'd keep it going. That's the way it was. It was really a fun year.

We got Don from Cincinnati. We got him in the trade that we got Harvey Haddix and Smokey Burgess. And of course, we got Vinegar Bend Mizell from the Cardinals. And Bill Virdon. He was with us before we got Vinegar, though. It was those four or five guys that really made the difference in our ballclub.

And Danny Murtaugh. I had about five managers I played for, but Murtaugh was the best. You knew where you stood with him. Also, he knew each individual player and what he could do in a tough situation. He knew what guy to put in at the right time, and who to take out. He was pretty good at that. He knew exactly what a guy could do in a tough situation. He knew what was inside them.

You knew where you stood with Murtaugh. He would talk to you. Some managers, if you didn't perform, say you had a bad day, you'd walk in, the manager's walking right at you and he doesn't say boo to you. You could've hit five line drives and guys made spectacular plays and yet the manager wouldn't come up to you and say, "Hey, you'll get 'em tomorrow. You'll get 'em. Nice going. You did a good job."

This is the classic example – Leo Durocher. You could tell he was a front-runner. When he was coaching third base, he'd go down and talk to the .300 hitter, but you think to a-.230, .240 hitter? *No way!* He ignored those guys. But he would go down and talk to the .300 hitter, while they were hitting, and offer encouragement. I saw that so much it made me sick. And I liked Leo. He was okay, but you've got to treat every ballplayer the same. Especially if you're manager. They'll produce for you, they'll come around.

That's all it takes. You have a nucleus. I mean the line between the good ballplayer and the great ballplayer is very fine. It's not that much of a difference, but all you need is maybe three or four of that kind of guy on your ballclub and you'll end up winning.

After the World Series, Ted Williams asked me, "How did you pitch to Mantle and Maris?"

I said, "Inside."

He said, "Inside! You're crazy!"

I said, "No. When I say inside, I mean about three or four inches off the plate inside, not where they can handle it."

Because both of those guys are anxious hitters. They want to swing the bat. So they see one coming in there and they've already committed themselves before they realize the ball is off of the plate. That's why it was important to know those hitters before I pitched against them. Because I'd never had the opportunity to see them play or pitch against them.

There were a couple of those guys – the report was not right! Moose Skowron was one of them! They said, "You can pitch him outside." Well, I did and he hit the ball. Yeah, you can pitch him outside, but you'd better be about four, five, six inches off of the plate. He'll chase that ball and he'll strike out. But they didn't say that.

He was one guy and Tony Kubek was another. They said not to pitch him inside. Well, I pitched him away, and the first time up he hit a ball that hit the third base bag for a base hit. And the next time up, base hit into left field. I said, "To heck with that report." I started going inside and I got him out.

In the World Series I was the first one, I think it was in the fifth game . . . I got the first hit. About the fifth inning. We weren't getting anybody on base. I got a double – thought I hit it good enough I might have hit a home run. I was more of a line drive hitter. I didn't hit the ball in the air an awful lot. That was in Yankee Stadium, down the line.

∎ ∎ ∎

I did everything I could to help myself when I was in the big leagues. I'd study the hitters. We did have meetings prior to every ballgame, and we'd go over the hitters. The grapevine. When I first got up there, we didn't keep charts on anybody. It was all memory stuff, you know, from other players.

And I could also pick up signs pretty well. Same way with the opposing pitcher. I'd say 80 percent of the time I could tell you what he was going to throw just by some of his mannerisms, either in his windup or the grip or the way he stepped, whatever.

I won several games with my bat. Ewell Blackwell, I remember beating him 2–1 one day. Had the bases loaded in either the seventh or eighth inning, and I ran the count 3–2. I was good enough to foul off a couple, three pitches, then he threw that big old sidearm curve of his and hit me right in the fanny. So I drove in the winning run. I can't say it was all that fun, but at least you won a ballgame, and I'd sacrifice that any time.

That was the fun part for pitchers, being able to get up there and take their cuts. But it's still a great game. It *still* is. Gosh, you know, I could be driving by a Little League game and want to stop and watch. I'm still a fan. You know, it's still in your blood. It just doesn't come out because you're retired from the game. The game doesn't leave you. You may leave the game or be forced away from the game. You just don't get it out of your blood.

And how some of these guys that have played the game, all of a sudden when they're out of it they just sever all ties with baseball. With players that they played with, everybody. They have nothing to do with it. And I think a lot of it is bitterness. Some of it. Because they weren't handled or treated like a person, like an individual who had feelings. The game today, as it was a little bit then, too, is very cold-blooded.

I think most players–and I'm no different than any of the other guys–want to be remembered as a competitor, a guy that gave everything he could to help win a ballgame or have a successful season. And that's what I think most players want to be remembered as, being a good competitor. Not being a guy who makes excuses. There are a lot of guys who make an excuse before the game why they're not going to win. And those guys are losers.

At the beginning of my career, when our team lost a lot, I just kept telling myself: "I'm not going to be the one that screws up. I'm not going to be the reason for losing this game. If we lose, I'm not going to be the reason."

It was very discouraging. I lost my first two games, both against Robin Roberts with Philadelphia. And the same guy made the same mistake, made the same error. I mean it was just like a rerun on the TV.

First two games that I pitched in. The score was tied, going into the seventh inning, either the seventh or the eighth – been so long I can't remember. I'm pitching. They had a man on second base, and with two outs, one of their guys hits a little looper into left field just over the head of the shortstop, and Rojek, Stan Rojek, goes back waving his arms, "I got it, I got it, I got it." And all of a sudden he *hears* Ralph Kiner, with his big feet, stomping in. So he stops and Ralph stops, and the ball falls in and the guy scores. I get beat 3–2.

And the same thing happened four days later in Philadelphia, again against Roberts. Same play, same everything. Yeah, big Ralph . . . but you couldn't blame him. He was trying to get to the ball, and of course when Rojek called, he backed off, and Rojek, when he heard him coming, he stopped, too.

That's the way my career started out, and it didn't change much over the years. For several years it was just like that. You just have to go out there and keep a positive attitude and just do the best you can.

I guess I was programmed for that early, because when I played in Meridian, Idaho, our high school team, if I didn't strike out everybody and hit, we didn't win then either. So it was nothing new for me, to have this happen.

But I think my outlook on life had a lot to do with it. After all, baseball is just a game. There are more important things in life than baseball. And I think that your attitude about life and keeping things in perspective is what's really important. Hey, when your career is over, that doesn't tell you where you're going, whether you're going up or down. It's how you live and how you get along with people and the way you've lived your life. Those are the most important things.

I can remember another ballgame. I don't remember the score, but I remember I had the bases loaded, and there were two outs, so guys were running. I had a guy hit a pop up – this was when Jack Shepard was the catcher. Jack was a brilliant student out in California. I think it was Stanford that he graduated from, but he didn't have good baseball sense, I didn't think.

But a guy pops up about three feet in front of home plate. And he's hollering, "I got it, I got it, I got it." Only he didn't get it. The ball hit three feet fair, he missed it completely, and because it was an easy out, the guy wasn't really running to first. So Jack picks up the ball, fires it past the first baseman, missed him completely, and then the right fielder picks it up and he throws it past third, and the guy that hit the ball circled the bases, cleared the bases. Nobody touched the ball.

Things like that happened to me during my career. You look at that and you look at the won-loss record and you say, "Well, he wasn't too good." But there weren't too many good things that happened on the field, either, a lot of years of my career.

But when we finally did start putting things together, that's when baseball was fun. Though it was always fun to put on a major league uniform, play with the big boys, so to speak.

Bob Cerv

September 19–20, 1994, Lincoln, Nebraska

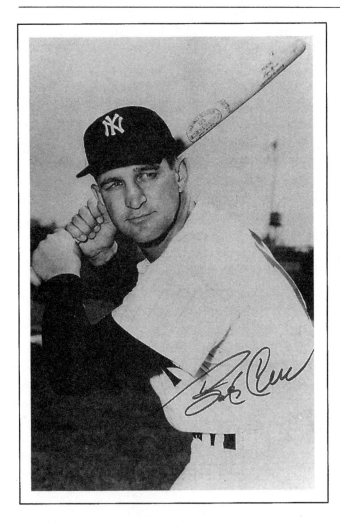

Bob Cerv played outfield from 1951 to 1962. In addition to playing nine seasons with the Yankees (six of which were less than a full season), Cerv played for the Kansas City Athletics, the Los Angeles Angels, and the Houston Colt 45s (now the Astros). A .276 lifetime hitter, Cerv played in three World Series for the Yankees. In 1958 with the Athletics, he hit .305 with thirty-eight home runs and 105 runs batted in.

Did you ever watch DiMaggio swing? I don't know how he hit the ball. How could a guy get as much power as he had? What did the work? The *bat* did the work. He made the head of that bat work.

Either you can hit or you can't. I don't think you can teach hitting. The only way you get to be a good hitter, I think, is you've just got to swing the bat, swing the bat, swing the bat.

When I was a kid, I used to go out to my grandfather's farm. They had walnut trees, and the walnuts would drop in the fall.

My grandfather would say, "Go pick them up!"

I'd whine, "I don't wanna do that."

So one day my grandmother said, "Grandpa, go make him a bat."

He had a shop and a lathe. He flattened one side of a piece of wood, and man, after that there never *was* a walnut on the ground. Hitting walnuts. I'd hit them into a little creek out there. I suppose it was maybe seventy-five, one hundred yards from where these trees were.

They also had big cottonwood trees on the farm. My grandfather hung a big chain from it—I don't know how he got up there—and he drilled a hole in a baseball, which he fixed to the chain. I'd hit that thing, and it would go way out there and come back. I'd hit that thing by the hours.

My uncle and dad played a lot of ball. And when I was a kid, I was always a batboy, shagged balls. Then, when I got older I started to go out to the farm during the summers and usually stayed the whole summer. Helped. There was work to do. Just to haul cobs, feed the chickens and hogs. The men were out in the field sunup to sundown. I lived in town, little town of Weston. The farm was about five miles west.

You had horses in those days. If you were a rich, rich farmer you'd have horses that you'd work a half-day, then take another set. Well, there weren't too many people like that, so you'd have to rest those horses two or three hours. So they'd go to work from maybe seven in the morning till noon, then give the horses about a three-hour rest and go again until dark. During the noon hour my grandfather always hit fly balls for my uncle.

They had, at that time, the Pioneer Night League. Wahoo was in it. There was probably six or eight towns. It was pretty good ball—semipro, but these guys were good. A lot of them were ex-pros. That's really how I got started.

About 1942—I was just about a sophomore in high school—I was sixteen, and I played Legion ball in Hastings. In fact, Yogi would come up to the tournament from St. Louis. They usually won it. He could hit that ball even then. Yog, he just had a knack. If he did something wrong, it was right. That's his whole life. I always thought the Lord took real good care of him.

Anyway, they needed somebody in the Pioneer Night League. I could hit the ball pretty well, so I started playing. Used to play two or three games a week, night games. And I did very well there and continued to play. Guys started going into the service – and they were needing more – and I played a couple of years there.

My dad was a truck driver most of his life. He *loved* to drive those trucks. After I was born we lived on the farm, oh, two, three years, then hit tough times around '29, '30. The bottom fell out. In the meantime, I had an uncle that had a business in Weston, gas and trucking, so my father started working for him and we moved to town.

When I was a kid – oh about '38, '39, in there – my dad drove a refrigerator truck. They hauled butter and, I suppose, chickens. Once a year, when I was about eleven or twelve years old, I got to make a trip with him, always to New York. And we'd always go to a baseball game. I saw Lou Gehrig hit three home runs in two games. A couple of years in a row, I got to see him play and I always used to come back and say, "I'm going to play for the Yankees someday." That was my motivation. I set that goal.

That's why I really signed with the Yankees. I could have signed with other clubs. I always wanted to be a Yankee.

But *years* ago, I was a Tiger fan. Because Wahoo Sam Crawford come from Wahoo, Nebraska, and that was in the county, seven miles east of where I lived, and I'd always heard about him.

I graduated from high school and went into the navy. I was on a destroyer. We were called the "Sacrificial Lambs." We would go out on picket duty, and then the kamikazes would knock hell out of us. I was aboard the USS *Claxton*, and on November 1, 1944, one hit us. It killed five guys and twenty-three got wounded. We were sinking when the USS *Abner Reid* come alongside. In two or three minutes, she sunk. We were the first ship to get hit by a kamikaze in the Philippine Campaign.

Then we went on, our squadron, up to Okinawa and all through the Philippines. We had just three of our squadron left. Five got sunk. A lot got sunk. You never read about how many got sunk.

After the second atomic bomb, we were heading back to the States. We'd gone from Hawaii to the Panama Canal to Guantánamo when we got orders to proceed to Washington, D.C., up the Potomac River. Our squadron was going to get the Presidential Unit Citation. And that's when I met Harry Truman.

Truman came aboard to give us the citation.

He says, "Is anyone from Missouri?"

No.

"Kansas?"

No.

"Nebraska?"

Yep.

So he came up and we shook hands. Then, in 1958 they had a Bob Cerv night in Kansas City, and Harry presented me with an embossed cover of the *Saturday Evening Post*. And he said, "I remember you. You were that kid." That many years later!

And he said, "Come around and talk to me sometime."

And I did. Hell, in those days they didn't protect them that much. I'd pull up, tell them who I was, they'd say come on in.

Heck of a nice guy. And the most ordinary guy. He liked you, he'd tell you; he didn't like you, he'd tell you.

■ ■ ■

In 1958 Roger Maris came over to Kansas City. Harry Craft was the manager, and Harry said, "Well, we got Maris and we got all these rumors that he's R.A." That's baseball talk for red ass. He said, "On the next trip you're going to have to room with him."

I said, "I don't care who I room with."

So we checked in and I'm up in the room, and all at once Maris says, "What the hell am I rooming with you for?"

I said, "Well, Rog, the skipper said he wanted to know what the hell makes you tick."

And he said, after a couple of days, "You know, I like you. You told me the damn truth." After that we were the best friends.

The next year we played together, and he was having a helluva year. He got to listening. I tried to help him. He was hitting over .300, then he had an appendix attack. And he made the All-Star team that year. Then, during the winter, he got traded to New York. After I came back to New York from Kansas City in '60, he said, "Let's get an apartment together."

We moved out to where they play tennis, Forest Hills. From our apartment we could see the tennis courts. He had a great year that year. Most Valuable Player.

In '61 Mantle stayed with us, the three of us. Everybody used to talk and we used to laugh at those stories, how they don't get along. And here they were living together. Nicest guy, Maris. And he got the bummest rap I've ever seen – and I used to *like* Cannon.

It was Jimmy Cannon. Cannon would say, "I'll get an interview with him!"

I'd say, "There's no damn way you're going to get an interview from him because he's out there working now."

Because when he went out in that field, he'd have already talked to those damn sportswriters for a half hour. Which he usually didn't do very much, anyway. He said, "I *need* the work or I'm not gonna do anything."

And the next day he got crucified, and after that he got crucified all the time. What Rog got mad at was when he got hurt that one year with his hand. He told me this later on.

An umpire had stepped on his hand at second base. Well, they went and took X-rays and said nothing was there. Finally, the last month of the season they said, "Oh yeah, you do have a broken hand." Well he had it the whole time. Oh, he just blew his top.

Then he had two hellish years with St. Louis and a lot of them said he should have been MVP that one year. But he didn't want it anymore.

He said, "I don't want anything, you guys. I've been through that."

What he wanted was to stay in the background. What he wanted was a beer distributorship. And he got one.

Rooming with them, hell, was just like rooming with anybody else. After games, you go home. Although Mantle, sometimes, didn't always go home.

It was a great year. It was a lot of fun. Both of them might have hit sixty or more that year. We were living together, and one would say, "Well, got to hit a couple to catch up to you tonight."

Then Mantle got some cold or something, and Mel Allen sent him to some doctor who supposedly hit the bone with the needle. Then infection set in and he didn't play much. He didn't play much in the World Series, either.

Maris never got the credit. He was a great outfielder. There weren't many better right fielders than he was. He just had a good arm. His ball was always soft, good stuff on it.

What really made me mad the year Maris hit sixty-one home runs was that he didn't get enough help from the PR department. Today it doesn't make any difference, but in those days they didn't want people from outside of their organization to break records. They wanted a Yankee to do it. I think that years ago each team had a certain type of guy they wanted to play in their organization. The ones that competed for the top. If Mantle had done it . . . he could've done anything, been fine. But Maris? Hey, he come from Kansas City.

• • •

I was twenty-five years old when I signed. I went to the University of Nebraska on the GI Bill. In fact, the last time they ever won Big Seven or Big Eight championships in baseball or basketball was 1950, and that's when I was there. I was the first baseball All-American from Nebraska and played guard on the basketball team. I was an eight-letter man, '47 to '50.

I was just inducted into the University of Nebraska Hall of Fame. This Friday I go into another one, for high school. When you get old, you get all these accolades.

Joe McDermott signed me out of Nebraska. I think that years ago he was with the Cardinals, and then he was with the Yankees. Years and years ago he signed Johnny Hopp, too, but he was with the Cardinals then.

He told me, "I'm positive you can play triple-A ball right away. It's not up to me, but I'll recommend it."

The Yankees were the only team interested in me that gave me a chance to go to triple-A. Well, I did go there and then I stayed, but I don't think I was expected to. I'm pretty sure the Yankees were going to send me down to Joplin, Class C. That's where Mantle was, and Whitey Herzog and Johnny Blanchard, a whole bunch of them. But I did so well. I think I hit over .300 the rest of the summer. I got there about July. I think I drove in over sixty runs. I had twelve doubles, thirteen triples, and fourteen home runs. Hit over .300. But they were a last-place club. Then the next year I led everything. I won the batting championship.

I don't know if you remember Joe Kuhel. He played for the Washington Senators. I never saw him play, but they said that he no doubt was the fanciest first baseman that ever played – at footwork.

He was the manager at Kansas City, triple-A. He said, "Bob, I know you just come out of college. Just try to forget everything you learned in college, and we'll try to help you."

And then there was a guy by the name of Jimmy Gleeson, his coach. Gleeson played for the Cincinnati Reds years ago. He took me under his wing and kind of told me what to do and how to do it. One time I was in a slump and he said, "Hey, do you drink?"

I said, "Not very much."

He said, "Well, tonight you're going to, because you're getting depressed."

So we went out and drank beer all night. God, I felt terrible the next day. But all at once I started beating the hell out of that ball. And he said, "See, that's what you needed to get relaxed."

But that's what the old timers used to do. Because if I got hurt and couldn't play, *he* had to play. He was a player-coach. He was old, in his forties.

He said, "You got to be relaxed." He'd always say, "You can't press."

Here I am 25 years old and they're treating me like a kid. But I *was* a rookie.

The next year I went up for a short cup of coffee. Mantle got sent down and I went up and never got to play. What the heck good does that do?

So I went down and I'd stay half a year and get sent back. Finally, in '54 my options ran out—they had to keep me or sell me. Well they didn't get rid of me until 1956, and that was my only self-satisfaction.

I knew I could play a little ball. I played three years at Kansas City—with the A's—and had over seventy home runs. In 1958, I hit .305, had 105 RBIs and thirty-eight home runs. Beat Ted Williams out of the All-Star position. He caddied for me. In those days the players and coaches chose. It wasn't like now, a popularity contest.

. . .

My first raise came when they raised the minimum salary from $5,000 to $6,000. And then if you got sent back to the minor leagues your salary went back down lower. You didn't get your major league salary down there.

Finally—I think it was in '56—hell, I had graduated, I had a degree, I could teach, coach. I had a couple of majors. I had an industrial arts major and that was always worth about $1,500 more in the schools—shop classes. Heck, with that $1,500 and with coaching a sport, you could get about $5,500. After all, I never did anything in the off-season. I always had a large family—we raised ten kids—and I always told my wife that we had enough money. I'd stay home and help take care of the kids, get to know them a little bit. So why the heck should I go to New York for $6,000? Although I always knew I would get a bonus at the end of the year, because they were winning pennants then. But then they finally gave me a $3,000 raise that year.

Then I got traded to Kansas City.

This goes back to late August or September, just before they could add some players. I don't know who it was, I think it was Slaughter come over. Anyway, that day was nasty in New York, humid. It was in the nineties and it felt like . . . That day I threw batting practice early. It was so hot that the guy that usually pitched after me couldn't go, so I went another ten minutes. Maybe I went thirty minutes throwing that day. Then everybody was just puffing and puffing. I made it to the dugout and was sitting there and everybody went in the clubhouse and Stengel came up.

He started talking. He'd always rattle on. And he went on, "Oh, I think we just got Slaughter." Some ballplayer or other. And he was talking about how great this guy was and then he said, "Oh, and by the way, one of you guys is going to Kansas City."

I'm the only one sitting there. I walked into the clubhouse and said, "Fellas, I'm not gonna be here next year. I'm going to Kansas City."

They said, "You don't know."

I said, "You wait and see."

The funny thing, Don Larsen and I *both* were supposed to go to Kansas City, but then he pitches the perfect game and they kept him. They could hardly get rid of him.

That winter I got traded. I was right!

■　■　■

My mom and dad used to come down to Kansas City to watch me play a couple or three times a year. Maybe more. Hell, there used to be trainloads coming down when we were in town.

I know when they had the Bob Cerv night in '58, that was the largest crowd they had in, what, a year, year and a half. Filled the place up.

That was the year I broke my jaw sliding into home base. I broke that on a Saturday, didn't play Sunday, had an off-day Monday, and played Tuesday night. Wired. The jaw was wired. In fact, I played with a broken hand *and* a broken toe. I don't think I hit a home run during the entire time I was wired up. Hurt too much when I swung hard. You just don't realize that you can't swing with your mouth tight.

In the middle of the '58 season, when I had my day, they gave me a $3,000 raise. And after the season was over – and I'd had a great year – they said, "Come on down, we want to talk contract." So we went in. Parke Carroll was the general manager. They had the comptroller there, the vice-president was there, they had an attorney there. I think there were five guys and myself.

Well, we started negotiating. I started out a little outrageous, but I knew what I wanted. I started out, "Well, I want forty."

"No way!"

We went back and forth, and finally they said, "You know, we'd maybe give you that but you struck out seventy-seven times."

I held out. I didn't go to spring training. I was with a sportswriter and he told me, "I think they're ready to sign you." So my wife and I got on a plane and flew down. Got in late at night and the next morning we go down to breakfast and Parke Carroll saw me and said, "Hey, come on up to my room."

Went up to his room and he said, "Here it is, thirty grand." He said, "Boy, we got a lot of publicity out of this, didn't we? Now we'll sell tickets!"

It's all business.

■ ■ ■

One thing about me, I could pinch-hit when I was twenty-eight, twenty-nine years old, where most guys had to be in their thirties or middle thirties, like a Mize, or somebody like that. Hell, when I was young I could do that. Stengel had me pinch-hitting right away. One time somebody told me I had thirteen pinch-hit home runs.

I don't know why I was so good – just went up and swung. I always liked the fastball. Maybe they threw the fastball, I don't know. I know I also had a pinch-hit home run in the World Series off of Roger Craig. In fact, somebody told me this year that I pinch-hit in the World Series and never made an out, three pinch hits. So you never know.

I don't know why. I was just put in that situation. I always said I was a pretty good first-ball hitter. And no doubt that was one of the reasons: I always looked for that good hummer. And I always could hit that fastball pretty good. And the philosophy always was, "Don't throw anything soft to that pinch hitter, because he's been sitting on the bench the whole game."

I liked the ball up and away. The fastball, of course. So I'd look for that hummer and usually rip it. I'd always try to swing hard at the first two, then cut down on my swing and try to make contact.

But I could hit the slider, too, I don't know why. Slider didn't bother me. Change-ups didn't fool me either, because I stayed back in the box. Somewhere I learned that. If a change-up is down, then you're gonna pound it into the ground, but not if it's up. I hit a lot of change-ups up. You had to stay back.

But with that slow "aunt Suzy," I didn't do too well. If I took it, they said it was a strike, and if I swung at it, they said it would've been a ball.

After a while, I conceded. I got a roll, pinch hitter, and I went along with it. Another thing, I got heavier and heavier—I mean weight-wise. And the legs got older and older. If I knew then what I know now, I would've got lighter and lighter. But in those days, as I always said, "The hardest push is from the table."

I suppose I could've screamed and hollered. What the hell, you had to do *something*. You didn't get a helluva lot of credit for pinch-hitting.

I know one night, we're playing in Detroit and big Bob Bruce is pitching. I think we were a couple of runs down and Stengel put me in to pinch-hit and boom, in the seats, three-run home run. Next day's headlines: Mantle Goes 3 for 4 as Yankees Win. Heh, heh, heh. Just *sometime* let's get it straight.

Cal McLish

April 15–16, 1994, Edmond, Oklahoma

Cal McLish pitched from 1944 to 1964, excluding his year of military service in 1945 and minor league assignments in 1950 and 1952 to 1955. In addition to playing four years with the Cleveland Indians, he pitched for the Brooklyn Dodgers, the Pirates, Cubs, Reds, White Sox, and Phillies. In fifteen full- and part-time major league seasons, he won ninety-two games, lost ninety-two, and compiled a 4.01 earned run average. His nineteen wins for Cleveland in 1959 were second best in the American League.

I was born in a barn, believe it or not. My parents were picking cotton for a farmer, and he had just built a big barn. We moved into that barn, me and my niece – my oldest sister's daughter. She was born one and a half months before I was. So I was an uncle the day I was born.

Then we moved into a dugout for a couple of years. Y'all don't know what dugouts are. It's a goddamn cave in the side of a hill. It's got a wooden door and grass growing on top of it with a chimney going through there. Then we moved down in the canyon just outside of Anadarko, a place called Washita, and we lived there until we moved to Oklahoma City in the winter of 1933. My oldest brother was driving a dump truck for some company, and he moved us up here in the back of a dump truck to Oklahoma City, about four or five blocks from Holland Field.

That spring – 1934, I was seven years old – after we moved to the city, the first time I saw the lights on at Holland Field I didn't know what was there. The whole sky was lit up. I wanted to see what was going on and went over there, and *goddamn*, guys running around, had uniforms on . . . hell, I didn't know *what* they were doing. But from that day on I was over there, looking through the knotholes, trying to sneak in.

I got to know the groundskeeper – he had two sons about my age, and I got to know them. Pretty soon I'm picking up pebbles in the infield with a bucket on my arm, hanging those tin scores on the scoreboard, shagging foul balls down in left field. Finally I worked my way up to ball boy just before they called the season off because of the war.

■　■　■

My father named me Calvin Coolidge Julius Caesar Tuskahoma – a president, a Roman emperor, and an Indian chief. My mother told me that he didn't get to name any of the other kids. He tried to catch up on me, but I think he was in the firewater.

I was thirteen years old when my father died. He was sixteen years older than my mother. When they met, he was working on a ranch down where my mother was living. He was thirty-two and she was sixteen.

I don't even think my mother went to high school. I know she didn't graduate high school. Just worked all her life. Hell, she worked pulling a cotton-sack when I was a baby. She raised all of us kids, didn't ever really make any money. She just worked her whole life. I don't think she ever made over thirty-two dollars a week.

When we moved to Oklahoma City, she worked for a cafe, and she got five dollars a week and whatever day-old bread she could bring home, and doughnuts, pretzels (I remember pretzels), potato chips (I remember potato chips). Then she worked in a bag factory close to where we lived. Walked to work, walked back home. Must have had a ten-block walk. In other words, we were very poor.

When I signed, I signed for a $1,500 bonus, and after what they withheld, I turned it over to her. I didn't keep a penny of it.

But as far as a childhood goes, I had a happy childhood. Spent all my time at the ballpark. Go down and get a nickel and go to the Friday-night movie. When the marble season came, I shot marbles. When top season came, I spiked tops. We played all kinds of roller skating games out in the street, hockey with a milk can. Played every kind of little game that you could play. Used to walk down the railroad tracks and pick up rocks and hit them with a stick. That's why I was a good fungo hitter. Gene Mauch will tell you I was the best fungo hitter he ever seen. Of course, I incorporated that fungo swing into my golf game. That's why my golf game isn't too good all the time.

We used to play softball at school. Never ate lunch, never took a lunch to school. Never had any money to buy lunch. But we'd go out and check out a bat and a softball and play softball during lunch break. Couldn't wait to get out there and do it. I'd rather do that than eat, although there were a lot of times I was hungry. But after that I never ate lunch all my life. I eat lunch now every once in a while, and I feel like horseshit the rest of the day.

We were poor, but like I say, there were a lot of people poor in those days. We had a lot of fun as kids. We built our own scooters–three-wheel scooters with ball-bearing wheels. We used to get up top of Tenth and Indiana; there was a big incline and we used to ride all the way down, a four- or five-block ride, then walk back up top and do it again.

Must have been thirteen before I ever had a bicycle. I rode around Oklahoma City one time backwards. On Grand Boulevard, which circles Oklahoma City. One day I didn't have anything to do, and I decided I'm going to ride my bicycle around Grand Boulevard. Sat up on the handlebars and rode it backwards all the way around. Come to a stop light and rode up to a filling station and rode around until the light changed.

One day when I was thirteen years old, my buddy came over and dropped his bicycle out in the front yard, and he came in the front door just as I happened to come out the back door. I saw the bicycle. I didn't know what it was doing there; I didn't know he'd gone inside. I got on it and started riding it a little ways, so I decided I'd ride it to Anadarko, which was about sixty-nine miles. Had a sister who lived there.

Summertime. So I pedaled down to Anadarko, 69 miles. Stayed three days with her, then pedaled it back home. Of course, there wasn't any traffic in those days. You'd find plums on the side of the road somewhere. Go up to a farmhouse and get a drink of water out of somebody's well. That's the way I grew up.

I played shortstop on my high school team. We were state champions my sophomore year. We played down at Norman, at the University of Oklahoma. We won the state championship. But the year before that, at Roosevelt Junior High, we had the same team playing hardball that played softball. We just switched our shortstop and pitcher: our shortstop in hardball pitched in softball; and our shortstop in softball pitched in hardball. I was a first baseman then. We won the state championship both in hardball and in softball.

When I was in junior high, the baseball coach thought that me and Leroy Jarvis were something special. Leroy was a catcher who lived across the street from me. He came up the same time as Joe Garagiola and Bill Sardi. Three of the top kid catchers in the whole country. And Leroy was probably ahead of the other two.

I guess we were a little bit more advanced for our age than other kids. We always had our gloves, we were always playing catch. We'd take it to the gym in the wintertime and play catch. *Boy*, you'd hear that mitt popping up there. I think our coach thought that we had a chance to be professional baseball players, so he wouldn't let me play football. I'm glad he wouldn't, because my bone structure wasn't football.

I guess it was always in the back of my mind that I was going to be a ballplayer. As a matter of fact, I told that to one of my teachers in high school.

I used to dive out the window and go across the street to hear the jukebox. He said to me one day, "You don't want to grow up to be a wooly." That's what he called guys who didn't care, who didn't make any plans for the future.

"You've got a good mind! You don't want to become a wooly!"

I said, "I'm gonna be a ballplayer."

That was my junior year in high school. Through my sophmore year, I played shortstop, first base. I really wasn't a pitcher till I started playing American Legion baseball. But I didn't dote on becoming a major league player. Then, of course, when the scouts came around, I thought of it.

That summer, in 1933, Jack Ryan, the Cardinals scout, had taken me and Leroy Jarvis to see the Cubs play a doubleheader in St. Louis. Those were the only major league games I had seen. But I'd seen every exhibition game they played down here at Holland Field. I'd seen the Yankees come through here. I saw Satchel Paige and the House of David, the Birmingham Black Barons. Plus I more or less grew up in the ballpark down there. I saw all the Detroit farmhands, the Cardinals farmhands: Howie Pollet, Virgil Trucks, Dick Wakefield, Hoot Evers, Birdie Tebbetts, Harry "The Cat" Brecheen, Al Brazle, Ted Wilks . . .

If you watch them, if you watch professional players' mannerisms, pretty soon it just ingrains in you. You don't throw like a girl and you don't step over here to throw over there. You watch 'em throw, and watch 'em take infield, and watch 'em hit. It grows in you, without knowing what you're really learning. But you're learning.

In 1943, the Cardinals also took me to St. Louis for the World Series, the Yankees and the Cardinals. I didn't know it then, but the reason was so I could go up and be introduced to Judge Kenesaw Mountain Landis.

There was a Washington Senators scout come through here, and he had us sign an agreement in Leroy Jarvis's mother's front room that we would go to Washington, D.C., for two weeks and work out with the big club. Work out with the Washington Senators. And we agreed to go. All expenses paid to Washington, D.C., and work out with the Washington Senators. Hell, it was a big deal! We couldn't wait. But it was just that, to work out, with a chance of *maybe* signing.

Well, what had happened, Joe Cambria, the scout, tried to make a contract out of it. The Cardinals had me come to St. Louis so I could meet Judge Landis and explain what happened. I told Judge Landis, "Well, we signed on a napkin in Leroy's house." And that's exactly what happened right there. But we're the cause, me and Leroy Jarvis, of that rule being written that you could not sign a high school kid till he or his class graduated.

. . .

I had just started pitching when Tom Greenwade signed me. He was a Dodgers scout before he went over to the Yankees. If you can picture Abe Lincoln, you can picture Tom Greenwade. Even the hat that he wore. Very serious guy. A good scout. Greenwade didn't want to sign Bobby Morgan, and Leroy and I wouldn't sign unless he signed Bobby.

It was Greenwade came through here one time and had a tryout camp. Bobby Morgan and Leroy Jarvis and I went to the tryout camp, and he was talking about signing us. The Cardinals had some scouts here looking at us. The Cubs had a couple, Pittsburgh had one. But we ended up signing with Tom Greenwade because he told me that the Dodgers were a coming organization. And he was right—on the money! Not meaning the Cardinals weren't, they already were.

I turned eighteen in my senior year in high school, and I thought I was going into the army. I had no idea that I might be playing ball the next summer. But in my senior year I get a wire from Branch Rickey wanting me to come to Bear Mountain, New York, for spring training. That's when they had spring training at the West Point Field House at Bear Mountain. They couldn't go south because of the war. That was in 1944. Ralph Branca came the same year, but a little later. Clyde King came the same year.

I went up to Bear Mountain with a pair of moccasins, a pair of jeans, Central High letter jacket, and a three-dollar suitcase I bought in a pawnshop down on Reno—that was the "bad" street in Oklahoma City in those days.

I walked into the hotel at Bear Mountain, and one of the first guys I remember meeting was Curt Davis, the old pitcher. He called me over—I'm thinking he was gonna say something I could learn from—and he says, "Hey, son, don't get caught out in the rain with that suitcase. All you'll be holding is the handle."

Then Wid Matthews took me and introduced me to Mr. Rickey. He was reading the paper in the hotel lobby. Branch Rickey was a very stern man. I remember the first thing he ever said to me, straight out to me in my face, was, "How's your teeth?" He kind of yelled it at me.

Meaning, in those days the first thing they did when they'd get a young ballplayer was they checked their teeth, because it was common knowledge that bad teeth caused bad arms. So he sent Clyde Sukeforth and me over to New York, to Brooklyn, somewhere by Montague Street where the office was, to see a dentist.

Then, later on, Mr. Rickey had me meet him down at Montague Street, and we went to a clothier and he bought me a suit . . . with a vest. I'm eighteen years old and I got a pin-stripe suit with a vest to go with it! Then we stopped at a soda fountain and climbed up on the stool and had a milkshake together. He was like a god to a guy like me.

Mr. Rickey wanted me to see if I could take a correspondence course to get my high school diploma. I came home and talked to my teachers, and they said I had no chance because I'd been up there for spring training for two or three weeks.

I wired Mr. Rickey back and he sent me a ticket, and I got on the train and joined the club in St. Louis. The first time my toe hit the rubber in organized ball – 1944 – Leo Durocher called me in from the bullpen: bases loaded and no outs in the seventh inning. Rube Melton started the game. I can't even remember what it was like. I was probably in a daze.

The first thing I learned to do when I got to Brooklyn was to ride the subway. I could go anywhere in that town on the subway. Used to go out to Coney Island, have a couple of hot dogs, then go back and get off at Ebbets Field for the ballgame. Go out to Times Square and listen to Frank Sinatra sing . . . all by myself.

In Brooklyn there was always something exciting going on. Every once in a while George Raft would show up in the clubhouse, Danny Kaye would show up in the clubhouse, Audie Murphy'd show up in the clubhouse. Probably many more, I just don't remember.

I would walk into Joe's restaurant on Montague Street. I didn't know how to order off the damn menu in 1944. What is linguine? I didn't know what linguine was. But I went in there one day and I had cream of chicken soup. It was the best-tasting goddamn stuff I'd ever eaten in my life. The waiter who waited on me a lot of times knew that I had trouble ordering. He knew how much I liked that soup – I didn't eat in there that much, mostly I ate hamburgers and hot dogs – but the time or two I went in there he didn't even bring me a menu. Says, "I'll bring you something." He didn't even tell me what he was bringing. When he brought it, I ate it. It was great, whatever it was.

Carl Furillo, every time he'd go out to eat at one of his uncles or cousins or someone, he always wanted me to go with him. You know, just to have a buddy go with him. He and I and Stan Rojek had a suite of rooms in the St. George Hotel. So I went with him a lot. Different functions and dinners and restaurants. The Italian community, in other words, loved Carl Furillo. Boy, those people could eat. I'd never eaten like that.

I haven't been to Brooklyn since the Dodgers left. I just got back from New York, though. I went to a Dodgers reunion – all the people that played for the Dodgers at Ebbets Field and are still alive. There's less than fifty of us left. You wouldn't realize that.

Anyway, I stayed with the club until August, when I got my draft call and went in the service. But what Tom Greenwade told me was true. He said that if you get drafted from a big league roster, when you come back they have to keep you on a major league roster for one year, and you won't get lost in the shuffle. Which was exactly what happened in my case. Because I had no business being in the big leagues when I was eighteen years old. Hell, I didn't know what a change-up was, or a curveball, or nothing else. Hell, I was just rarin' and throwin'. I *could* throw strikes. I *could* throw the ball over the plate. But that was just about the extent of my knowledge of pitching at that time.

I went overseas for twenty-three months. When I came back, the Dodgers had to keep me for a year. Come back in July of '46 and was with them the rest of that year. Went to spring training with them in Havana, Cuba, the next year, 1947. Robinson, Campanella, and Newcombe – they all came down.

Jackie would destroy a pitcher on the bases. He'd make them balk, he'd make them throw to the wrong base. He'd do everything. I thought a lot of Jackie. Hell, he came through here one time, some kind of promotion, playing golf. I took a ride out there just to say hello to him. He saw me: "Coolidge!" Most of the guys called me Coolidge, because that was my middle name. I liked Jackie.

And I liked Roy. Roy Campanella was kind of an enlightened spirit. He'd never forget you. Of course, you're around a guy a few weeks in spring training and then two weeks in the season and you get to know a guy. You don't forget them. I don't forget many guys that I played with. Some of them are hard to recognize now. But I guess I look as old to them as they do to me.

Anyway, my arm was bad that spring of '47. I'd hurt it overseas – not war related. About a month after the war was over and we found out we weren't going to Japan, we scratched out a baseball diamond inside the Salzburg, Austria, racetrack and started playing division level baseball. That's where I hurt it.

So I went over to Pensacola, where they had all the minor league teams. They sent me over to play around the infield – second, short, and third. They sent Tommy Brown over to play first base. I played, oh, fourteen or fifteen games there for Pepper Martin's team. He was the manager of Mobile, a double-A club. I was a switch-hitter, and I think I could have become a hitter if I stayed with the Dodgers.

When the season started, of course, I had to go back to Brooklyn because I had another half-year. Burt Shotten was the manager. Two weeks later I was traded to Pittsburgh, and they didn't know anything about my playing a position. They acquired me as a pitcher.

I stayed in Pittsburgh until my year was up in July. Pittsburgh bought a pitcher from the Yankees named Mel Queen, Mel Queen's dad. In the deal, they had to send a pitcher on option to Kansas City, a Yankee triple-A club, so I went to Kansas City on option. The next year I played for Al Lopez in Indianapolis, the first year he managed in the American Association. And that winter I was traded to the Cubs. Frankie Gustine and I got traded for Clyde McCullough and Cliff Chambers.

I stayed in the Cubs organization for about seven years, most of the time in Los Angeles. One year–half a year in '49 and '51–I was with the Cubs, but the rest of the time I was in Los Angeles. Then I got traded from Los Angeles to San Diego, and that winter I was purchased by the Cleveland Indians. That's how I got to the American League.

■　■　■

Actually, the war and being on the Dodgers without minor league experience probably saved my whole career. Because I don't know where I would have wound up. I had a little bit of an edge because I went to the service *from* a big league roster, came back out of the service *to* a big league roster. They know more about you if you're on a big league roster than if you're in A ball or B ball, I guarantee you.

But I became a pitcher when I was in the Coast League. Pitching to smart hitters is how I learned. Pitching to the Billy Hermans and the Cookie Lavagettos and the Jack Grahams and the Minnie Minosos and the Al Rosens and the Suitcase Simpsons, the Les Flemmings. You bet I learned! I learned from good hitters.

I wasn't a very good pitcher. It was hard for me to impress a manager. After I'd hurt my arm and came back from the war, I threw pretty hard again, but I wasn't what you'd call a power pitcher. Pitching out in the Coast League, in Los Angeles at Wrigley Field where it was 345 feet in the slots in left center and right center, it dawned on me, in other words, that I had to change my style of pitching. I knew that I wasn't going to be a Bob Feller.

So I started learning little things, putting a little tail on the ball, as a guy by the name of Ralph Hamner told me one time. He pitched for the Cubs and the White Sox a little bit, tall thin guy. He'd throw more ground balls than anyone I'd ever seen. So it started dawning on me that if I'd learn how to do that maybe I'd be a better pitcher. Watching him pitching and talking to him is what got me to change my whole perception of pitching.

I was about twenty-one or twenty-two. I had never pitched below triple-A baseball, so I was learning at a pretty good class of baseball all this time. I took my lumps, but I had the determination, I guess. If I was low man on the totem pole, I figured I'd work my way up. That's the way I used to think about it.

And that's the way I did at Cleveland. Hell, when I got there they had Feller, Wynn, Lemon, Garcia, Score, Houtteman, Mossi, Narleski, Maglie. Good God, I thought, what in the world's going on? Of all the clubs, I wouldn't have thought it would be Cleveland! As a matter of fact, I was pitching in Venezuela when I got the news. Winter ball in Caracas. I asked, "Who? Cleveland? Oh, God!"

I *knew* what kind of pitching staff they had. But the only thing I could do was work my way up and that's what happened.

My career was pieced together so much: part of a year when I shouldn't have been there; part of a year when I come back with a bad arm; part of the next year waiting for my year to be up so I could go out and pitch a little bit. Then when I came back to the Cubs after I won twenty games in the Coast League in '50, I wasn't impressive enough to get in the rotation and stay in it. And when Cleveland bought me, I only started a couple of games that year. I worked out of the bullpen when they could use me.

In '57 was when I really started pitching – starting, relieving and doing everything, because they had a rash of bad arms. But '58 was really the first year that I started taking a regular turn, other than the Coast League. I got in the rotation and stayed there. I was 16–8 in '58.

Really, when I started pitching good was when Joe Gordon took over the club. Frank Lane had gotten rid of Bobby Bragan. But the night of Bobby's last game, I pitched in Cleveland. It's a 1–1 game going into the bottom of the ninth inning, and Ted Williams hit a home run off me. Beat us 2–1. And Bragan always said that I'm the one who got him fired. He said it jokingly.

But Joe Gordon was sitting in the stands and he says, "That guy's pitching for me!" We hit it off right away. He saw that game and he liked the way I pitched. So I responded real good to Joe Gordon.

Plus, we had a pretty good club. We had some pretty good hitters. Colavito, Woody Held, and Tito Francona had pretty good years that year. None of us was hurting for runs. Although when Gordon took over in Cleveland, there was one stretch where I pitched fifteen one-run games, and some of those the runs were unearned.

But I never considered myself a shutout pitcher. If I come down to the late innings with a big lead, well, I'm not gonna pitch a guy the same way that I would in a jam. Because you save that – something else that you learn. Why would you do that? To humiliate a guy just to pitch a shutout? I'm not gonna lead the league in shutouts, and I know that.

A good example. One time in Cincinnati, I got 'em beat 6–0, and they send Jesse Gonder up to hit. Well, I know later on they'll send Jesse Gonder up to hit again, and it might be a game where I *need* to get him. I didn't have to get him this time. All right, I let him hit a fastball. He hit it out of the ballpark. But the next time I'm facing Jesse Gonder, I may not have a 6–0 lead. So I'm gonna save what I'm gonna get him out with for the next time. I don't know if the next time happened that particular year, but that's the way I thought. I knew he was their guy on the bench. I know I'm not going to humiliate him and I know that I'm not going to show him what I might use if I *have* to get him out.

That's the way my mind works. Had to be smart. Had to be, because my stuff wasn't that good.

But before that '59 season was over, I gave up my last start. Frank Lane called me into Joe Gordon's office Friday night. I had won nineteen games. They told me that they'd like me to give up Sunday's start to Herb Score, so there wouldn't be any pressure on him. Seems like quite a while after he'd been hit in the eye, but he had had some problems. So I said, Sure. I was doing it for Herbie.

I *thought* I was doing it for Herb. Find out later on that, hell, they had already decided to trade me. So I gave up my chance to win twenty games. I packed my stuff and left Friday night, and Sunday I'm here in Oklahoma, and we score twelve runs in Kansas City. So it was possible that I could've won twenty ballgames. But if I had, it didn't mean nothing because records didn't mean nothing to me at that time. I never think about those things. I never do. What the hell, I figured I was lucky to be there as long as I was.

So that's when I got traded to Cincinnati, the first year they had the interleague trading. Cleveland had some good arms coming up then: Gary Bell, Mudcat Grant, Jim Perry, Hank Aguirre, Dick Tomanek. So I can understand why they would trade me—I must have been thirty-four then. But it kinda kicked the legs out from under me, having to go to another league.

If I'd have stayed in the American League, I don't think it would have hurt me as bad. The kind of pitcher I was, for me to have an advantage I had to know hitters very well and pitch accordingly.

But I went over to the other league. And at that time it was a little bit better league than the American League. I thought the difference was that the National League had more guys that could run, throw, field, hit and hit with power. The American League had a lot of guys that could hit the ball with power—Killebrew, Jim Bob Lemon, Roy Sievers—but they weren't complete ballplayers like Clemente and Robinson and Mays and Aaron.

There was a difference, no question about it. The big swingers hitting the dead-fish pitches gives the pitchers a lot of advantage. I had more success with big swingers, power hitters, than I did with the Bobby Richardsons and the Harvey Kuenns, guys that would put the ball in play, solid contact hitters. I had a lot of trouble with those guys, more so than with the big swingers.

Although one day I threw four home runs in one inning. It was in Fenway Park. It sounds like sour grapes, but I wanted to start, and Kirby Farrell started Bud Daley, a left-handed pitcher. Hal Lebowitz, a writer from the *Cleveland Plain Dealer*, said, "Well, McLish has been doing everything for you." And I had been.

But Farrell said, "Ah, I been working him too much."

So the Red Sox get to Bud Daley right off the bat for four or five runs. Now, who gets up in the bullpen but me, and I'm supposed to be resting.

So I came in and finished up that inning. The next inning I throw a change-up to Gene Mauch, fastball to Ted Williams, walked Jackie Jensen, then Dick Gernert hit a curve, and Frank Malzone hit a slider. Four home runs: one was on a change-up, one was on a fastball, one was on a curve, and one was on a slider. Kirby come to the mound and I was mad because I thought he ought to let me pitch to the next hitter, Pete Daley, the catcher.

But I wanted to start. I always thought I was much better as a starting pitcher. Put me in the rotation and let me take my turn, let me have my bad games, because I would pitch more times good than I'd pitch bad if they would leave me alone. And I pitched better when people left me alone. For some reason that was hard to get across to managers.

The way it worked out, if I got started off good I could go nine innings. I'd keep whatever I had, I wouldn't lose it. I think I had fifty-seven complete games out of the ninety-two wins and ninety-two losses I had. I could *go* nine. If I got by the early innings I never lost many games in the latter part of a ballgame. By then you know what your pitches are doing, and I never actually got tired. Maybe hard throwers get tired, but with my style of pitching I never got tired. I felt just as good in the ninth inning as I did in the first. When you're in a rhythm, in a groove, you don't get tired.

But Cleveland had all those good young pitchers and needed somebody to play second base, and they got Johnny Temple from Cincinnati. I wouldn't have cared where in the American League I went. I felt I could have carried on.

So I had to learn all the hitters all over again. Then, the next year, I go back to the American League with the White Sox. I can't use this as an alibi because I don't like to do that, but the year in Cincinnati and the year with the White Sox I was at my lowest ebb physically that I could possibly be in. I knew that I needed a double hernia operation, but I wouldn't get it because I had a chance to be a starting pitcher. Coming from 16–8 and 19–8, I felt like I didn't want to get away from where I was. In other words, I guess I was trying to fake it. But I was very physically run down.

I don't remember what a double hernia does to you, but I can remember when I was running it always felt like a chore. My strength was sapped. Always felt groggy. I pitched two years needing an operation, which really set me back. But when you were a pitcher like I was, you don't like to give up what chance you might have. So I didn't tell anybody.

I stayed up there in Chicago that winter, '61, and had it repaired. So now, the next year in spring training with the White Sox, we're in Sarasota and I'm feeling so goddamn good I'm like a racehorse again. I'm running footraces with Herb Score and Bob Shaw out in right field. Sprints, thirty or forty of them a day. Running with the pitchers.

Then I got traded that spring to the Phillies, and I come back and had a good year. I was 11–5. The next year I was 13–11. We did have a great ballclub and an excellent manager in Gene Mauch. I felt like I was on my way back. Then I hit the rotator cuff injury. That's what finished me. Right at the tail end of the '63 season. Came to spring training in '64 and I could hardly throw. Gene Mauch gave me all that spring and until the hot weather came.

I coached four years in Philly after I got done playing. Two of those years I was an advance scout. I think I might have been one of the first guys they sent ahead of the club. So I was two years there, seven years with Montreal, and seven years in Milwaukee. So it was sixteen years I coached. Threw a lot of batting practice. Good coaches can throw a lot of batting practice.

■   ■   ■

I think I was a good pitching coach, because I left the guys that were pitching good alone. Most pitching coaches get their name in the paper. The reason they get their name in the paper is because they *want* their name in the paper. I told every pitcher that I was ever around, "When you pitch good, *you* did it. Don't mention my name to the writers or anyone else. You did it. When you pitch *bad* don't mention my name, either.

"I'm here to help you on those days that you pitched bad, because I *know* what you do when you pitch good and I *see* what you do when you pitch bad. I'm here to help you get back over here."

That's what a pitching coach is for, and that's what I've told every pitcher I've ever had. I never had a pitcher that didn't like me or that didn't take my suggestions, but I was very careful *not* to overcoach or overteach or to blow my own horn and have my name in the paper every day.

Pitching comes down to velocity, movement, and location. That's the only three things a pitcher has to deal with – velocity that you throw the ball, the movement that you put on the ball, and where you throw the ball.

Movement can come down to natural movement. Left-handers have a natural tail on their fastball. Some pitchers have a natural hop or sink or whatever. Then induced movement, what you have to learn to put on the ball yourself. If you don't have natural movement, then you have to learn the pressure to put the sink on it, put the slide on it, put the cut on it, put hop on it. And then there's the location where you throw the ball. That's the only three things that a pitcher has to deal with. And I've always told pitchers that.

Get it clear in your mind. I want pitching to be clear to you, I don't want there to be a fog in there. You're 60 feet 6 inches away and you've got to throw it over that plate.

If you go strike one on the hitter, you now've got two chances to make a good pitch, a pitch that he doesn't like to hit. You can do it with a fastball, you can do it with a change . . . whatever you want, but you have two chances to make a good pitch to get strike two, to keep from giving him a pitch that he likes to hit.

Now if you do *that*, you got three chances to make a good pitch, with whatever pitch you want to throw and wherever you want to throw it. If you get ahead of a hitter the plate widens, and now you can make him chase what I call balls-that-look-like-strikes. You can throw it off the plate, whatever. Because the idea of pitching is to make a guy hit a bad ball, make them swing at balls. If you get ahead of a hitter, you can make them chase bad balls because the plate widens when you get two strikes on a hitter. That's all in my book.

I've written a seventy-page manual about pitching, things that I know about pitching. Not many people can do that. Part of coaching is to point out certain things to improve a pitch, or control of a pitch. When I see a guy throwing the baseball, I would never change his delivery per se, but I will point out things that will help him improve a certain pitch or his control. You don't actually ever say, "Hey, you've got to throw sidearm, or you've got to . . ." You'll point out if a guy is pitching across his body. You'll point that out because it's hard to step over there and throw over here. And usually if a guy does that he can't hit the outside part of the plate. Common sense tells you the toughest pitch to hit is a baseball on the low outside corner. I mean, Ted Williams come out with a diagram, and I'll believe anything *he* says about hitting. So you have to point out things like that, because you don't want the kid to fail. But sometimes guys use that as an excuse.

I based everything I tried to tell a pitcher on pure logic. Things that I heard from hitters and things that I heard from pitchers. Logic. I have a very logical mind. Back-and-forth pitching is a guy that throws fastballs, curves, change-ups. He destroys hitters from front to back. Sandy Koufax was a back-and-forth pitcher. An in-and-out pitcher is a guy that throws a sinker, a slider, change-ups. He works a hitter inside and outside.

Then if you feel you have to be both, I'll tell you how to do it. Tell you how important it is to learn to throw a curveball on the first pitch because most times hitters are taking. Most hitters want to hit the fastball to start. They're looking fastball. They gear their hitting on fastballs. So you're a dummy if you're gonna throw fastballs to everybody on the first pitch because there are so many good first-ball fastball hitters.

If you learn how to throw a curveball, strike one, it doesn't have to be your best curve, just an aim-strike curveball. The hitter takes it. That's what we call "curve for effect." Now you've put "curveball" in the hitter's mind: "How do I know that he ain't gonna come back with another curve? How do I know that he ain't gonna come back with a back-off curve and get me out in front where I fall on my face?"

So you teach a guy: If you learn to throw a curve strike one and you come back with your fastball, which doesn't have to be a Bob Feller fastball, his bat's gonna be a little bit slower because you've got that curveball in his mind. That's why so many balls are fouled back or fouled to the opposite field, because they don't get the head of the bat out there like they would on a first-ball fastball, because you have put curveball strike in their minds.

There's three ways you pitch inside. You pitch inside to people that are vulnerable inside, hitters that like to extend their arms. You pitch inside for strikes to get him out. Then you pitch *off* the plate to get in a guy's kitchen, to move him off the plate to set up your pitch on the low outside corner, your next pitch. Now, how far you come inside determines just how bad you want that to happen. You come inside, you play chin music, or you knock him on his ass, one or the other. But you're gonna get him out with the next pitch on the outside part of the plate.

Well, this last one is gone because they'll run you out of the ballgame. But you can still do the first one and you can still do the second one. So if a guy fully understands *that*, he's ahead of the game.

I can explain all these things to anybody that wants to listen. I defy them to beat it down. I can beat down any guy that wants to argue with me about pitching because it's based on logic, common sense.

I saw Paul Waner get his three thousandth hit. He told me, "You put a guy on the mound with a twenty-two rifle. First one's by me, second one's by me, but when I see him start his finger I'm going to start the head of the bat. He ain't gonna get the third one by me."

You see what he's saying to you? First one's by you, second one's by you. I'm gonna start the head of my bat on the third one, if that's all he's gonna throw. Now, say he had thrown a change-up on that third one, instead of the fastball. Well, Paul Waner would have been too far out here when the ball wasn't halfway to home plate. So he's trying to tell me how important it was to have a change-up, and how important it was that you can't stand out there and throw three fastballs by a hitter.

Nolan Ryan spent most of his career on two pitches, fastball and the curve. The day he's not getting his curveball over, the hitters spit on it and wait for the fastball, anticipate the fastball, sit on the fastball. That's why he didn't win more. Think how many he could have won. He was a .500 pitcher up until a few years ago. He come up with a helluva change-up the last few years he pitched. I just wonder what he would've done with his velocity if he had learned that when he was young.

Some pitchers don't want to learn what pitching versus hitting means. That's come clear to me after so many years.

One of the biggest faults a pitcher can develop is overstriding. They get some little guy with short legs and his stride is so big I couldn't jump as far as his stride, and they wonder why he can't throw a good curveball. You can't throw a curveball by overstriding. You've got to get up on top and pull it down to throw a good curveball. You can't jump way out there, because everything goes down and your curve goes up, over, and down, and it's just there for somebody to whack. Then they wonder why they're not successful.

Certain things you've got to learn if you want to be a big league ballplayer. I've seen a million good arms go down the drain and a lot of them wondering why. Because they think it's gonna happen; they don't *make* it happen. A lot of guys, it ain't gonna happen. If you're blessed with a Tom Seaver arm, it's gonna happen. Because they're gonna give you every opportunity in the world to do it.

That's why I admire Bob Tewksbury, for instance. The guy throws strikes and knows how to pitch. He had to know how to pitch because he doesn't throw hard, he doesn't have that kind of stuff. Evidently, knowing how to pitch means something to him.

Greg Maddux doesn't have overpowering stuff, he knows how to pitch. Tommy Glavine knows how to pitch. Mike Mussina was my number one pick the year I went to see him. I drove from Roanoke, Virginia, all the way to Montoursville, Pennsylvania, and back to watch him pitch. The day I saw him throw, he could have pitched a big league ballgame and he wouldn't have been embarrassed.

I always thought this: If you take it in this ear, you can let it go out this ear. If you listen to someone that's teaching logic to you, you can always close your mind to some guy that's not. You can hear a lot of voices, but if you listen to the words, what the guy's saying, you can take the guy that suits you better.

. . .

I had to go to the minor leagues and learn. Trial and error. And I pitched a lot to do it. You've got to have innings to learn how to pitch. You start enough ballgames like I did in the Coast League – I pitched 230 innings, 240 innings a year – and you learn.

I was very green, very raw, no question about it. But I persevered, if that's what they want to call it. Because I *loved* it. Damn, I loved it so much! You have to. I couldn't wait to get to the ballpark, get the uniform on, go play catch or play pepper, hit ground balls, hit fungoes. Something to look forward to every damn day, like a New Year's Eve party.

I always looked forward to going to the park. I used to even enjoy pitching batting practice. Kept my belly off. Kept me in pretty good shape. Turned it into a game – see how many strikes I could throw in a row. Fun, it really was fun.

Watching a ballgame, from the very start to the finish, *that* is fun. Really watching Roy McMillan play shortstop or Bobby Wine play shortstop, and know what they can do, and learn by watching them and seeing how they do it. Such a rhythm. Not by the numbers: go out and catch the ball, turn, then throw it. But catching the ball *while* you're turning and throwing, all those little things that people don't see. And then realize how good a guy is, when maybe another guy *doesn't* realize how good he is. The accuracy of the arms, throwing to the right bases, all that kind of stuff.

Years ago we used to stay out and watch infield, because you didn't want to miss watching those guys throw, Snider, Furillo . . . but especially Furillo. Now nobody watches. Colavito's arm might have been stronger. Rocky Colavito had the strongest arm I've ever seen. He could pick up a ball and throw it nine miles, but Furillo got rid of it quick and accurate.

Jim Hegan, the catcher, was a very smart guy. He would make me use all my pitches, even if I wasn't getting one of them over. I think he felt that I was the type of pitcher that had to use all of my pitches. In other words, he would never narrow me down to one or two pitches. If a pitch wasn't working right away, he thought, "If I can make him use it, then pretty soon he'll have it working." He was smart like that. Very smart receiver. Not much of a hitter but a good receiver.

I appreciate talent. In the meantime I don't appreciate some of the things that you see that's come into baseball. When it first started . . . I know it happened a time or two back in Ted Williams's day, where he had crunched one and maybe didn't run hard to first base because he knew it was gone. It happened back then, a time or two, I know it did. But now you see it, it's off the wall and the guy hasn't left home plate. It's like "in-your-face" stuff. Guy cranks one and then stands there and watches it go out. That's like he's sticking his success in your face. He doesn't do that when the pitcher strikes him out or he hits into a double play. But they get away with it now.

I like the professional type of players, the guys who would never do things like that. The home run trot? Bush, is what we used to call it. Bush! Just run around the fucking bases like Lou Gehrig did. Like Jimmy Foxx did. Like Minnie Minoso did. Like Robin Yount and Paul Molitor did.

My little nine-year-old grandkid was pitching down here the other night. This little kid comes to the plate, sticks his hand up to the umpire for time, and starts fixing the box with his foot. Nine years old, now, and every single time it was a ball he walks over here, takes a couple of swings, goes back over here and starts fixing the box again. And then they wonder why the games last so long.

This is a nine-year-old kid, he's seen all that on television, and he thinks that's really beautiful – instead of wondering how to put the bat on the ball, or instead of how to throw the ball to first base on a ground ball, or how to get under a pop fly. He's got all this stuff figured out, but the rest of it probably don't mean a thing.

I don't think fundamentals are taught quite as good as they used to be. You *had* to learn them. The one thing I always heard was – Run every ball out to first base. It's one of those things that all fans *expected* you to do, back in those days. Well, maybe the fans are changing, but I still hear people in the stands say, "Why didn't he run that ball out?" Fans resent a guy not running out ground balls, fly balls. That's one thing that a fan, who may not understand anything else about baseball, expects to see. They expect to see a guy busting his ass to first base.

You'll see it some, with a guy that knows he doesn't have a lot of talent, that knows he *has* to do that if he wants to get anywhere. But those other guys thinking, "Oh, I'll be there, it's coming." Then pretty soon they wake up and it never got there, because they didn't do anything to make it happen.

That's the way I see it.

Milt Bolling

February 18–19, 1993, Mobile, Alabama

Milt Bolling played shortstop in the American League from 1952 to 1958. In addition to playing five seasons with the Red Sox, Bolling played with the Washington Senators and the Tigers. The brother of Frank Bolling, a second baseman with the Tigers and Braves, Bolling hit .241 lifetime. He has been a scout with the Red Sox since 1967.

I don't know why Mobile is such a rich place for ballplayers. I can re-member the scout that signed me, George Digby. He called me one year and he asked me, "You ever heard of a guy named Hank Aaron in Mobile?"

And I said, "No."

He says, "He's supposed to be a good player."

I said, "Where's he live, George?"

Well, it turns out he only lived a few blocks from me. We lived a block and a half this side of the railroad tracks, Hank Aaron lived maybe a block and a half on the other side. Never heard of him, and he's only a year younger than I am.

Right by the house we had a football stadium. And there was a big wooded area and we used to go back there and have clay battles with the black kids. Never knew who they were. It was all fun. We'd have our caves. Probably throwing against Hank Aaron and never knew it.

Ed Scott, who scouted for us for a long time, lives here in Mobile—in fact, I hired him for the Red Sox when I was working in the front office—he signed Hank Aaron originally for the Indianapolis Clowns. You know, today, whenever he's honored, like the Hall of Fame, Hank Aaron always flies Scottie in for the ceremony. That's unusual. Just be-cause the guy gave him a chance to play ball with the Indianapolis Clowns. All these years . . .

We used to come back after the season and Eddie Stanky would manage us, all the guys who played pro ball here. We'd get up a team and we'd go out and play on a Sunday afternoon for money against the black team out here.

The first time I ever saw Aaron play, we had a pitcher named Pete Wojey, pitched a little bit in the big leagues with Detroit and a long time in the minors. We went out and played the black guys one day, and he struck out seventeen. I mean he was smoking. But one guy hit three home runs off him. It was Aaron.

He was playing shortstop against us that day. He had just finished his first year with the Indianapolis Clowns. As hard as Wojey threw it, the farther Aaron hit it.

I don't know what it is about Mobile. We didn't have any youth pro-grams. In our years it was high school baseball and a little semipro. Black kids? I don't know where they played, because they had Central High School, and back then it was segregation so you didn't play the black schools. And they didn't get much publicity in the papers, so you never knew who they were. I guess they probably just played sandlot ball on their parks like we did on ours.

When I first started going to college, I went to Troy State. One day George Digby came out to school. He says, "Jackie Robinson's All-Stars are playing the Birmingham Black Barons. How 'bout going to the game with me tonight?"

We're two of the few white people there, and we're sitting way out in the bleachers. I'll never forget this. Larry Doby is on third base and Campanella is the hitter. Campanella hits a long fly ball to center field, almost to the fence, and the guy catches it in center field and Doby tags up. He could walk in. Well, he's just trotting and here comes this throw and he's about twenty feet from home. And Doby is out! He just stopped and looked at center field, puts his hands on his hips and looks out there. And we looked at our scorecard and all it said was *Mays*.

And George Digby said, I'll never forget it to this day, "Man, if the Red Sox'd sign a black player, I'd sign that guy on his arm alone."

This was '49, and the next year–I guess George must have mentioned this to the Red Sox–because they sent some guy–I think it was Larry Woodall, caught a little bit in the big leagues–to look at Mays, but he winds up signing Piper Davis.

I don't know if you've ever met Piper. Piper's a great guy. He was thirty-three years old at the time. I was at Scranton, Pennsylvania, that year, and they sent Piper in there to Scranton. Piper could play any position. Well, they finally moved him to first base, and that's the month he's leading the league in hitting and they released him. I guess they found out how old he was. I don't know what happened. That was 1950. He was the first black guy the Red Sox had signed.

. . .

I was only seventeen when I signed. They sent me to Class B– Roanoke, Virginia–and I was overmatched right there. I should've started in Class D. I was the youngest guy in the Piedmont League. I could play defense up there, but I'd never been to spring training. All I'd seen was high school pitching. When you got to Class B in those days, you'd been playing for three, sometimes four years. They just smoked me! Only hit .180-something. I cried every night.

Mike Higgins was my manager, and Mike changed me right away. I step into the batter's box, scared to death, got in my batting stance, and Higgins said, "You can't hit like that, son."

I said, "Okay." I didn't know! He put me right on top of the plate, like he hit. And, man, I broke bats on the first three balls in batting practice. Then, after that, every manager I ever played for changed my batting stance to the way he hit. My first year in the big leagues, under Boudreau, I hit like he hit.

There was only one guy let me alone – Jack Burns, when I was with Scranton. And I hit .290 or right at .290 that year, and the Eastern League was a tough league to hit back in those days.

You know, I used to play with the men, semipro, when I was sixteen years old. A lot of guys had played pro ball, a couple had played a little bit in the big leagues. I had no problem hitting the ball around here. I can remember this old-timer – in fact, he was the police chief and he'd played a little pro ball – telling me, "Don't ever let them change your batting style." But here I am, I've just got into professional baseball, a southern boy who was brought up to respect authority. Yes sir and no sir. You didn't doubt anybody. Today a kid would probably say, "Let me try it my own way."

I probably would have had a shot at making the club in '52. That's when they started their youth movement: all those older guys – Doerr and Pesky and Dom DiMaggio – with Boudreau as the manager. But I missed spring training because I had to stay in school. The Korean War was on and I was in ROTC. If I'd have left, I would've been drafted.

I wasn't eligible until June 15 that year. They sent me to Birmingham, then they called me up around the first part of September. Then the next year I went to spring training and made the club and was the starting shortstop. I went 4 for 5 opening day in Philadelphia in '53. Boston had a whole Pullman carload of writers and radio guys traveling with the club. Took you a couple of years to find out who everybody was. But, yeah, I went 4 for 5, and one writer came up to me and said, "You think you can keep that up all year?"

Right! And I'd be the first guy to hit .800.

They're just rabid fans up there. I think that if you hustle, they'll appreciate you. Sure, they'll boo you sometimes. That's the toughest part about playing professional athletics. You expect to get booed on the road, but getting booed at home . . . You know, when you're really trying, but you still boot one or strike out in a critical situation . . .

I had never seen a big league game till I played in one. When they called me up, the club was in Detroit. About the sixth inning, Boudreau got mad at the guys on the field. We were losing. Virgil Trucks was pitching – he pitched two no-hitters that year – and I'm sitting on the bench. I've never seen a big league stadium. I'm sitting there with my hat on one nail, I don't know where my glove was, and Boudreau says, "Get in there, Bolling."

Well, the club's already on the field. The players are out there. Johnny Lipon's been in the big leagues five, six years, and he sees me come out and he's cursing.

I say, "Look, he told me to come out here."

Lipon wasn't mad at me, but here we are playing in Detroit, where he had played a long time, and he was embarrassed. Why didn't he take him out before he went on the field, rather than put him in an embarrassing situation? I got to face Trucks. He walked me the first time and I breathed a sigh of relief, because he throws hard. Then I had to go up against him in the ninth inning again, and I got a broken-bat single over the shortstop's head. I was one for one. I should have quit right there.

We went barnstorming one year, after the season, and we were up in Wythesville, Virginia. Bad lights, a Class D town, and we were playing some kids that were Class D and C ballplayers. So Trucks went over to them and said, "Look, I'm pitching. I'm gonna throw it in there, let you guys hit it, and we're gonna get this game over with."

Well, about the third hitter hit a line drive, and as Trucks followed through it hit him right in the butt. The next seventeen guys did not even foul a ball off under those lights. He just smoked it by them. I felt so sorry for those poor kids.

Boudreau would do a lot of things I could never understand. Like Nellie Fox would come up with a man on first. Okay, left-handed hitter should be thinking about pulling the ball. If he singles, the guy goes to third base, cause if he singles to left, you've got first and second.

Boudreau says, "Go three steps off of second base."

I said, "Lou, he's gonna hit it over there."

"That's what I want him to do," he said. "I want him to go to left. You've got his mind thinking the opposite of what he should be thinking of doing. He should be thinking about pulling the ball to get the man to third base. Now he sees you with that big hole between third and second, he's gonna try to go that way. All he's gonna do is go first and second, and if he makes a mistake, you get the double play. You put the second baseman way over, and even if the ball is hit to third base you can still cover and make the pivot."

We'd do things like that. Back then he started charting pitches. Everyone thought he was crazy and he finally dropped it. But he was innovative, way ahead of his time. He started the Williams shift.

Boudreau was a good teacher. I liked him. He tried to help. The older guys'd have nothing to do with him, but the younger guys . . . He was good for younger guys, who respected him because of what he had done. So you listened to him. Older guys sort of undermined him. Guys like Lipon and Hoot Evers. Professional jealousy in some respects. From what I hear, he wasn't an exceptional athlete. I think he lacked speed, but he knew how to play. He used his head. He knew how to play position. Plus he was a good enough hitter.

•   •   •

Jimmy Piersall was my roommate. See, I'm a Catholic, Piersall's a Catholic, and when I came up in '53, he'd just gone through '52 with all the mental problems. He'd had the shock treatments. He was with me at Birmingham that year. Double-A, Southern League. He remembers none of that.

I was sort of a laid-back guy. I was still in college. They thought I might be a steadying influence, and they asked me to room with him. I said okay.

Man, that was the toughest thing I ever did in baseball. I mean, we just didn't have the similar backgrounds and hadn't been brought up the same way. There's a lot of stories I could tell, but I could never say them in public, because I wouldn't be like a Jim Bouton. I don't understand – things that you learn in private about people, I just could never say them in public situations. I just don't think it's right.

Piersall's problem was he had to be the center of attraction. We'd go to a restaurant after a game and nobody'd recognize him, and there was some sort of a scene that he'd be recognized. You know, crowded elevator? It'd be the same way. He'd liable to blurt out anything. And everybody'd turn and look at him. He was okay after that. He'd got the attention.

Ted Williams was there. And Piersall was a good player, but nobody was in the class with Ted Williams, and of course Jensen came later, another good player. And Piersall was trying to get his share of the limelight, and he'd do things – even then, after he was supposedly healed – to be noticed. That, and because of his background . . . he came up in a lot of poor circumstances. That, and the dollar meant a lot to him.

But we got along. If I see him today, he still calls me Roomie, I still call him Roomie. But, there were just a lot of things he did that I didn't approve of, and although I tried to be a steadying influence on him, *nobody* could be a steadying influence on the guy.

I'd just go to Tom Dowd, our traveling secretary, once a year and say, "Look, Tom, man, I gotta get outta there."

He says, "What do you mean?"

I says, "Look, just give me one road trip."

So he would, and nobody'd room with Piersall. He'd room by himself, and he'd come to me, almost crying, and he'd say, "What's wrong?"

And I'd say, "Man, I don't know. You have to ask Dowd." I didn't want to tell him. It got to be too nerve-wracking for me. But I did it for three years. I'd sleep with one eye open at night, as I used to kid him.

The funniest thing was in '52, the year we played together at Birmingham. We had another guy on that club named Windy McCall. He had a cup of coffee with the Red Sox. He went to spring training with the Red Sox, say in '51 or '52, and he told Ted Williams he could strike him out. He was screwier than Piersall . . . Those two on the same club? Man . . .

We were in New Orleans, and the president of the league was there. McCall's pitching, Piersall's in center field, I'm at shortstop. We used to leave our gloves in the field back in those days. And Piersall, before he'd go out to center field, he'd stop and talk to me and tell me how to play shortstop. (They tried to make a shortstop out of him, in spring training in '52. That's what he told me always caused him to go off to have his problems, trying to make a shortstop of him.)

So McCall's warming up and he turns around and sees Piersall talking to me. He tells Piersall, "Get your blankety blank out in center field where you belong."

And Piersall – he's a nice-looking guy, he's got a big smile – tells him, "Blankety blank, yourself. Mind your own business." Well, Piersall hadn't reached his glove yet. So McCall takes the ball and throws it at him, and Piersall ducks and the ball rolls all the way to the center field fence. The umpire, at second base, says, "Jimmy, go get the ball."

"Hell, no!" he says. "I didn't throw it. Let McCall go get it."

I mean, these guys are teammates!

Umpire says, "You go get it."

Piersall says, "Let McCall go get it."

Finally, Piersall picked up his glove and saunters out there. He gets to the ball and throws it to the guy on the scoreboard. So McCall throws another ball at him. And Piersall turns around and throws *it* to the guy on the scoreboard.

Guess who they threw out of the ballgame for throwing the balls away?

About a half-hour later, maybe less, we saw Piersall up in the stands. They had the knot-hole gang back then, where they let kids in free and they all sit together. Jimmy's leading them in cheers: "We want Piersall."

Another time in New Orleans, we're in between games of a double-header. You'd play all night games and a doubleheader on Sunday in the South. Man, you talk about guys would melt.

You know, you get hungry between games, and you get the club-house guy to get you a hot dog. Well, Piersall, he said he's gonna get it himself, but he only had his athletic supporter on. And he walks right out like that and gets a hot dog.

He'd stand on the corner – any corner – in every town we'd go to: Chatanooga, Little Rock, New Orleans. You used to have these little photographs – autographed – and he'd stand out on the corner, giving them away, so people would know who he was. He'd get all kinds of write-ups from all kinds of papers, and the next morning he'd be in the clubhouse, "Man, look at this article, look at this article." As if all he was looking for was the publicity.

Remember big Frank Thomas, the guy who played with Pittsburgh? He played right field for New Orleans. Piersall, one time in Birming-ham, was carrying two water guns in his pocket, and every time we'd change fields he'd – squirt! squirt! – shoot Thomas in the face. Thomas lasted about three innings. He grabs him and picks him up, one hand – Thomas was strong – right off the ground. Picked him up and shook the hell out of him.

Boston sent him down in '52. He had played at Birmingham, and he'd had an outstanding year there the year before. The people loved him. So he's coming back, and he's supposed to get in that night about eight o'clock. Our games start at eight. They were going to meet him at the airport with a squad car, get him to the ballpark – he was going to dress in the squad car – and come out to the ballpark and play. Well, right before eight o'clock it started raining. There was a delay, the game hadn't started. Well, along about eight thirty, we hear this siren coming. The lights are out in the stadium. The tarp's out on the field. We hear this siren coming, and the car comes right out on the field. They turn on all the lights. Piersall goes to the mound, and the people went crazy. So, we start to play the game. I'll never forget, in Birmingham, then, if you hit a home run you got fifty bucks, or a suit from this department store if you hit this neon light on top of the scoreboard. But if you broke it, it was a thousand bucks. I think we were playing Memphis. First time up, Piersall misses that neon light by less than a foot. It's in play, but the center fielder thought it was a home run and he took it and threw it out of the ballpark. He was that mad.

I tell you what, though, he could play. Good defensive outfielder! But then he hurt his arm in '53 or '54.

We used to play the Giants, a charity game once a year for the Jimmy Fund in Boston. Then we'd play in New York the next year for some other charity. They had contests before the game, you know, like throwing, home runs. . . . And Piersall and Mays had a throwing contest from right field. Mays threw first. Piersall had a good arm, but he didn't have the kind of arm Mays had, and he tried to stretch it out. You know Jimmy, he's an actor. He'd put on all the time, always trying to get the limelight. So if he hurt himself you'd think he's just doing it to get sympathy from the fans. But that day they were throwing from right field. And he threw, and boy, the ball just died, and he grabbed his arm and it looked like somebody shot him. He staggered up against the foul pole in right field in Fenway, and he just started rolling, rolling down the wall and holding his arm. And we're all sitting in the dugout: "Look at that crazy act!" We're figuring that he just couldn't throw with Mays and he didn't want to embarrass himself, so he was trying to get out of it. He'd roll. Fall down. Get up and roll again! It was hilarious. Of course, we thought he was just trying to jake out because he knew he couldn't throw harder than Mays. But he did hurt his arm, and he never did throw well after that.

But he threw well enough to play. His first year, '53, Tommy Umphlett was our center fielder and Piersall played right field. I saw him, two days in a row, go in on Vernon around the foul pole. First day he went in a row and got a home run off him. The next day he went in two rows and got a home run off of him. And he could hit. Good enough: He'd hit his .270, .280.

In '52, that's when he had all his mental problems. It was about July of that year that he was thrown out of a ballgame in Birmingham. I saw the movie *Fear Strikes Out*, and it just didn't really . . . You look at the numbers, all the numbers are very high numbers. A lot of the players wouldn't lend their names to the situation, the movie. . . . Maybe it was professional jealousy. Piersall had offended a lot of people.

Anyway, he got thrown out of a game in Birmingham. They take him back to Boston to get these shock treatments – I think he had something like nine or ten shock treatments – and that was the last we saw of him.

In spring training the next year, '53, we were playing the Philadelphia Athletics, and Johnny Mackinson, who had been our teammate in Birmingham the year before, comes over and he's talking to Piersall and me before the ballgame. When he leaves, Piersall says, "I don't remember him."

During the season we'd go into different towns – he had played a little bit, you know, with Boston in '52 – and we'd see people who acted like they knew him, and he wouldn't remember them. He comes to realize, finally, that anything that happened in 1952, the year he had the problems and the shock treatments, he didn't remember anybody that he had met that year. If he had known you prior to that he'd remember you. I don't know whether it ever came back.

Yet he handled it so well. He had a nice personality. He liked people, and he met people well, and he overcame it. I give him a lot of credit for that, because that had to be a difficult situation. He had a large family of his own, which he was trying to support. I think that's why he was worried about making money all the time, because he had a lot of outside pressure on him. Never met his father. Knew his wife, Mary; Mary was a nurse.

. . .

When I first saw Williams in '53, middle of the season, he had just come back from the Korean War. He's gotta be in his middle thirties. He made it look so easy. He was like a big leaguer and we were all Little Leaguers. I mean, that was the difference in his hitting and the rest of us.

Of course, he thought he made himself a great hitter, but it's an ability, like God gives you speed or a good arm. He's gotta give you that eye-hand coordination to be a good hitter. But Williams, I don't know if he really believes in God, but he had some ability to go with it. Because he used to tell me, he'd say, "You do everything right up there but hit."

"What's wrong with you?" he'd say. "Look, the first pitch they're gonna throw you's a fastball. He's gonna try and get a strike on you with a fastball. Rip it!"

Well, I go up there, foul it off, even miss it, come back to the bench – he had a very foul mouth – he'd start cussin': "Told you what was coming!"

I say, "Yeah . . ."

He says, "Why didn't you hit it?"

I said, "I didn't *try* to miss it!"

He couldn't understand that. He was the kind of guy who'd keep you on your toes, especially at batting. But it was intimidating, because he could not understand why a person couldn't do a certain thing, especially with the bat. In fact, we had a catcher named Sammy White, and Sammy had a terrible swing. But Sammy was his own man. You weren't going to tell Sammy White anything. When Sammy'd get in batting practice, Williams would turn his back and walk away.

He'd say, "I'm not going to look at him. He'll just put me in a slump."

Used to be, in the clubhouse, we had these little boxes of sand to spit the tobacco juice in. Williams would get his fly rod out and he'd throw one of those things all the way across the clubhouse, and he'd say, "Man, I might not be the best hitter in the world, but I'm the best fisherman."

Frank Sullivan, that big right-handed pitcher we used to have, went bonefishing with Williams one time. He says, "Man, I caught a lot of bonefish, but I'll never go again.

"Williams steered the boat, and said, 'He's over there, there he is, over there.'"

And if he missed casting it where he's supposed to, Williams'd get all upset. He said, "Man I caught a lot of fish, but I was a nervous wreck."

.   .   .

I played one year with my brother, '58 in Detroit. They had Billy Martin and they tried to make a shortstop out of him. They got me over there to back him up. They brought him over from the Athletics. Frank was at second. Billy was always a fiery guy when I played against him with the Yankees. Of course, the Yankees always won back in those days. In Detroit, we finished fourth that year, and he wasn't a leader on that club. I don't know if it was because they weren't out front winning. A lot of the players were disappointed. He really didn't have that leadership quality that he had shown with the Yankees, on the field, especially. I don't know whether he didn't feel he could win there or what. I liked him, but he wasn't the real rah, rah, hustle guy he showed you in New York. But they definitely had him out of position when they had him at shortstop. He didn't have the arm for that.

But playing with my brother . . . we never even thought about it. We'd grown up together, played ball together. Just four brothers that ever played combination in the big leagues. I never knew that until a year or so ago. You've got the Ripkens, the O'Briens at Pittsburgh in the '50s, and the Hamners with the Phillies played for just a short time, like Frank and I did. I read it in the paper one time, but they didn't have Frank and I in it. I said, "Well, Frank and I did it." Then Ernie Harwell – he noticed it, too – and he mentioned us on the air.

A guy can be the best defensive player in the world. I don't know if you remember a guy named Willie Miranda? I don't think there's ever been a better shortstop to come along. He couldn't hit .200, but man, he could do everything with that glove. He and Luis Aparicio. He just couldn't hit, so he couldn't get in the lineup to play enough. Probably had more range and a better arm than Aparicio.

That was my last year, '58. I wound up going back to the minor leagues. I was only twenty-eight. I had a couple of bad injuries. I wasn't a real good hitter and I hurt my arm, and I just couldn't throw very well to play shortstop anymore. I got real discouraged, mentally. You know when you have a certain ability and all of a sudden you can't do it, it really gets to you.

It was actually my rookie year. In '53, we were playing the White Sox in Chicago. I was on first base, and I think Kell hit a ground ball and I started to slide into second. Nellie Fox told me to hold up and I should've gone in and slid. But I didn't, and my spikes caught and I flipped all the way over the bag and popped something in my ankle. All the ligaments were torn.

Today, they'd cast it, but back in those days they just wrapped it and put me on a crutch and said, "Wait ten days. You'll be able to play."

This was around the first of August, and I was hitting about .270-something. Lipon hadn't played all year, and his arm was really shot. They didn't have anybody else to play short, so Boudreau kept rushing me to come back. When I got back out there, after about ten days, I was really limping. But back then, they thought you were jaking all the time. So I tried to play, and when I did I couldn't put any weight on the foot to throw. I was throwing different and I hurt my shoulder, and I never could make my ball carry anymore. My ball would always sink. The next year my arm didn't bother me, my shoulder didn't bother me, but I could never find my groove again to make my ball do anything.

I'd finished school, I'd gone in a training program for a big company, and they wanted me to come and work for them. And then the Giants finally got me the winter of '58. I wrote Chub Feeney a letter and said, "Look, I'm just going to quit. I don't feel I can do it anymore."

He said, "Well, we're going to make a second baseman out of you."

I probably would've gone back and then gone in the expansion as a second baseman, cause I was still young enough. But the big thing that happened in '58 was when I was with Detroit. McHale was the general manager, and in July he came to me and said, "The Phillies want you to play second base over there."

I said, "I'd like to go. I'm not a good high-ball hitter, and that's what kills me in the American League."

You know, back then—strike zone now is belt and below on everybody – but in the American League they could smoke you up high. In the National League, I thought I could go over there and see if I could hit better over there.

He says, "No, I can't let you go with Martin here. We need you to be the backup infielder for your brother *and* Martin."

Then, about August first, they bring up another shortstop and sent me to the minor leagues.

But, you know, that's just what happens. And I had a family, and I just felt it was coming to an end because of that. I was discouraged.

I was out of baseball from '61 to '65, and when Dick O'Connell was made the general manager, I wrote him a letter, and I said I don't really care about getting in the baseball end of it, but I'd like to learn the business end. So he brought me back and he put me in his job, that he had.

Been with the Red Sox forty years, scouting down here in Mobile since '67. I'll be sixty-three the end of this year. I've given them till 65, and if they don't fire me by then they can have it.

When I signed, I never even thought about making the big leagues. I just thought that playing professional baseball was a job, and if you didn't have a job, and you weren't educated, you went home and worked in a factory and carried a lunch pail, as they said.

And guys were glad to see baseball start again because, you know, it was easier than carrying the lunch pail. That's why you had a lot of baseball teams: a lot of guys kept playing baseball in the minor leagues till an older age because there was more money and it was an easier lifestyle than working in a factory.

I think what determines what you look for in a ballplayer are your past experiences. You compare the kids you see today with the guys you played with or against. They've got to light me up. That's the way I scout. He lights me up, I come back; if he doesn't light me up, I don't go back. That's why, whenever I talk to kids, I always tell them, "Look, if you're interested in professional baseball, hustle *every* time in *every* ballgame. You're only going to bat three or four times. Run to first as hard as you can. Run everything out, don't loaf. Because that scout may be sitting in the stands on that day, and if you don't show him your abilities he's going to walk out on you not knowing if you can play."

Most guys who play in the big leagues, 90 percent of us, I'd say, are average ballplayers. We're no better than the guy in triple-A or double-A. We got a break and maybe took a little more advantage of it. Maybe our mental aspect was a little bit better playing the game. Maybe we dedicated ourselves a little bit better. But as far as physical ability, we weren't any better than those guys.

MILT BOLLING

You know, we all knew that when we finished we had to go to work. We always knew we had to have something else to fall back on. You always prepared for that, or made contacts. That's why you always treated people nicely.

Tito Francona

June 30, 1994, Beaver Falls, Pennsylvania

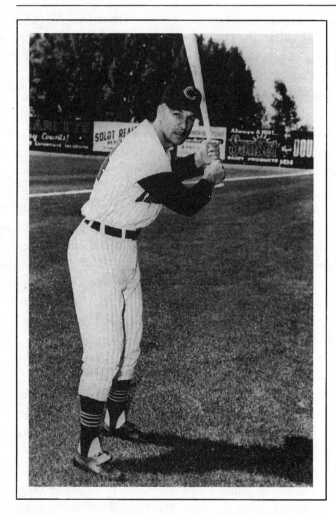

Tito Francona played outfield and first base from 1956 to 1970. In addition to playing six years with Cleveland, Francona played for the Orioles, White Sox, Tigers, Brewers, Cardinals, Phillies, Atlanta Braves, and Oakland Athletics. A .272 lifetime hitter, he hit .300 or better three times. While he was forty at-bats shy of qualifying for the batting title, his .363 average in 1959 was highest in the American League. He is the father of Terry Francona.

I always remember the first game I played in the big leagues. I went out to the ballpark early in the morning, about eight o'clock. We had a one o'clock game. It was Boston. I put my uniform on, then walked around the field to get acclimated. I was sitting in the dugout, and all of a sudden I see this big guy coming out of the Red Sox dugout. Number 9. Ted Williams.

He walks across the field and comes into our dugout and says, "Are you Tito Francona?"

And then he starts telling me about hitting.

When we're done I'm wondering, "How the hell does he know who I am?"

Never mind, I found out. My roommate was Harry Doorish, who played with Boston in the '40s. He called Ted Williams up the night before and told him I was going to be there early. So *Williams* came out early. He made me feel comfortable. Gave me some tips.

I never watched many big league games before that. The Red Sox were taking batting practice, and I was off on our side of the field with my back to home plate. All of a sudden everything got quiet. I turned around, and Ted Williams was taking batting practice. Our whole team ran behind the batting cage to watch this guy hit. Sportswriters were watching him.

They hit about five minutes for each ballplayer. He'd hit five minutes, then everybody went back to doing their business. About twenty minutes later, same thing: everything got quiet. I turned around, he's hitting. Everybody runs to the cage.

This was the first season after he got back from Korea. I remember the sportswriters used to rag him a lot. One writer I remember in particular called out, in a heavy Boston accent, "Hey, Ted, you can't get around on the fastball anymore!"

He was hitting. He turned around and he looked at that guy and he said, "Jesus Christ couldn't throw a fastball by me."

If anybody could say I'm going to hit .350, I think Ted Williams could. He was the closest thing to a machine. I've seen Musial, Mantle, Aaron, Clemente. I used to call them "struggling hitters." They were going to hit .300, but they had to struggle to do it. Even Musial. With Williams it was automatic.

I was at an old-timers' game a few years ago in St. Petersburg, Florida, and he was managing our team. We were taking batting practice and he walked in from right field. Everybody ran towards him. I was sitting in the dugout and I said, "Ah, I'm not going to bother him."

He walked right by everybody and sat down beside me in the dugout and said, "I want to talk to you."

Everybody was carrying balls and they wanted his autograph – I'm not an autograph hound – and he's sitting there signing balls. He signed one for me and slipped it in my pocket. He made me feel good. He made me feel important.

. . .

My real name is John, but my dad started calling me Tito. I think it means "little one" in Italian. I was small. I went all through school, and nobody knew my name was John.

Like every normal guy, I played Legion ball and high school ball. A guy named Jim Weaver signed me for the Browns. There were a few other ballclubs interested in me.

I had gone down to Johnstown, Pennsylvania, and worked out at their tryout camp. I hit for about six hours down there. I was the only guy hitting. Everybody else was shagging. Man, I had blisters! They signed me. I got a $5,000 bonus, $2,500 before the season, $2,500 after the season. Then, a couple of days later, I was on my way to York, Pennsylvania, Class B.

When I got into York it was too late for me to play in the game that night. But here was the guy whose place I was taking – they were going to release him that night – and they'd just told him he would be there all year. He had a wife and two kids. But that's how baseball goes.

This was one of the first times I'd ever been away from home. That night I checked into this old hotel and the hotel burned down.

I finished out the 1952 season in York. Geez, we had a good ballclub. A lot of those guys moved up within two years to triple-A. I was the only lousy ballplayer on the team. I hit .228. But of everyone on that team, I was the only guy who went to the big leagues. They went to spring training, a lot of them, but nobody else ever made the big leagues.

Then, in 1953, I went to spring training with Thomasville, Georgia. I had a real good spring and I thought I was going back to York, but they sent me to Aberdeen, South Dakota. I never heard of Aberdeen, South Dakota. I was disappointed. I thought I was going backwards. But they said they wanted the manager up there to work with me. And that's where I met my wife. In Aberdeen, 1953. We got married in 1956.

After the '53 season I went into the service for two years. When I got out in September, the Orioles – the Browns had moved to Baltimore by then – sent me home for a few weeks, and then I went down to

Columbia with Brooks Robinson, Wayne Causey, and another bonus ballplayer named Bob Nelson. I had a pretty good season down there – about sixteen or seventeen home runs, and I hit about .290.

That spring – that's when they started these early camps, spring rookie camps – they had around twenty young kids there, and they were chopping them off every day. But I had a good spring and they carried me right into Baltimore. I never thought I'd stay long. I was always trying to get five years and the pension plan, but I wound up getting fifteen years.

I went to the White Sox after the '57 season. A big trade, about twelve guys. I opened up in right field. My health wasn't good, but nobody knew about it. I had been playing winter ball in Puerto Rico. I went to bat one time, swung at a pitch, and fell down. Got up, got my composure, swung at another pitch, and I went down again. Something was wrong.

So they took me to the doctor, and the next thing I know they're handing me a plane ticket home. What the hell's going on here?

I came home and I went to the doctor, and he diagnosed it as hepatitis. I was doctoring in Aberdeen, South Dakota. After about a month and a half, it was worse than when it started. So I called Chicago. They ran a complete physical. They said, "We don't see any hepatitis. We see a slight liver infection and we think something's wrong with your heart."

I said, "What am I supposed to do?"

They said, "Go to spring training. If you fall over dead, we'll know you had a heart attack."

■   ■   ■

I started out in '58 with the White Sox, then was traded to Detroit. They figured, let's get rid of this guy, he's damaged goods, but they didn't let anybody know.

The day I got traded, the man that traded for me, the manager, Jack Tighe, got fired and Bill Norman took over.

It was a Sunday. Jack Fisher and I got traded for Ray Boone and Bob Shaw. We were in Chicago. I went over to Detroit on Tuesday and went in to Bill Norman and introduced myself.

Norman said, "What position do you play? I didn't make this trade."

Then Bill Fisher and I walked in to the trainer, and Bill told him he was Tito and I told him I was Bill. For two weeks the trainer was rubbing my arm down thinking I'm a pitcher. I didn't play much over there.

In the spring of '59 I go to spring training with Detroit and we've got nine left fielders. And Norman was trying to push a guy he had down in

Charleston. He'd had a good year down there and Norman was trying to push him for the job. So I didn't play in any games.

Then one day he told me, "I'm gonna give you a chance to play." We had a long trip from Lakeland to West Palm Beach. He left all of the big guns home and took the scrubeenies. I get down there and I don't even get in the game. I was livid.

I was standing by the bench and Norman comes by. He looked at me and says, "Heh, you travel two hundred miles and don't play . . ."

My wife was back in South Dakota; she was pregnant with Terry. I had gone to school that winter while we were living up there, and I figured I had better change my vocation. I decided to quit and go back to school.

When I got back to the hotel I started packing. My door was open, and a sportswriter whose room was right across from mine saw me and asked, "What are you doing?"

I said, "You see the situation. It's a big joke here. I'm just wasting my time."

He said, "Let me write a story about you. Wait a day or two."

So he writes this story, and Frank Lane, the general manager with Cleveland, read it. Frank used to buy *all* the papers. He had Larry Doby over there and Larry was towards the end of his career, and he thinks, "Maybe I'll offer them Larry Doby."

Joe Gordon was the Cleveland manager then, and Joe had seen me play in the Pacific Coast League and said he liked what he saw. So they traded Doby for me.

Now I'm trying to get from Lakeland to Tucson, and the Tigers' traveling secretary won't give me any money. There was a guy from Youngstown who I knew from back home, a sportswriter who happened to be down there visiting. He said, "I'll help you out." And he did.

When I got to Tucson the writers started: "Where do you think you're gonna play over here?"

They had Minnie Minoso as the left-fielder, Jimmy Piersall as the center fielder, and Rocky Colavito as the right-fielder. Vic Power was the first baseman. Hey, I didn't make the deal! But they got on me a little bit, seeing that I said I was going to quit in that article.

So Joe Gordon said, "I want you to go down to the batting cage every day." And he worked with me.

I used to uppercut the ball; he wanted me to tomahawk it. He said, "I don't know where you're gonna play, but I think you can help us out as a pinch hitter."

So I'd go in the batting cage every day and Joe would work with me.

Then he said, "Minoso will play five or six innings, and then you pick him up so you can get some at-bats."

I was satisfied with that role.

When the season started, we got into some crucial situations and he used me as a pinch hitter. The first seven times I pinch-hit I got six hits. And I won ballgames.

One of the first times, I hit a home run in the tenth inning. We were playing the Yankees. Cal McLish was pitching for us. It was no score, and they score a run in the ninth or tenth inning. Everyone's down-hearted. We get a man on base in the bottom of the inning, and Joe Gordon looks down the bench and says, "Anyone bat against this guy?"

I can't remember the pitcher's name but I said, "Yeah, I batted against him."

He said, "What do you think?"

So I went up and hit. It was a Friday night. I remember because they gave a car away every Friday night. Big crowd. Always a big crowd when Cleveland played the Yankees. Hit a home run and the people went wild. And when they raffled the car off, they called me out of the dugout to pick the winning ticket.

Then a couple of games later, here I am, six for seven and every-body's saying, "Hey, you've got to play this guy someplace."

It was June. We were playing a doubleheader in Cleveland, second game, and the shadows were going over the pitcher's mound. Jim Pier-sall came out of center field and said, "I won't play."

So Joe Gordon says to me, "Can you play center field?"

I said, "Hell, yeah. You put Piersall in the bullpen to tell me how to play the hitters." And he did. And that's how I got into the lineup.

That '59 Cleveland team was a very good ballclub. We should have won that year. We were in first place most of the year, and then we were playing the White Sox and they wiped us out seven games in a period of two weeks.

I remember one game we lost. I was playing center field and Minnie Minoso's playing left field. The White Sox had the bases loaded and Sherman Lollar was the hitter. He hit a high fly ball into left center field, near the fence. I went back and I was calling for it when Minnie called me off of the ball. We had a sellout crowd in Cleveland Sta-dium – I think we had sixty thousand or seventy thousand people there – and Minnie's calling me off. He's calling me off, and the ball hits in his glove and pops over the fence. I was stunned. I think if I wasn't so stunned I could have reached up and grabbed the ball before it popped over the fence. They gave him a grand slam home run on it. It should have been an error.

That was one game. Another game, George Strickland, our best defensive ballplayer, muffs a double-play ball in the ninth inning.

The first series they wiped us out four games in a row, and we thought we were out of it. Then they went into a slump and they lost five or six in a row. If we could have just played .500 ball we could have won it.

I thought we had the better team. But, you know, they had Aparicio leading off. He'd get on, steal second, then Nellie Fox would bunt him over to third and a ground ball would score him. They'd one-run you to death.

But that was a good year for me. Things went well for me. In '59 I'd hit a couple of good balls, then I'd dump one or two into left field or right field. I hit twenty home runs and batted .363.

But I didn't have enough at-bats to qualify for the batting title. I had about 399 at-bats and you needed 477, including walks, sacrifices, and sacrifice flies. I probably had a total of 430-something.

The whole year I was playing with a pulled hamstring. I'd go out to the ballpark early in the morning limping. I couldn't even walk. Chuck Tanner was with us, and Chuck said, "Tito, you've got to push yourself. Play hurt. Don't let anybody get your job."

So I'd go out there, get in the whirlpool, twenty or thirty minutes, walk around, come in, then right before game time I'd wrap that thing. Well, it got to the point where my leg started to turn black. The trainer said, "Tito, you've got to sit out a couple of games." I hated to because I had an eighteen-game hitting streak.

We were playing Washington. Pedro Ramos was pitching and Joe Gordon asked me to pinch-hit. I went in and made an out and that broke the streak. But I came back, and I think I got an eight- or ten-game hitting streak right after that. When we got down to September, they moved me up in the batting order to get more at-bats, but I had to sit out. Then the last two or three games of the season I didn't play—we'd clinched second—and I lost about twelve at-bats there. But it was close.

When I look back now, it would have been so important to win that batting title. But then I was just so happy to be playing. Everything was going so good. Everything just went well for me. I had a lot of confidence, had a quick bat.

I had a couple of other good years in Cleveland. The next year I came back and I hit .292. I hit the ball just as well, but I didn't have that luck. In '61 I hit .301, drove in eighty-five runs, hit seventeen home runs, and made the All-Star team.

Frank Lane broke up that team. He tore it apart. He got rid of McLish, he got rid of Rocky, Score, Power, Minoso, Russ Nixon. If Frank didn't like you . . . There's the story about J. W. Porter, who was there before I got over there.

J. W. was keeping a log, like he was writing a book. And Lane saw him one day and said, "What are you writing?"

Porter said, "I'm writing a book."

And Lane said, "Well, put this in your book: You just got traded!"

Then Gabe Paul replaced Lane. I think 1961 was my best year. I figured, well, this should be about a $10,000 raise. Gabe Paul came in and said, "You're gonna play for the same thing."

I said, "What?"

He said, "We're not making any money."

I held out. I finally got a raise of $3,500 and a rental car to drive to spring training. I told him, "Gabe, when things go bad, don't forget me."

The next year I didn't hit as well. I played for the same salary. Then, the next year, Birdie Tebbetts came over and he was trying to build a new team and I didn't have a good year. I don't know, I hit .230, .240. Something like that. Gabe put the ax to me. He cut me about $5,000.

I wasn't Tebbetts's style of ballplayer. I remember, we always had meetings. I said, "You know, Birdie, if I'm hurting you, you're hurting me. The best thing you can do is trade me."

He wasted a year or two like that, and eventually I ended up in St. Louis. Stan Musial was the general manager. I was the first ballplayer he ever signed as general manager.

■ ■ ■

Paul Richards was sharp as a manager. Then he became a general manager. I don't know what the hell happened to him. He got bitter. That's when the strike came in and Marvin Miller was coming in.

I dream of him a lot. Of Richards. He gives me nightmares. They've never been good dreams. It's always that he's getting back at me. Or I'm going up to bat, and as I get to the plate he sticks a pinch hitter in for me. I've never had a dream where he said anything good to me. I don't know why.

My wife used to get upset with me: "Why can't you forget this guy!"

And that's just it. He was such a great manager. And then he became general manager. I remember when I had this meeting with him when I was with Atlanta.

I told my wife, "I just can't live with myself." I'd got cut three years in a row. Then I broke my thumb in Montreal and I asked him if I could go home. I went home three times, and they wouldn't pay the bill. So when I talked to the owner, Bill Bartholomew, and Richards together, Bartholomew said, "We've never had this situation."

I said, "I had it with Richards when I was in my second year with Baltimore. I broke my hand. They took care of all the expenses and let me go home."

I just lit into him. I told Bartholomew, "I'm going to use language I've never used before." I called Richards any word I could think of. Richards got up and walked out. Bartholomew called him back in.

I just said, "I'm unloading!"

Bartholomew said, "Boy, did you!"

I said, "You guys can do what the hell you want to do with me. I've got this out of my system."

Then next day I was gone. They sold me to Oakland. I didn't think they'd get rid of me. They were in the running. But I would have done the same thing if I were him.

We'd just got into St. Louis. Phil Niekro and I were roommates. The phone rang. It was Luman Harris, the manager: "Richards sold you to Oakland."

I hung up and said, "I'm not going to Oakland."

Phil said, "You've got two or three paychecks."

I said, "Phil, I've been thirteen years, I've had it."

I was playing with a bleeding ulcer. I'd been eating baby food all summer. I had a hard time getting my thumb in the glove.

Phil says, "You can't go."

Then the phone rings. It's Charley Finley. This was in the morning. Finley says, "You've got to be out here for tonight's game. We're playing Baltimore. We're battling for first place."

I said, "Charley, I'm ruling the roost. I've really finally got some-body where I want them. One of you guys is gonna get hurt. I'm going home."

He said, "You can't go home."

I said, "I can do anything I want."

He talked to me for an hour. I told him, "This guy owes me all this money. Three years over here I lost $9,000. I have my suitcase packed and you want me to go out there for six weeks? I don't have a car, my wife and the kids are home. I've had it, Charley. I can't even get my hand in the glove."

He said, "Oh, you'll help us, you'll help us."

I hung up on him.

The phone rings. It's him again.

He made everything good. He picked up the nine grand. He got me a car. He bought me $500 worth of clothes. I told him, "Okay, Charley, I sold my soul. I said I wasn't gonna do this. I wanted to go home, because I'm hurt."

So I went over to Oakland and I just picked up right there and was doing well. Hank Bauer was the manager, and he said, "I'm gonna play you till we're out of this thing."

Then Finley started in on next year. He had DiMaggio, who was a coach out there, come down and talk to me.

"You know, Charley wants to keep you here at the end of the season, get your ulcer taken care of."

I said, "Nah, I'll finish the season and I'll go home."

Then he said, "Charley wants to send you to the Mayo Clinic after the season."

I said, "You know, Joe, I'm tired of this baby food. As soon as the season's over I want to go home."

Then I notice that Joe always has this white stuff on his lips. I said, "Joe, are you chewing Maalox pills?"

He nods yes.

I said, "You have an ulcer?"

He said, "Yeah."

I said, "When you get your ulcer cleaned up, I'll go."

I went home at the end of the season and saw my doctor. He told me that all I had to do was watch my diet, which I did, and I've never had any problems after that.

But Finley is still calling me at home, and he finally talked me into going back.

Finley said, "We've got a good team."

I said, "I know it, that's the only thing that's bringing me back."

And that's when Reggie Jackson becomes a holdout. He killed us. He struck out time after time.

■ ■ ■

Charley Finley told me one time, "You know, you'd be a good manager."

I said, "Yes I would, Charley."

He said, "You ever think about it?"

I said, "Yes."

He said, "Would you like to manage?"

I said, "Yes."

He said, "Well, we'll keep you in the organization."

I said, "Wait a minute. There's only one place I'll manage, that's in the big leagues. I wouldn't go back to the minor leagues."

He said, "Why do you say that?"

I told him.

Back in about 1968, when I was with Atlanta, in the middle of the season, toward August, we were playing an exhibition game with our farm team in Richmond. I got up that day, it was one hundred plus degrees. Drove to the airport, and the plane's air conditioning wasn't working.

We got into Richmond and got on a school bus, no air conditioning. Got to the ballpark, I looked up and saw the lights. Dark. We had to dress in shifts. Dust flying. Two showers. The clubhouse was dirty.

I told myself, "Tito, when you get that urge to manage, think about this day. Is this what you really want?"

I told myself that if I manage it'll be in the big leagues, not even triple-A. I've always remembered that. That's why I never went back.

But I think Terry, my son, likes managing. He has good rapport with his players. If things go right for him, I think he'll be in the big leagues one of these days. Of course, you never know because there are only so many jobs. And it's pretty tough now that you've got guys making $1 million.

He seems to enjoy it, and his ballplayers seem to enjoy him. He's thirty-five. He tries to preach to them. They're so close to the big leagues, so much money that could be made out there if they just work hard at it. He said it feels good when they bring a kid up.

I was in Tucson last Thanksgiving. Terry lives there. They had the winter league running, and the White Sox general manager, Ron Schuler, was in town. He called Terry and said, "Come on out to the ballgame, and bring your dad."

So we went out there. We're having a Coke and he said, "I'm going to tell you something but don't say anything. You're about to read how Michael Jordan wants to play baseball."

I've told Terry, "You're the luckiest guy in the world to manage him." The exposure and the experience. Some big league managers don't get this kind of exposure. It's tough, every place they go *he's* there—and people are there.

Terry has a good rapport with him off the field. But he told him, "When you're on the field, I'll treat you just like any other ballplayer."

I was going down to Birmingham this year at a time that Jordan didn't know if he would stick it out.

Terry told him, "You can't quit. My dad's coming down to see you play!"

Terry fined him fifty dollars one game because he flew his own jet.

Postscript

I'm not a collector, but an unmistakable "find" arrived in the mail two summers ago: an autographed photo of Roger Maris. A friend came across it while settling the estate of his recently deceased aunt. Never much of a baseball fan, my friend said that he thought I would appreciate the memento.

The photo, in black and white, was taken in Cleveland in 1960, Maris's first season with the Yankees. Maris is in the foreground, and the photographer has caught him completing the follow-through of a practice swing against a batting tee, which is out of focus and appears to be spinning in a circle. In the background, an unidentifiable Indian is playing pepper with players outside the eight-by-ten window of action.

It's not hard to guess the probable hour of the day or the time of season. There are a few hundred shirt-sleeved fans scattered in clusters throughout the lower boxes. The undersides of Maris's muscular upper arms reveal a mature golfer's tan, say, midseason form. There's an earnest expression on Maris's face. His eyes are focused entirely on the tee, and there's a slight grimace on his lips. Otherwise, he seems remarkably loose, relaxed. He is still more than a full season away from breaking Babe Ruth's single-season home run record. He is confident. He is still twenty-five years old.

■   ■   ■

The only time I ever saw Roger Maris play was the year before this picture was taken, 1959. Maris was in his final season with Kansas City, and I was a six-week boarder of my aunt and uncle and my cousins, Steven and Iris, living in the back of their candy store in Brooklyn.

The memories from that summer remain vivid: of an eternal fountain of egg creams and the slow, luxurious afternoons at the Coney Island Baths and the salt air. I fell secretly in love with the exotic Olivia Buffolini, who lived in the house behind Charley Chiu's Chinese

Laundry. It was a visceral world for a twelve-year-old from the distant country of Hartford, Connecticut.

Mostly, though, 1959 was memorable for all the Yankee games Steven and I took in. We'd ride the subway to the Bronx for a Friday night game, then spend the night with my grandmother. She lived in a rent-controlled, three-room apartment on Morris Avenue, across from the old Bronx High School of Science. On Saturday, we were back at The Stadium.

More than any other, one game stands out in my mind. In fact, from that entire summer I can recall no other game but this one. I don't remember who pitched and I don't remember who won. Only the color of the game, and the image of the Kansas City right-fielder, remain.

The Athletics were in town for a weekend series. Our bleacher seats on Saturday were in the front row, adjacent to and on the center field side of the Yankee bullpen. We were so far away from the action out there that we grew involved in the smaller worlds around us. In the bullpen, Clete Boyer (Hector Lopez was the regular Yankee third baseman that year) and Duke Maas were waging guerilla warfare with paper clips against anyone within striking distance. And I seem to remember Ryne Duren passing money into the stands for hot dogs, just like a paying customer – but this may be a matter of age and all that I've read since then.

By the third inning, a few fans sitting near the foul pole became musically involved in the game. Whenever Kansas City right fielder Roger Maris took his position in the bottom half of the inning, they sang out in unison, "Ma-ris, cha, cha, cha." And Maris, his back to the stands, punched out the beat in the air with his glove.

As soon as Maris finished warming up and the inning began, Steven and I directed our attention to the bullpen, occasionally looking back to the field to follow the arc of a long fly into the acres before us. By the middle innings, Maris had assumed the role of conductor, leading the right field chorus in an up-tempo hymn to himself. In the top half of the seventh inning, Maris doubled off the bullpen fence in right, and the entire right field choir, probably two or three hundred strong by now, rose up and cheered wildly like some precursor of the dreaded "wave." When Kansas City took the field in the bottom of the inning, the chorus reached a magnificent crescendo as Maris took his position. He grinned, doffed his cap, and in one grand and elegant gesture he bowed to us all.

In December of that year, when I read that Maris had been traded to the Yankees, I couldn't have been happier. Though I was disappointed

over the loss of Hank Bauer (Norm Siebern, Marv Throneberry, and Don Larsen also went), I was convinced, based on that one game and all that had taken place off-stage, that Roger Maris was actually a version of Bauer, a hero I was losing.

In 1960, the year of the photo before me, Maris batted .283 and hit thirty-nine home runs. He led the league with 112 RBIs and a slugging average of .581. He was named the American League's Most Valuable Player.

Everyone knows what happened the following season.

■　●　■

Twenty-three years after he broke Babe Ruth's record, on the afternoon before the 1984 Cracker Jack Old Timers Baseball Classic, I met Roger Maris in the players' hospitality suite of the Hyatt Regency Capitol Hill hotel in Washington, D.C. One of my jobs was to arrange interviews with ballplayers for members of the press who were in town to cover the game.

Maris was sitting with ex-Yankees Hank Bauer and Bill Skowron. The three wore identical flat-tops: It was like a reunion of drill sergeants. But they were gracious to the point of the ridiculous: They introduced themselves to *me*, and invited me to sit with them. We talked – I sat, they told stories.

At the time, it never occurred to me to mention that afternoon back in '59. Years had passed, and baseball was no longer a game I played; now I claimed to "understand" it. I read more baseball than I saw, and my reading seemed to take me ever farther from the field.

I knew Maris had cancer. But he looked good, and his spirits, as we say at such times, were excellent. We talked awhile longer, then Maris rose, put his arm around my shoulder, and said, "Let's go." And we were off to the interview sessions.

Well into early evening, the press loved Roger Maris as they never had before, certainly not during the 1961 season. That day, Maris was funny and patient and wise about the game of baseball and, in particular, his assault on Ruth's record. Distance from the event had given him perspective. Despite – and because of – his illness, he was that kid outfielder from Kansas City once again, filled with an unmistakable joy for living and for the game by which he once earned his living.

If you're old enough to remember the drama of the 1961 American League pennant race, then there's no need to remind you of the image we were left with of Maris by the end of that hectic chase. But for whatever we were told, in 1984 (and for probably as long as anyone can *honestly* remember) Maris was nothing at all like the picture the press had painted throughout most of '61. He was not surly. He was not aloof. And he was not unworthy. He was genuine, considerate, and thoughtful. He remained in the press room until the last questions were asked and, in the mind of each reporter, satisfactorily answered.

I thanked Maris for his time as I walked him through the lobby and the hoards of autograph hounds. He signed every card, photo, and baseball. Just before the elevator doors closed to take him up to his room, Maris thanked me, Lord only knows for what.

■ ■ ■

What happened later that evening could only have happened to Roger Maris. A security guard turned away Maris and his family from a hotel reception held in the ballplayers' honor. Apparently Maris was without his invitation and name-tag, though his crewcut, if nothing else, should have been unmistakable. In a hotel lobby-turned-paradise for card collectors, should not Roger Maris, at any age, have been identifiable as, at the very least, a ballplayer, even to the most benighted security guard?

According to one story, Maris accepted the rejection without incident. He and his wife and son dined quietly in the hotel's rooftop restaurant with its night view of the capitol and Washington's lighted monuments.

Later I learned that Maris was deservedly put out. But I also learned that there was no arrogance in his annoyance. Rather, it seemed that the incident was something he'd almost, sadly, come to expect. Which is to say that Maris did not appear to take what happened personally. The guard, no doubt, should have known, should have been informed – somehow. But he was only doing his job. In my mind, at least, the way Maris handled the situation makes him an even bigger hero for what he had in common with the rest of us whose invitation has ever been revoked at the threshold by human error.

■ ■ ■

The year the photo of Maris arrived in the mail marked the thirty-fourth anniversary of Maris's sixty-one home runs. No one since has come close. In 1991, the commissioner of baseball (*not* Bud Selig) removed Ford Frick's asterisk, a monument of human error, from Maris's record. Unfortunately, the ruling came six years too late.

And so is this story too many years too late. Maris deserved to be reminded of the impression he made on a few hundred fans on a July afternoon at Yankee Stadium in 1959. He could not have known that the image of him we took away from the park that afternoon was of a ballplayer who enjoyed the game and who cared to share that enjoyment. At the very least, Maris deserved to know that. For everyone in right field that afternoon, for Ford Frick and that security guard – for the found photograph – I regret not having told him so.

This book is really for Roger Maris and for all the wonderful players who, like him, are no longer among us to tell *their* stories.